HOW
TO
DO iT

OR *The Lively Art of Entertaining*

BY ELSA MAXWELL

R.S.V.P.: ELSA MAXWELL'S OWN STORY

HOW TO DO IT, OR, THE LIVELY ART OF ENTERTAINING

ELSA MAXWELL

HOW TO DO iT

OR *The Lively Art of Entertaining*

RIZZOLI

to Maria

FIRST RIZZOLI EDITION PUBLISHED IN THE UNITED STATES OF AMERICA IN 2005

RIZZOLI INTERNATIONAL PUBLICATIONS, INC.
300 PARK AVENUE SOUTH
NEW YORK, NY 10010
WWW.RIZZOLIUSA.COM

ORIGINALLY PUBLISHED IN 1957 BY LITTLE, BROWN AND COMPANY

FOREWORD © 2005 SIMON DOONAN

2005 2006 2007 2008 / 10 9 8 7 6 5 4 3 2 1

PRINTED IN U.S.A.

ISBN: 0-8478-2713-5

LIBRARY OF CONGRESS CATALOG CONTROL NUMBER: 2005900671

Author's Note

WHEN my publishers commissioned me to write a book on the art of entertaining, I hesitated for some little time before I signed the contract.

The art of entertaining has been for me such a special, personal matter that I didn't at once see how it was possible to reduce what I had learned during the past forty years to a formula concise and simple enough to appeal to my readers' intelligence, interest and curiosity. In other words, I must transmit to you my way and techniques of entertaining. This must be done not so much, perhaps, by any fixed system of rules as by my personal experience and the know-how of a unique, highly specialized expert, as I suppose I am at this moment of writing.

I will ask the indulgence of the many millions of women who know me throughout the world — for this is primarily a woman's book — and at the same time be grateful if they learn a little of how to enhance the charm and beauty of their lives, homes and surroundings.

E. M.

Contents

Simon Doonan

VEN IF YOU TOOK MARTHA STEWART, Julia Child, Two Fat Ladies, Regine, Suzanne Bartsch, Nigella Lawson, Diane Brill, Carmen D'Allessio, Pat Buckley, Amy Sacco, and Phyllis Diller and threw them all into a giant blender, you would still fall short of producing anyone as compelling and scrumptious as the late, great, über-hostess Elsa Maxwell.

The most enthusiastic and sought-after party giver of the first half of the twentieth century, Elsa Maxwell leaves all the other bash-throwing broads of history in the dust. She was not only ingenious, creative, witty, musical, highly intelligent, and extremely naughty, but, most importantly, she was also rather fat.

Miss Maxwell's Falstaffian corpulence was by far her biggest asset, literally and figuratively. Permit me to explain: Her chosen milieu was the world of international high society, a world where you could never be too rich or too thin. Chunky, rule-breaking, nonthreatening Elsa Maxwell charged in and trampled all the old rules governing this uptight, food-disordered monde. She gave all the aristos, swans, and moguls carte blanche to have fun. To those of you who might accuse me of exaggeration, let me remind you that we are talking, for God's sake, about the woman who is widely credited with having invented the scavenger hunt! With her love of costumes, games, and general silliness, Elsa tore off the constricting girdle of convention and released the hot air from upper-echelon society.

Despite her appearance, Elsa Maxwell was, it must be emphasized, no raspberry-blowing vulgarian. "She looks like a cook on her day off!" said Diana Vreeland of her old pal as she recalled her frolicking on the beach in Antibes in her book *Allure*. She then sharply reminds us that Elsa "had no doubt just been dining with kings—always kings."

In *How to Do It*, Elsa Maxwell reveals herself to be a social-mountaineering monarchist and an unrepentant name-dropper of massive proportions. The words Cole Porter, King Paul of Greece, Winston Churchill, Queen Ena of Spain, and Maria Callas fall from her lips like so many flakes from a vol-au-vent crust. Even her recipes were famous: Aren't you dying to try Claudette Colbert's Snails or Mrs. Darryl Zanuck's Fudge? So committed is she to demonstrating her proximity to the famous that she even drops names one has never heard of: Who, for example, are the John Gunthers? And what about the Munns of Palm Beach?

Like so many socially ambitious types, Miss Maxwell was not highborn. She once described herself as "a short, fat, homely piano player from Keokuk, Iowa, with no money or background, [who] decided to become a legend and did just that."

In *How to Do It*, Elsa Maxwell exposes her rough and ready background via a brutal honesty. She pulls no punches when it comes to stating her pet peeves.

CHILD ENTERTAINERS AT PARTIES: "Pure poison."

ACTRESSES: Food-phobic killjoys whose profession "assesses glamour largely in terms of tape measure and scale."

GLADIOLAS: "Some flowers seem to have been designed by nature to adorn hotel lobbies."

DRUNKS: She sternly advises any would-be hostess "to order the offender off the premises in no uncertain terms, and to be prepared to back up the order with a discreet show of bodily force if necessary." For a female drunk Miss Maxwell gets more specific: "Simply go up behind her and give her pearls a twist."

Her most damning commentary is reserved for those who bore. According to Miss Maxwell, a bore is the "vacuum cleaner of society, sucking up everything and giving nothing." Bores "put you in a mental cemetery while you are still walking." The thing that seems to irk La Maxwell most about the bores she has encountered is their unwillingness to confess their crimes: "Under pressure people admit to murder, setting fire to the village church, or robbing a bank, but never to being bores."

Pearl-garroting aside, only a fool, or a bore, would read this book looking for useful tips. *How to Do It* is really more of a psychological case history than a guide to entertaining. Here, unfurled for the world to see, is a vivid and endearing self-portrait of a world-class attention junkie. When Miss Maxwell denounces her chum Margot Asquith as "an exhibitionist, a sensationalist who adored having the limelight focused on her at all times," we get the distinct feeling that the pot is calling the kettle beige. From the very first chapter, Miss Maxwell has no problem comparing herself to all the most noteworthy women of history beginning with Eve and somebody called Queen Hatshepsut. All right, already, with the royal name-dropping!

Were her monarchy-infested and celeb-encrusted parties as much fun as she makes them out to have been? With the incredible and gifted Elsa Maxwell at the helm, one suspects they were pretty damn good. Was she as much fun as people say she was? Probably about a million times more so. This is, after all, the woman who, when the repossessors unexpectedly took away the piano from her little house in Montmartre, entertained her guests by slapping out an entire opera on her ample thighs.

HOW TO DO iT

OR *The Lively Art of Entertaining*

CHAPTER I

Renewer of Hearts

I SUPPOSE I should know a little about the art of enter-taining. I've been at it long enough. On and off for forty years I've been giving parties, some 2000 in all — big parties, little parties, fantastic parties, spectacular parties. Parties in New York, Hollywood, London, Paris, Monte Carlo, Cannes, Biar-ritz, Venice, Egypt. Parties reported in almost every news-paper and language under the sun, including Hindustani, Sanskrit, Chinese, and Arabic. (If I knew what they said, per-haps I wouldn't mention it!) Parties simple, parties gargan-tuan — but always gay parties, amusing parties, enjoyable parties. Above all, enjoyable. If I have a boast, it is that. For whatever the party — wherever the place, whoever the guests — I can truthfully say I have yet to give a dull one.

I know that for many people giving a party is a penance. For me it is pure happiness, pure pleasure. I love giving parties. I always have. I always shall. I have given them spontaneously, on the spur of the moment, or I have planned and staged them with all the strategy and tactics of a battle, together with a loving care and affection. When I eat my cake I like to enjoy it! Either way, people seem to find they like my parties, that I give good ones, that they want to come to them again and again. In short, that my parties are successful.

How has it all come about? How has a simple love of gaiety, a love of enjoyment and of wanting to bring enjoyment to others, earned me the title of World Party-Giver No. 1? I didn't ask for this mantle of champion party-giver; the world has pinned it on me. To me entertaining has ever been second nature, merely "doing what comes naturally." I've done just that, and had a world of fun doing it. But with what reason? To what purpose?

Perhaps the answer lies in history.

"We are part of what has gone before," says that exquisite writer and wit, Oliver St. John Gogarty. "Portions and parcels of the past guide us and carry us on. . . . What we call the present is only a suburb of the past."

I believe that. I believe that in my predilection for bringing into the world a little more laughter, a little more color, a little more warmth, I am merely following in the footsteps of others; I am just another page in the long history of entertaining — a story that began, let's face it, in the Garden of Eden, when Eve gave the first party of all with only an apple!

Since poor Eve unwittingly involved us in the fall of man, there have been hundreds, thousands of women — and men — whose place in time is forever marked by the bright stamp of pleasure they left on a not always pleasant world. They were not all good hosts; some of them were downright bad. But the spirit that moved them was the same: to amuse, to divert, to lighten hearts and hopes.

A great queen has been described by a phrase that puts the *cachet* on it all. She was Hatshepsut, who ruled Egypt nearly two thousand years before Christ. Queen Hatshepsut had many titles, among them "Bestower of Years, Goddess and Lady of All Lands, Renewer of Hearts."

Renewer of Hearts! That is the one that appeals to me — an

appeal in no way diminished by the strong likelihood Hatshepsut wrote it herself. The phrase sings through the ages, touching the countless generations of people who have wakened one morning and thought, "I think I'll give a party — the best party ever!" I like to think that I am simply a twentieth-century addition to that gaudy, wonderful crew — a sort of latter-day "Renewer of Hearts."

It was in Egypt one winter that I first became acquainted with my fascinating Hatshepsut and, caught up and imbued with the excitement of the incredible past about me, began to wonder if "portions and parcels of the past" had not indeed unconsciously guided me since the time some ten years before when I had begun to weave my little tapestry of entertaining.

What parties Hatshepsut gave! There was the one honoring the return of her expedition to the Land of Punt — Somaliland as we know it.

The five great-sailed and -oared galleys came home laden with ivory, gold, ebony, cassia, myrrh, green monkeys, greyhounds, leopards and, most precious of all, aromatic gum trees which would provide incense to honor the great god, Amen-Ra. (The gum trees were planted in the garden of the temple at Thebes, where they flourished and duly produced an abundance of fresh incense. Indeed, when I was there one of the supposed roots of the trees was pointed out to me.)

For the celebration, Hatshepsut, like any good hostess, planned ahead. She had sent artists with the expedition to make on-the-spot sketches, and these she had reproduced in sculpture and mosaics in her temple, so that the travelers at her party could live again in the scene of their triumph. She knew the importance of creating a pleasing backdrop for her guests, the enchantment of make-believe.

As keeper of the state purse, I'm sure the canny Hatshepsut kept an eye on expenses; but she had the queenly advantage of not having to engage high-priced entertainers for her party. Dancing girls and musicians were fixtures at her court and guests were treated throughout the feast to the eye-filling sight of beautiful girls with lilies in their hair swaying to the rhythms of harp and flute and that considerably less melodic disc-and-wire instrument, the sistrum.

For her party Queen Hatshepsut dressed as a queen should, in a flowing, richly-colored robe, her long hair braided and curled, on top of her head a lump of sweet-scented unguent which must have been tricky to balance, though a great aid to good posture. So she sat, regal in her great carved, claw-and-ball-footed throne, while the lesser of her guests made do with the fold-away chairs whose progeny may be seen today at our best church suppers. Lying down while eating was never the chic thing with Egyptians that it was later to become among the Greeks and Romans.

Men talked politics and money. Women talked eternals. Women who were strangers to each other observed custom: How many children? they asked politely. . . . And how difficult were the confinements? . . . Doubtless it broke the ice.

No post-dinner letdown marred the rollicking pace of Hatshepsut's party. For those who drank and ate too much — and that was most of the guest list — a vomitorium was handy; eat, drink, and be sick seemed to be the Egyptian idea of a perfect party. Then, digestive problems solved, they could get to the more colorful diversions of the evening, such as tossing a handful of virgins into the Nile to appease the gods' and the crocodiles' appetites. (To the Egyptians, nothing was too good for a crocodile. They considered them sacred and even bedecked their necks, like dowagers, with collars of emerald.)

Hatshepsut was no wager of wars, no bloodstained conqueror. To me, it is significant that a woman who so clearly attached importance to the art of entertaining made her reign noteworthy by still nobler arts, chief among them the art of peace. She brought tranquillity and beauty to an age strange to both. Her temple at Karnak is among the wonders of Egypt, and one of the great obelisks she built, the highest and finest of its kind, still stands.

I like to think that such a woman spent *her* post-dinner hours in quieter pursuits than a bit of good-natured human sacrifice. Once I came across her backgammon board, and felt a glow of personal friendship between us. She, too, must have enjoyed an after-dinner gamble as I do. (In point of accuracy I must add that I believe it was a draughts board. No matter; I have won and lost a few dollars at that, too.)

Externals change, but the human heart does not. It's an old truth and one we all rediscover from time to time in our lives, yet never have I been made so vividly aware of it as when I stumbled on the records left by this ancient queen and realized fully for the first time how ageless and honored is the heredity of entertaining. Four thousand years ago, could not Hatshepsut have chosen to reward the achievements of her travelers merely with titles and lands, the customary royal perquisites? She could have; no doubt she did. But she didn't stop there. She added to her thanks the most heart-warming gesture of gratitude a woman can make: she gave a party.

Run a finger down history's long index; note the great periods; and note, as I have — to my pleasure, and with perhaps a forgivable bit of smugness — that they were all periods in which women figured importantly, and the art of entertaining rode high. (I shall have to except the years of Victoria's reign. Unquestionably they were great years, yet during them entertaining as an aid to cheer rode somewhere well below the Plimsoll line.)

The Greeks, in the heyday of their greatness, greeted each other with the words *Chaire! Komos!* ("Rejoice! Revel!") They did just that. Celebrations honoring their numerous gods and goddesses were as much a part of their lives as breathing. During these festivals — and they occurred just about as often as it took to recover from the last one — whole cities spilled into the streets, dancing and drinking, feasting and loving and singing, shouting their joy to Zeus and Dionysius and Aphrodite, most of all to the fates that had made them Greek and therefore blessed among men.

It was not, sad to say, a period in which the average woman could show her best party-giving hand. Married women were virtually house-bound by a patriarchal society, yet it was a society in love with pleasure and, as such, forced to acknowledge that, without women, pleasure was a pretty empty pursuit.

Drinking clubs were one alternative. There a Greek gentleman found other conveniences than a chance for a friendly tipple. He might dine, for example, on such delicacies as shark meat and eels, make a ritual of conversation, and contemplate to his heart's content the singular talents of the auletrides — the dancing girls who played the flute and sang.

For rich men there was even fairer game. The glamour girls of Greek society were the hetaerae, those remarkable women who found the only independence possible to them by staying single, using their beauty as nature intended, and adding to natural endowments the pretty arts of conversation. They were the true hostesses of their time, and proof enough — if proof be needed — that, however much men may profess to scorn the sex it dubs "weaker," they still cannot get along without women — and, in particular, women who know the whys and wherefores of entertaining. Indeed, a few Greek men had the grace, even then, to acknowledge the superiority of women as social fence-menders. Thus in Aristophanes' great play, *Lysistrata,* we have that wily lady bringing about the signing of a peace treaty that men had sought unsuccessfully for years. How did Lysistrata do it? Why, with wine. She simply got them all a little drunk and so happy they'd sign anything.

It was the Romans who finally restored to women a place of honor at the banquet table, if only at the foot. Perhaps the men of Rome were simply conceding a truth learned from their Greek predecessors — that you can't keep a good woman down. The fact is that women serve men well, and men well know it. It may be going too far to suggest that any or all three of Caesar's wives contributed measurably to the great dictator's greatness, yet it is surely not inconceivable that at his table the right dish put before the right ambassador at the right time might have gained favor where favor was sought. Caesar could hardly have taken time out from wars and conquest and law-making to learn whether a guest preferred his flamingo tongues with or without garlic. Women could, and did. Who can say what political mishaps were averted, what appeasements arrived at, simply because Calpurnia put her talents as a hostess to work?

I must say she went overboard, by modern standards anyway. If, for example, there were to be twelve honored personages at dinner and each had a different preference in food, twelve different dishes would be served. To each his own: shellfish ragout to one, sheep's head to another, and so on down the list through shark's liver, whole spit-roasted lamb, scallops and oysters, sea urchins, snails. As a hostess I can't say I recommend catering to the individual palate of each and every guest, but

I do most heartily commend the spirit that moved Calpurnia: like Hatshepsut, she sought only to please her guests. And in doing so, she pleased herself.

Nearly a thousand years passed before there came again a civilization with the capacity for living life in a manner Queen Hatshepsut would have applauded. The Renaissance burst like a phoenix from the murky ashes of the Middle Ages and brought with it a galaxy of men and women more dazzling than any the world had seen before or is likely to see again.

Lorenzo the Magnificent, Leonardo, Michelangelo, Gutenberg, Columbus — the very names spell greatness. Yet to me it is the women of the Renaissance to whom their twentieth-century sisters owe the loudest salute. Roman women had taken a few bold if hesitant steps towards emancipation, but their gains had all but disappeared in the wasteland of the Dark Ages. Now again appeared women with the wit to perceive that a permanent position in the back seat obscured the view. Moreover, they had the brains to do something about it.

Isabella d'Este was scarcely out of her teens when she assumed virtual rule of Mantua (her husband, the Duke of Mantua, wasn't very bright) and was shortly being called *la prima donna del mondo* —"the first lady of the world."

Isabella set the style for Renaissance women. She was an accomplished poet and writer of prose, she played the clavichord and lute and danced with such airy grace she was poetically credited with having wings. She drew the finest painters and poets and musicians to her court, and built an imposing collection of manuscripts, statues, and paintings. She also collected dwarfs. She was, in fact, so mad about dwarfs that she went to considerable expense to have a six-room suite built to their measure in the palace, complete with chapel. Understandably this foible did not catch on, but her otherwise exemplary social conduct did. Women took avidly to culture. They studied the arts, perfected dancing, trained their voices. They cultivated all the most seemly elegances of manner and speech and, determined to hold their own, sat with stiff upper lips when their husbands' talk shifted from the polite to the ribald.

The result was that men gave ground. In deference to their obdurate ladies, they now took to the practice of fine manners and fine talk. *Bel parlare* became as admired among men as it was among women, and this new awareness of beauty reflected itself in their clothes, their personal grooming, the very food they ate. The Renaissance man became a gourmet of the first order, even learning to appreciate the advantages of the new-fangled fork. His rough-and-tumble sports gave way to the more genteel pastimes of cards, chess, dancing, fencing. Yet with it all he lost none of his vigor, his masculine aggressiveness. He'd been a rough-cut stone. Now, with women wielding the buffer, he simply acquired luster. And it lasted. Thanks to Isabella and her sisters in bond, the mannerly arts were with us to stay.

One use Isabella didn't think of for her dwarfs was serving them for dinner. That whimsy was reserved for the ever-resourceful French when their own great age arrived. In the eighteenth century, elegance and wit were the keynotes of the French court, and chefs applied both to their cuisine. A dish that never failed to draw cries of delight was an enormous cake from which dwarfs jumped out on cue to entertain and titillate the guests.

The eighteenth century was not, in fact, as all-fired gay as is popularly supposed. There were endless bloody little wars, stiff taxes, wretched poverty among the peasants. Yet few but scholars identify the period with hard times. To most of us, the century brings to mind the glitter of Versailles, apogee of the life beautiful — with its mirrored halls, its marbles and crystal and gilt, its swan lakes set in perfumed parks where stately fountains played and bejeweled and beribboned ladies and gentlemen strolled to the melodies of violin and flute.

Certainly it was a time for greatness, and it met the challenge with many great men. Yet of all the names that dot its history, none shine brighter than the women who lent it glamour: La Vallière, Madame de Montespan, La Pompadour, Du Barry. Today when we think of the Revolution we are apt to think first neither of Robespierre nor of the luckless Marat, but of the still more luckless Marie Antoinette and her irritable advice to "Let 'em eat cake!" (What she actually said, if she said it at all, was: "Let 'em eat brioche." No matter. In a story, it's endurance that counts.)

What is fascinating and to the point in all this is that, though wars are fought, famines endured, monarchs overthrown, it is the givers of pleasure, the bringers of beauty, the gay at heart who endure. These are history's darlings. Now I have no intention of defending the disdainful and rather stupid point of view that brought on Marie Antoinette's callous little epigram, nor even the ostrichlike attitude of the other pleasure-loving ladies of the French court. The kindest thing that can be said for them is that they didn't know any better. What politics they understood were power politics. Their world was the satin-cushioned world of privilege by divine right. Yet for all the extravagance of their balls and tableaux, their intentions were good: it was their timing that was out of kilter.

History has a way of dishing up the cream and ignoring the milk. So if in giving you this pocket-edition peek into the great periods in the history of entertaining I have touched only on the rich and royal, it is simply because in those days you had either to *be* somebody, or at least able to afford a big splash, before you were considered qualified for posterity. Yet the high and the mighty have no monopoly on pleasure. Far from it. In the final analysis, it is not the *who* but the *why* that counts in entertaining. It is not the money you spend, nor the prestige you may reap — it is what is in your heart. More, it is what you leave in the hearts of others.

Of all the parties I have given, there is one that stands out in my memory as perhaps the most rewarding of all. Certainly it was the smallest. I had a guest list of one! Yet never have I known a happier fulfillment in my role as hostess than I did on that evening when I entertained a girl I had never seen before, and may never see again.

Her name, let's say, was Alice. Alice was young, a widow, and having a heavy time of it making ends meet in the Brooklyn flat she shared with a friend. One day I received a letter from her. She knew, she said, how much I love music, that I went often to concerts and the opera. She had read in my column about the places I dined and the people I met. "Oh, once, just once," she wrote, "to spend an evening as you do!"

So I invited her to do just that.

I booked seats at Carnegie Hall for a concert Toscanini was to conduct. Before the concert we dined at El Morocco and Alice had the time of her young life watching the parade of Hollywood and Broadway and society that came and went. People stopped at our table to chat: Walter Winchell, Leonard Lyons, a former governor of Pennsylvania; and when, as we were about to leave for our concert, Alice came face to face with Betty Grable I nearly had to assist my little friend into our taxi.

I don't think two people ever had a better time. It was a

beautiful evening, an evening surrounded by elegance, from the perfection of the food on which we dined to the perfection of the music we heard; and when it was over Alice told me she had never spent a finer, happier few hours in her life. Well, she no more than I. That night there was not one, there were two hearts renewed.

Now I am aware that it is a far cry from a Theban temple to El Morocco. Yet I like to feel that what Queen Hatshepsut accomplished on a long-ago night in Thebes, I too accomplished that evening in New York when I was able to bring to a lonely young woman some of the beauty, some of the elegance, some of the romance, if you will, she so yearned for. For there is romance in elegance; and today, I am sorry to say, there is far too little of both in the routine of our daily lives. Yet I sincerely believe that by entertaining we can all bring the romance of elegance a little closer.

Party-giving isn't simply a matter of trotting out the best china, the wedding-present linen, and hoping for the best. It is loving. It is giving. It is sharing. It is everybody's chance to light a little candle in the sometimes gloomy corners of the world. Someone has said that life itself is a party: you join after it's started and you leave before it's finished. Well, when it comes my turn to leave this longest of all parties, I can hope for no better epitaph than the one the late Frederick Lonsdale, a little prematurely to be sure, once wrote for me:

"She knocked on the door of history," he said, "and made a part of our century gayer with her entertaining. Hers was the fame of a thousand and one nights — and never a dull one."

And should someone care to add to that, "Renewer of Hearts," I hereby submit my heartfelt thanks.

CHAPTER II

Analyzing Some Parties

YOU can throw away that book of etiquette if you wish me to be your guide to the secrets of successful entertaining. I'd say that slavish adherence to the dos and don'ts of etiquette as laid down by the rulebooks has doomed more parties than anything else. Time and again outmoded conventions of etiquette are the reason parties are so terrible, so boring, such flops, why so many people find custom hanging like wet seaweed on their hands.

I am not talking about the etiquette that prescribes simple good manners. Abandon the tried-and-true precepts of courtesy and tact, and you will make yourself about as endearing socially as a typhoid carrier at a house party. No, what I declare war on is the etiquette that ordains a fixed, inflexible pattern on the way in which this or that kind of party must be given — the etiquette that states, for example, that hot breads may *never* be served at a tea where there is dancing, that before a dinner the hostess *must* remain standing, thereby keeping the gentlemen on their reluctant feet, that when the guest of honor leaves *all* must leave, whether they or the hostess like it or not. What should a party be, in heaven's name? A good time, or an exercise in discipline?

Rigid standards of procedure are all very well for royalty and high officialdom. They are fatal to the party given with the pure and unbeguiled aim to please. Queen Victoria was an imposing jewel in the British crown, I know, but she threw a pall of stiff-necked etiquette over two continents that clings to the traditionalists among us to this day. I had tea once with that Queen of Etiquette, Emily Price Post. I found Mrs. Post charming, but her party wasn't exactly gay. Nothing creative has ever yet come out of blind obedience to custom. Yet still today I know of people who entertain — if that is the word — in the same joyless, stodgy, oh-so-correct fashion that turned nineteenth-century drawing rooms into the overstuffed shrines to boredom they were.

It was the monotony of most people's parties that drove me to invent my own. Early in my party-giving career I made up my mind to break the rules that bound entertaining to formula dullness. I dare say that often enough I've done the wrong thing, at least by conventional standards, yet in party-giving as in everything else it is results that count, and I have no intention of being modest about the results I've had. I give good parties, and they are good because they don't conform, they don't hew to the line of hidebound precedent. They don't, in short, bore.

Give people what they don't expect is my advice if you would succeed as a hostess. Throw out all the rules, except those that discretion and good taste demand, and you will swim to the top. Don't try to keep up with the Joneses. Make the Joneses keep up with you — if you care at all about the Joneses. Take the lead. Put your imagination to work. Nowadays the tendency to conform is an appalling threat to individuality. Get off the assembly line, I say, and turn out parties that are custom-made to *your* personality, *your* taste, *your* pocketbook.

That old bugbear, money, is the most common defense I hear from women who are afraid to give parties simply because they can't afford to entertain on a gilt-edged scale. Nonsense. All the money in the world doesn't make a good hostess. If wealth were all, Barbara Hutton would have put me in the shade years ago. Money doesn't make a good party. You do. If I were to give ten thousand dollars to some people I know and tell them to spend it all on a party, the party would still be a flop. But if I were to ask Cole Porter, for instance, to play host to a Dutch treat party, guests to bring their own food and drink, all would be a-bubble till break of day. In entertaining as in finance there is a sort of Gresham's Law at work; in entertaining it is not bad money, but money badly spent, that will condemn the most expensively backed party to social oblivion.

I have given parties when I hadn't two pennies to rub together — and I haven't so many more now — crazy, childish parties like the one at which a group of cabinet ministers had the time of their sedate lives blowing feathers off an outstretched sheet. True, I have also given parties that would have cost others tens of thousands — parties for kings, statesmen, for assorted nabobs from the arts and from society; yet, I repeat, it was not the sum at the foot of the bill I didn't always get that made them good parties. It was because they were different. They offered the unexpected. When I give parties I like to surprise, to astonish, to *épater* or delight, as the French say. Certainly, also, there is the ever-present determination to top the last party I gave.

"Where in the world do you get your ideas?" is a question I am often asked. Well, to that I can only answer, "Out of my head," and that is a piece of equipment on which I have no monopoly. Anyone can find a novel idea if he'll only go looking for it. To illustrate, I am going to tell you about some of the parties I look back on with special affection because each was, in its own way, unique. Let me first, however, anticipate those who will complain, "It is all very well for Elsa Maxwell to give such parties, but how is it possible for me?" I agree that some of these parties were on a generally prohibitive scale. Yet I say again. In party-giving it is not money but imagination that counts. I used my imagination when I planned these parties. And there is not one of them in which the basic idea could not be adapted to the facilities of the average household and budget. Later on I will make some suggestions as to how.

I suppose it must be my lifelong devotion to the cause of unseating riders of very high horses that accounts for my predilection for leveling devices at parties: games, contests, fancy dress are all great levelers. No one, for instance, is going to stand long on dignity while he is engaged in demonstrating his technique at dunking doughnuts into coffee, which was the sole purpose of one party I remember with pleasure.

The uninhibited twenties, which have come to be associated with all sorts of sinful goings-on among the rich, were, as a matter of fact, the heyday of the innocent pastime at parties. Nowadays party games are commonly left to the children, while their parents content themselves with the statelier diversions of dining, drinking, looking at television, occasionally breaking the routine with excursions onto a dance floor or to a card table. All very pleasant things to do, but how very much more fun can be had from life by climbing out of the adult rut now and then, doing something delightfully *un*adult for a change. "Make me a child again just for tonight" is a wish that psychiatrists no doubt view with pain; but, take it from me, acting on it is the greatest mental therapy there is. What is more, when a party is joined in some gay and lively enterprise, however foolish, there is a lot less senseless drinking done, and a lot more enjoyment for all as a result.

Well, there have been all kinds.

There was the game I staged in London one year in the twenties that began on an ominous note but resulted in a fad that was still going strong into the forties when the war apparently shelved it. Lady Diana Cooper, Blossom Forbes-Robertson, and I hit on the idea of organizing a treasure hunt and sending the invitations out in the form of an anagram. There was only one hitch. Not knowing how many people would be able to decipher the message, we had no idea how many would turn up. We needn't have worried. So many cars converged on Lady Juliet Duff's house in Belgrave Square, where the hunt was to start, that the police arrived wanting to know what was going on. We all had visions of being arrested as public nuisances, but then, just as we were about resigned to being carried off to the nearest police station, out from a car stepped a fair-haired young man and the law disappeared like the mists at morning. It was the Prince of Wales. So we carried on, the party was the hit of the London season, and when I returned home in the fall I found the idea had gotten here ahead of me. Treasure hunts were all the rage.

There was my cooking party in Hollywood — this the result, during my first visit there in the early thirties, of my outspoken views on the quality of the local cuisine. The food in most of the houses and restaurants I visited struck me as uniformly bad, and I blamed this state of affairs on the fact that apparently no one out there knew his way around a kitchen well enough to make toast. This was denied on so many fronts that I decided to put a hand-picked group of people, all claiming to be good cooks, to the test: I invited ten top stars to have it out with chafing dish and spoon at Mike Romanoff's. Through Mike I ordered a great variety of foods, which were spread out on a long table with other necessary equipment, and when the contestants arrived they were ushered to one of the chafing dishes, equipped with aprons and chefs' caps, and told to cook whatever they liked. This experiment, I should add, was also in the nature of a calculated risk: whatever came out of those chafing dishes that night was to be dinner for the whole party. As it turned out, it was a risk worth taking. With one exception, my ten glamorous chefs produced dishes worthy of a *cordon bleu* — and the first prize, ladies, went to a man: Clark Gable. At this remove I don't remember what it was Clark cooked — something to do with eggs, I believe — but I do remember that, whatever it was, it was divine. Ronald Colman ran a close second to Clark among the men, and in the women's division Joan Fontaine and Claudette Colbert did their sex proud.

There was my painting party in Paris, which in my book has two stars to its credit for uniqueness: for one thing, it lasted a solid month — surely the longest party on record; for another, it started the craze for amateur Sunday painting that is with us still. If I had nothing else to feel proud of, I am proud of being able to claim credit for launching the vogue for a purely aesthetic hobby at a time when the conception of art for art's sake was fast losing ground to the conception of art for the sake of the dollar.

The idea for the party came to me when my friend, Countess

Mimi Pecci-Blunt, an admirer of art and a hard-working philanthropist, was casting about for a means of raising money for a pet charity. Why not, I thought, make her happy on both counts? We would ask fifty women, the cream of Paris society and amateurs all, to paint pictures, and at the end hold a money-raising exhibition of their work. Mimi fell in delightedly with the idea, and together we transformed the drawing room of her house on the Rue Babylon into a gigantic atelier, crammed with easels, canvases, palettes, brushes, paints, smocks. Here, every day for a month, fifty of the most fashionable women in the world, faces and hands daubed with paint, toiled away with varying degrees of artistry. Princess Marina and Princess Elizabeth of Greece, I remember, both painted beautifully, as did Daisy Fellowes, Millicent Hearst, and Mimi Pecci-Blunt herself. Mine was a horror. I have never had the smallest talent for painting or drawing. But uneven though the contributions were, the exhibition was such a success that the late Virginia Vanderbilt later brought the entire collection to New York, where it was shown at, I believe, the Wildenstein Galleries, and repeated its Paris performance by raising a very tidy sum for charity here. Meanwhile, *Town & Country* magazine had covered the progress of the party in Paris, gave it a great spread, and the nationwide rush to the art stores was on.

There was the barnyard party at the Jade Room of the Waldorf in New York, which gave me the pleasure of indulging my passion for paradox when I converted the most luxurious ballroom in the world into a scene so authentically bucolic that even the hogs I brought in for the occasion felt at home. There were apple trees, a well, hayricks draped with red flannel underwear, farmers in straw hats and overalls, beautiful dairymaids, three cows, those hogs — twelve enormous beasts — even a hog caller imported from Ohio for me by Len Hanna. Actually only the hog caller, his charges, two cows, the hayrick and the red flannels were authentic. The trees with apples sewn on the branches were very convincing fakes — just how convincing I hadn't realized myself until I caught sight of the late George F. Baker trying to climb one to reach an apple. The well yielded beer instead of water. The farmers were my men guests. The beautiful dairymaids were beautiful young society women gotten up in their own elegant versions of what the well-dressed dairymaid wears. And the third of the trio of cows was a very lifelike papier-mâché copy of the two real ones, her chief distinction being that she gave champagne and whisky instead of milk. Anyone who knew how to milk a cow was invited to help himself at this novel bar. Amateurs were barred out of consideration for the real cows. All three animals looked so much alike that, with champagne flowing freely, not everybody could be trusted to tell the difference. (Some years later in San Francisco, incidentally, I put this same stunt to profitable use at a benefit: experienced milkers paid twenty-five dollars for the privilege of showing what they could do.) But the biggest surprise of the evening was the hogs — or, rather, the performance put on by the hogs. They'd been kept penned behind a screen at one end of the ballroom, and when the hog caller went into his act at the other end, letting out that weird cry that only hogs seem to understand, they all came running, so fast that some of the beautiful dairymaids who were sitting on the floor were taken completely unawares and had to scramble, screaming very authentically, to safety.

There was the time I planned a party for the first of May

and turned it into a fitting celebration of the day by making a
living Maypole of Mrs. John ("Fifi") Fell, who stood centered (and scared to death, she told me later) on a small high
podium in the middle of the ballroom floor, while the hand-
somest men there, each holding the end of one of the long
satin streamers fastened to her gown, danced about in a circle,
winding the ribbons around her. Later, since May Day seems
to call for dancing, I put on a waltz contest which Mrs.
Lytle Hull, then Mrs. Vincent Astor, won by unanimous decision of the judges. Her partner? A young man named Ray
Bolger.

There was the year in Venice when old-guard Venetians —
not yet used to the antic ways of the Americans who had
only recently begun to invade the city en masse, thanks to my
promotional efforts at the behest of the tourist-hungry city
fathers — were rocked back on their patrician heels when I
gave a dinner for the late Princess Mafalda, daughter of the
late King of Italy, on a string of gorgeously draped barges
towed to and fro on the Grand Canal. This was one of the
first, but by no means the last, samples of party-giving, American
style, that at first startled, finally captivated Venetian society.
A few years later Linda and Cole Porter sent eyebrows up with
their Red and White Ball at the Palazzo Rizzonico. Knowing how lazy people are about dressing up for a party, at the
witching hour of midnight the Porters brought the mountain
to Mahomet by giving all their guests the most wonderful red
and white paper costumes to wear. Then, following my oft-
repeated enjoinder to keep the surprises coming, they released a flight of acrobats who turned our stomachs upside-
down by performing on the parapet and on wires strung
across the top of the Palazzo courtyard. There have been many

others since, equally stunning and novel. There isn't much
that will startle a Venetian now.

Let me now step aside and say that two of the most beautiful
parties I can remember were parties I didn't give. In Paris in the
early thirties — in July, 1934, to be exact — Baron Niki de
Gunzburg, a rich young White Russian, now an editor of
V*ogue* magazine, gave a party on an island in the lake in the
Bois de Boulogne which was unmatched for beauty in my experience. He called it the *Bal des Valses*, and it was supposed
to take place in Vienna. All the guests wore costumes of the
period. Prince Jean de Lucinge was Franz Joseph; his wife
("Baba"), the Empress Elizabeth; and Denise Bourdet and
Niki himself were the star-crossed lovers, Maria Vetsera and
Archduke Rudolf. For reasons that now elude me I chose to
go as Napoleon III.

There is a restaurant on the island, le Pavillon des Îles, and
when you give a party there the whole island goes with it.
Niki had had the restaurant and surrounding grounds lighted
and decorated by the French decorator, Monsieur le Baron,
who added a final note of elegance to the whole by having
white velvet carpeting laid from the entrance of le Pavillon
right down to the landing at the water's edge where, at 10:30
at night, guests arrived in little rowboats. That crossing must
have been quite a sight — all of us standing up in the rowboats because our costumes didn't allow room for sitting down,
while the astonished boatmen ferried us toward the island
from which blared the music of the two alternating orchestras,
one playing Vienna waltzes, the other *tzigane*.

One of the amusing incidents I remember about that night
happened at supper. Princess Marina of Greece, one of the
most beautiful young women I have ever seen, was sitting

at my table. She was living in Paris then with her parents, Prince Nicolas of Greece and the Grand Duchess Helen of Russia, and not having an easy time of it. During supper Marina turned to an American friend who had just arrived from Hollywood. "I am so tired of being poor!" she said. "I wonder if you could get me a film test in Hollywood?" It might just have come about, too, except that later in the summer Princess Marina went to Dubrovnik on the Dalmatian coast for a holiday, and there met another holidayer — Prince George, afterwards Duke of Kent. They fell in love and were married before the year was out.

If it was difficult in those free-and-easy days to persuade people to put on fancy dress, it has now become next to impossible. Even so, I still do what I can to dress up my parties. For example, when I gave a ball recently to honor Stavros Niarchos I decided that, since it was he who made my cruise to the Greek islands possible, I must pay him a fitting tribute. So I asked all the women to wear a headdress or tiara, synonyms of elegance, and to my amazement two thirds of them actually showed up in tiaras. Mine, incidentally, would have been at home at Niki de Gunzburg's *Bal des Valses,* as it had belonged to Empress Elizabeth of Austria. Harry Winston, the jeweler, lent it to me, and it was the most beautiful thing I have ever seen — all diamond roses, exquisitely entwined. With it, at Mr. Winston's suggestion, I also wore the Portuguese diamond which one of the Kings of Portugal had sent into Brazil, and which finally reached New York. This was a single diamond of great purity and weight, valued, I believe, in the neighborhood of half a million dollars. So with these two adornments I had, for the first and, no doubt, last time in my life, roughly a million dollars on my person.

Another recent party at which elegance was the keynote was a dinner I gave in the Empire Room at the Waldorf a few seasons ago — a party that was strictly a labor of love because it was in honor of a man I love dearly, Cole Porter.

Now it has always seemed to me that if you are going to give a party to honor a friend, the honor ought to be expressed in more tangible ways than simply where you seat him at table. Since this was to be Cole's party, I tried to think of what I could do to please him. What would make the party particularly his? I know Cole very well, and, tenderer sentiments aside, there are three things about him that key him as a personality. First, there is his music. Second, his gaiety. Third, his extreme elegance. So what did I do? For music I had birds, some two hundred of them, singing their heads off in airy, decorative cages. (Later I gave the birds to the women guests as favors.) For gaiety — pink. Pink flowers, pink balloons, plumes of pink feathers. For elegance — ah, what is more elegant than a man in a white tie? All the men were asked to wear white ties; and for offenders who didn't or wouldn't or forgot, I had spares at the door which they could don before entering the ballroom. What's more, they loved it. Looking their elegant best tickled their vanity, and it certainly added to the pleasure of the evening for the women.

Actually, of course, the most rewarding parties to give or go to are those that not only give guests a good time, but also serve a good cause. I have taken active part in more benefits than I care to remember, and I have loved every one of them. The biggest, I think, was a benefit at Madison Square Garden before World War II for Chinese Relief, when 16,000 people crowded into the Garden to watch, among other unusual sights, a Floradora sextet featuring Clifton Webb, Bea Lillie, and Elsa Maxwell.

More recently I had a wonderful time turned out as Catherine the Great in the pageant of empresses at Mrs. Lytle Hull's Imperial Ball to benefit the Hospitalized Veterans Service. I was in regal competition, with Maria Meneghini Callas, a real beauty, as my old friend, Hatshepsut; Faye Emerson as the Dowager Empress of China; Arlene Dahl as Poppaea, wife of Nero; Mrs. Frank Hunter as the Empress Maria Theresa of Austria; English actress Margaret Leighton as Empress Eugénie; Mrs. Lawrence Copley Thaw as the Empress Josephine; and Mrs. Bertrand Taylor III as the woman of today, embodying all the attributes of all the Queens. As I don't regard myself as in any way a queenly figure, and hardly pin-up girl material, I was a little surprised when *Time* magazine bypassed all this glamour and ran only my picture when it covered the ball.

But the benefit that is dearest to my heart is the annual April in Paris Ball in New York. I suppose there is an element of parental pride here, for I was one of the ball's originators and I have watched it grow from a fairly modest beginning into the largest charitable undertaking of its kind in this country. It had its start seven years ago, the year Paris celebrated her 2000th birthday. Alexander Manziarly, French consul-general in New York, Claude Philippe, head of the banquet department and vice-president of the Waldorf, and I lunched at the Pavillon one day to discuss putting on a party at the Waldorf to honor this historic event, and to raise money for French charities here. We discussed some of the organizations we might help, and I am glad to claim credit for naming the French Hospital in New York as one of the beneficiaries. It was poor, badly in need of money, and the balls have helped it enormously.

So the plans took shape. Bernard Gimbel agreed to be our treasurer, and he has remained our treasurer. Valerian Rybar was, and is, our decorator. I was general *entrepreneuse*. But one man alone did, and has continued to do, all the real work, and that is Claude Philippe.

We called that first party the 2000th Anniversary of Paris Ball, and it was such a success that the following year we decided to make it even bigger and better, hold it in the Grand Ballroom of the Waldorf, and call it the April in Paris Ball. It has been growing in size and importance ever since, making more money each year. Five hundred people attended the first ball. At the last, there were 1200, and the net take for the French charities was $130,000.

One April in Paris Ball I have special cause to remember. I believe it was the third, when someone hit on the idea of bulking it up still larger — with elephants. John Ringling North agreed to lend us some from his circus menagerie, and Beatrice Lillie and I agreed to ride them. Unfortunately, if that is the word, it didn't turn out that way. Bea and I dutifully went around to Madison Square, where the circus was quartered, to practice, but the elephants had other ideas. They would have none of us. So it was decided that, rather than risk our necks, we would follow them on foot in the parade around the ballroom — equipped, for reasons that will be obvious to anyone who has ever spent time with an elephant, with dustpans and brooms. On the night of the party, when the time came to go on we went to the anteroom from which we were to make our entrance — I costumed as a maharajah, Bea as my favorite — and found our monstrous charges waiting. Maybe they were just nervous. Anyway, they had misbehaved quite horribly, and Bea and I felt obliged to do what we could in the way of tidying up. We had barely finished when a charming voice called in from the doorway to ask what we were doing. We turned, blinked, and stood mute, unable to reply. It was Queen Juliana of the Netherlands.

Mrs. W. C. T. Gaynor had always been an ardent helper with the ball, and the following year when I found I had to leave early for France I asked her, with Claude Philippe's approval, if she could take over for me. I was sure the ball would be in good hands, and it was.

Understandably, it is today a less intimate, personal affair than in the beginning. Now it is so big, so commercial, that it is necessary to treat it objectively. No matter. The object was to raise money for the French, and that goal has been bounteously achieved. Mrs. Gaynor, assisted by Mrs. Henry Hyde, has gained each year in experience, and her efforts have earned for her the one thing she wanted most: last year in Paris General Catroux presented her with the French Legion of Honor.

So there you have, in sum, eleven parties, each different from the other, each designed to suit a particular moment or place or problem or person. Each, as I admitted earlier, was elaborate by average standards and expensive by any standard. Yet analyze them and you will see that at the core of each was simply a novel idea.

The treasure hunt? This is a game that can be organized on any scale, for any number, any time — indoors or out, on foot, by car, on horseback.

The cooking party? No need for fancy fixings. Lay in a supply of good simple foods and challenge would-be cooks to see how ingenious they can be in using them to create different, interesting dishes for the party dinner. (Never mind if the resulting menu isn't in ideal balance. One eccentric meal never hurt anybody.) Prizes to the winners? Something new and inexpensive in kitchen gadgets. And if you want to ensure a concerted effort by all hands, announce that the cook voted least good must wash the dishes.

The painting party? Make it a drawing party instead, if you don't want to invest heavily in art supplies. Set up a still-life subject, give each guest a drawing pad and crayon, have each artist contribute a quarter to a common pool, select an impartial panel of judges, and award the pot to the best artist to do with as he sees fit.

The barnyard party? Ask your guests to dress for the farm, and do what you can in the way of props to set the appropriate scene. For an indoor party, vegetable arrangements, perhaps, in place of flowers, and miniature scarecrows as table decorations — easy to make yourself from scraps of cloth and straw from the kitchen broom. For an outdoor party, hay spread on the grass, wonderful to sit on — perhaps a life-sized scarecrow in the background. Perhaps, indeed, a real-life scarecrow — which is the guise in which Cecil Beaton came to my barnyard party, complete with crows.

The Maypole party? It could be copied just as I've described it.

If it's elegance you're after, my Tiara Ball and my party for Cole both contained the basic ingredients: white ties for men, headdresses for women.

As to the two benefits I've mentioned — both drew on history for their themes, and that is a bottomless source. Go far and wide — or stay at home: look into local history for a gay or dramatic event to commemorate when you want to appeal to civic pride and purse.

Imagination, ideas — they are what make a party. They are what will make you as a hostess.

CHAPTER III

The Art of the Hostess

ANATOMIZE the character of a successful hostess and the knife will lay bare the fact that she owes her position to one of three things: either she is liked, or she is feared, or she is important. I began in the first category and I hope I'm still there, although there are evidently some who think I now overlap into number three, if the incidence of attempted gate-crashing at my parties is any criterion. But being important, being feared, are scarcely winning attributes. If I thought people came to my parties only because they felt they "must" or because it was "the thing to do" I'd strike them off my guest list in a minute.

It is true that hostesses who enjoy their reputations because of their importance probably number more than all the others in the world. Naturally a woman who enjoys the undoubted advantages of money and position has it in her power to be a good hostess, whether she be mayor's wife or President's lady — but whether or not she succeeds is a matter of her own personality and how she exploits it. The acid test of all entertaining is the extent to which guests enjoy themselves. No matter how important a woman is, if she does not provide her guests with a good time she can abandon any claim to being a good hostess.

Position alone cannot make a good hostess. A likable personality can — and here we have an intangible. For such a personality cannot be categorized. She may be clever or stupid, pretty or plain, from any income bracket and any walk of life. Likableness is no respecter of pedigrees. Some women, and men too, seem born with an aptitude for inspiring affection that is as artless and effortless as breathing. They radiate a kind of natural magnetism that is wholly unanalyzable. Certainly it has little to do with wit or intelligence. How often you hear people say, "I know she's pretty silly, but I like her." I've said it myself and I do not normally hold much brief for lightweights, yet I know many woman so naturally endearing that none but the most captious cares that they cannot hold their own in a conversation on anything weightier than the new letter in Dior's alphabet. Not, I hasten to say, that innate likableness is the exclusive property of delightful idiots. But brains alone are no guarantee of success in the social field. If intellect were all that counted I'd have been looking for a new line of work long ago!

On the other side of the coin there are women whose intelligence only enhances their natural charm. Surely one of the most engaging women in the world today, irrespective of position, is Elizabeth of England. The Queen, I feel sure, would have possessed the same qualities of serene, unaffected sweetness and warmth mixed with wisdom that have made her loved the world over whatever her birthright. The same is true of the Queen Mother, whose calm courage in the face of the panic brought on by the Blitz set an example to millions of mothers and wives during the Battle of Britain. The Queen Mother has only to enter a room to make her charm felt. And, of course, the bright, beautiful, *méchante* Princess Margaret needs no build-up from me as a charmer.

There is no doubt that wherever Princess Margaret goes she scatters a special magic. I came to know her quite well when we took part together in a production of *The Frog* put on in London in the summer of 1954 by Judy Montagu to raise money for needy children. Princess Margaret was co-director. After the first rehearsal the cast was assembled and asked to sit in a circle on the floor to discuss rough spots in the performance. I tried dutifully to lower my bulk to the floor, but the Princess instantly sensed my distress and, smiling, offered me a chair next to hers. Maybe I'd have made it, but her considera-tion saved me from possible disaster. I have heard that when she gets angry she is rather frightening. This I do not believe. A princess with her sense of humor might feel anger, but she would never show it. Margaret loves gaiety, courts it, and has been undeservedly criticized for it, for with it all she works hard and conscientiously for her country and certainly deserves the few extra hours of relaxation afforded by her intimates. To my knowledge she seldom manages more than three hours of sleep a night, yet she is able to appear each day at whatever function the court calendar requires, fresh, radiant, bright of eye. Added to all this, she is talented. She plays the piano and sings beauti-fully — and, gentlemen, she can cook. Often after rehearsals we would creep back to Judy's tiny doll's house in Trevor Place (where two fat dogs take up as much space as the guests) and Princess Margaret would roll up her sleeves and scramble eggs. Very good eggs they were, too, for she loves to cook and has a true flair for it. Come to think of it, I doubt if this singular young woman could do an unbecoming thing if she tried. Even marry.

Another princess of the blood who is liked for herself is Queen Ena of Spain, and so is the Duchess of Kent. Position, environment, training do of course contribute to the easy charm of manner these royal ladies bring to their appearances in public, yet they present to the public eye only what is their natural manner in private.

Royalty has no prerogative on charm. Two American hostesses who have it in abundance are my lifelong friends, Millicent Hearst and Mrs. William Woodward, Sr. Both Millicent and Elsie have the inborn faculty of giving friendship freely and so, in return, receiving it.

Perhaps you are one of the lucky ones — born likable. If so your success as a hostess is assured, for you know when you entertain that your guests are at ease with you and therefore with themselves and therefore happy. But if you are one who finds easy friendship difficult — perhaps from shyness, perhaps from fear, perhaps from an unduly prejudiced mind — then you must do your level best to root out the trouble.

Entertaining is an important part of all our lives, and I say this from no personal bias. My television appearances have resulted in hundreds of letters pouring in to me from all over the country, and I have learned from them that, by and large, women understand very well the value of party-giving. A party is more than a few people getting together to eat and drink and gossip. In its way a party is a miniature forum. It is an occasion when ideas may be exchanged, quarrels patched, news disseminated, business discussed, politics argued, charities organized, crops prayed over, babies viewed, recipes exchanged, remedies appraised, marriages made — or sometimes broken! A party is, in short, a sample case of the art of living together and it devolves on the women of the world to keep it on view. No woman who wishes to be part of a community life can avoid having to entertain now and then. Therefore she should make it as painless for herself as possible. She must feel sure of herself, and she will only feel sure of herself if she is also sure of entertaining in an uncritical climate.

Easy enough to say — the shy woman argues — but how can

I feel sure of myself, when the very thought of giving a party reduces me to a quivering mass?

Well, I can answer that best by saying that one of the shyest women I know is a woman who has not only overcome shyness — she has triumphed over it. That is Katharine Cornell. Out of the theater Kit has never been able to get the best of her shyness. I have been to her parties and I know that she feels about first-night guests exactly as she does about first-night audiences: sheer terror. But let her confident performances once on stage be a lesson in Spartanism to you who shrink from a few guests in the parlor. All it takes is a sense that your audience is with you. Not long ago in New York, for example, I was having lunch at the Pavillon when I glanced up to see Kit standing in the entrance. Only a night or two before I had watched her bring great beauty and authority to the brilliant though wordy and often difficult, lines of Christopher Fry's *The Dark Is Light Enough.* Now here she stood in Henri Soulé's unalarming doorway looking poised, lovely — and absolutely scared to death. When she first glanced around the room and saw nothing but strangers, her timidity was as plain on her face as a pallor. Then she spied me. She came at once to sit with me and my friends, and the minute she found herself with people she knew and could relax with, her shyness disappeared.

Fear, too, can be overcome — if that is your particular millstone. Everyone is afraid of something. Afraid of doing the wrong thing. Of saying the wrong thing. Of being laughed at. I say everyone — but I'm afraid I must make one exception: I must plead myself guilty to never having experienced this particular foible. In me, self-confidence amounts to original sin. I am sure it is a mistake of nature, some sort of overlooked omission in my make-up, but the fact is that I have never had any doubts about myself whatever, nor any shyness. Of course this assurance has been a great advantage to me as a hostess, for having no misgivings about myself I have no misgivings about my parties. I automatically sell my parties to myself, and through myself to my guests.

But if I am the exception, a lifetime of experience has taught me the rule. By and large even the most successful people approach a new situation in a state of enervating doubt. What kind of impression will I make? they ask themselves. Am I suitably dressed? Will I be able to keep up my end of the conversation? Will they like me? Lack of confidence in one's own ability to cope is, in fact, so general a complaint that I cannot think why misery, which is said to love company, doesn't simply sit down with itself and enjoy the fellowship. In any case, you who suffer as hosts because of stunted self-confidence ought to derive some comfort from the knowledge that, nine times in ten, those seemingly all-of-a-piece people you meet and boggle at cultivating are every bit as scared of you as you are of them.

Failing all else, try devising a mental defense or two. One man I know of hit on an ingenious trick — a man, incidentally, who looked the very model of composure. Not so.

"Whenever I feel myself in danger of being overawed by people," he said, "I simply undress them mentally. You've no idea what an edge it gives you to be the only fully dressed one in the room!"

Human nature being what it is, I can't say I recommend this particular gambit as general practice, but the thinking is sound. It is simply the psychology of ridicule fancifully applied. Everyone, after all, feels superior to what he can laugh at.

Less easy to overcome than shyness or fear is prejudice, and that is as it should be. Have your prejudices, by all means: it would be a sorry comment on the species if we were not all able to exercise our individual powers of discrimination. Our likes and dislikes are, after all, what peg us *as* individuals. We do not all like olives or baseball or tatting or the color red, nor do we all like people for the same reasons. What is caviar to me may be cyanide to you, and vice versa. Friendships must be circumscribed by personal taste, just as are the clothes we wear and the food we eat.

The trouble is that while most of us are willing to experiment from time to time with new styles in dress and food, we tend to shrink from experimenting with new styles in people. "She and I have so much in common," we say of someone we like, and settle contentedly into the protective shelter of shared tastes. This is natural enough. Common interests are a bond, of course, and if your subject happens to be collecting old fans or the conservation of the whooping crane you are naturally going to be drawn to a fellow fan collector or whooping crane enthusiast. But it is a mistake to seek friendship only within the limits of common interest. "So-and-so is awfully nice, but so *dull*," you say of someone else, meaning usually that So-and-so's interests differ from yours and that it has probably never occurred to you to give the poor dullard a chance to show his own colors.

Parties are people, and the greater the variety of people, the better the party. For this reason the clever hostess will widen her sights to cover many fields. When you meet new people don't allow trivialities to get in the way of discernment. Perhaps you don't like women who paint their fingernails green or men who part their hair in the middle. That is your privilege. But try not to glue the blinders on too tightly. Minor idiosyncrasies do not necessarily herald major faults. Take the trouble to investigate before you judge a new acquaintance. Your first impression may have been right, or it may not. Learn to evaluate people for what they are, not what they seem at first glance, or what So-and-so has told you about them. Your best friend isn't necessarily your wisest counselor when it comes to appraising character. Set your own standards of what you like and admire in others and have the courage, once you've decided a friendship is worth making, to be loyal to it. "I can't think what you see in So-and-so," from a carping friend, should find you with all guns loaded.

Just as tastes in people differ, so do tastes in parties. So, for that matter, do talents in hostesses, and the first thing the good hostess learns is where her particular party-giving talent lies. Some women are good at one form of entertaining and poor at others. One woman may give perfect dinner parties, but fail when it comes to a private dance. Another may excel at a dance or a fork supper but lose her touch in the more intimate atmosphere of a luncheon or dinner. Few hostesses are good at all forms of entertaining. I think that I, for example, should fail miserably as a week-end host. In line with the old proverb that house guests are like fish, smelling after three days, I'm afraid I'd be sick of the sight of my guests by Monday morning. Actually, this is not a theory I've been able to put to test — for, never having had a home of my own, week-ending is one form of entertaining I have experienced only as a guest.

The only sure way to discover your particular métier as a hostess is by trial and error. Obviously, there will be occupational considerations: the career woman, or the woman who is her own cook, bottle washer, and family sergeant-at-arms can hardly be expected to feel her sparkling best at the end of a hard day. For her, the informal week-end party, such as a backyard barbecue where husband and guests can join in the cooking — or, failing a back yard, a simple buffet — is logically the most comfortable and laborsaving way to entertain.

Or why not a week-end luncheon? It seems to me too bad

that these hectic times have all but relegated mixed luncheon parties to the status of anachronisms in this country. Speed cultists that we are, it has become virtually impossible for the average man to take time from his business day to relax at luncheon: the blue-plate special and be quick about it is by and large standard midday procedure for him. But there is no earthly reason why a luncheon should not be arranged for a Saturday or Sunday, when men could be included. There is, in fact, every reason to recommend it to the busy career-or-house-wife hostess. In the first place, luncheon is an easier meal to prepare than dinner, because the food served at lunch is always simpler and less varied than at dinner. Then, too, guests do not linger after luncheon as they customarily do after dinner, thus gaining precious hours for the hostess. But quite apart from simplifying the hostess's task, a luncheon party has a personality all its own that is different and charming.

In New York these days, there is a group of hostesses who like to entertain at luncheon for precisely these reasons. They are busy women, concerned with economizing on time without sacrificing pleasure. Margaret Case, for one, a senior editor of *Vogue*, is a sturdy defender of luncheon parties: "They seem to offer an opportunity to create an especially relaxed, intimate atmosphere," she says, and she is right.

Margaret has lived a good deal in London, where the custom of lunching at home is still a pleasant survival, and where it is possible — as it is not in most American cities — to count on men to put in an appearance, weekday or no weekday. Of course London is a compact city, with residential areas close to the business districts and to Parliament and the embassies and Fleet Street, so that men needn't waste valuable time getting to and from these parties as they must in our big cities. But more than that the English — and, indeed, all Europeans — look on the midday break as precisely that: a break. And they treat it accordingly. They make it a time to relax, to refresh, to re-tool, as it were, for the working hours ahead. I am all for that. In fact, if anyone should ask me I should be delighted to launch a new Woman's Party for the Return to the Leisurely Lunch Hour in America. However, as this is not a platform apt to sweep the country with any great success, I will compromise by urging women to return to the graceful custom of company for lunch, calendar permitting.

Still another short-form method of entertaining which has died of neglect is the mixed afternoon tea. Gone With the Cocktail Party might be the epitaph on the grave of this gentle custom, and for this, too, I must blame men. Apparently it is no longer considered quite manly to be caught in public after five o'clock in the afternoon with anything less stimulating than a glass of 90 proof and soda. Just why the average man should feel he is putting his virility to question the minute he picks up a cup of tea is beyond me, but it is a fact that he does and that because he does tea parties per se have now passed irrevocably into the realm of women. This is too bad, for while most women enjoy the aura of elegance that hovers about a tea table they would enjoy it a great deal more if there could be men around to decorate the scene. But modern late-day entertaining has arbitrarily divided itself into two camps: the tea party without men, or the cocktail party with. Why not a compromise? Why not an afternoon party where the sexes meet halfway — tea for the women, a bar for the men? Of course the men might on occasion find their territory under invasion, but let them worry about that.

Not that I have anything against the all-female tea party, although that is a specialized form of entertaining and one not all women enjoy. Personally I'm all in favor of an occasional get-together with The Girls, although I can think of little drearier than a steady diet of afternoons surrounded by nothing but great gaggles of women. Still, an absence of men from a party has its merits now and then. Left to themselves, women will let down their hair, become less self-conscious and consequently more enjoyable. All the same I see no point in herding women together simply for the sake of a good gossip or to guess the price of each other's hats.

If you would segregate the sex, let there be a better reason. A tea is fine if it does duty as the monthly committee meeting, or serves as a recruiting rally for a pet charity, or celebrates an engagement or an expected baby or some other vital statistic. Or if it merely provides solid diversion. Card teas are always fun; playing for prizes or money stakes, or just for the love of the game, puts teeth into what otherwise might be no more than a few tepid hours of talk and food, agreeable though both may be.

The food one traditionally serves at teas is, in fact, a point in their disfavor for the self-help hostess. Variety is always the keynote, and this practice is further complicated by the need most women seem to feel to compete for catering honors when they entertain at tea. Perhaps they feel that they are compensating for the absence of men by going all out to titillate the palate, or perhaps it is simply that there really *isn't* anything very exciting about a plain cup of tea and exciting food makes up for it. Whatever the reason, all this stress on abundance has an unfortunate tendency to spiral, so that the woman who gives a tea one week and serves a half-dozen different kinds of sandwiches is almost certain to find herself at a neighbor's tea the next week taking her choice of no less than a dozen.

Competitive entertaining in any area is not only nonsense; it is self-defeating. No hostess whose main concern when she gives a party is to make an enviable impression is going to be able to forget it for one minute, with the result that she becomes self-conscious and that, willy-nilly, her self-consciousness rubs off on her guests so that all guards go up and no one is happy. I may be sounding awfully like Elsa the Glad Girl with all this insistence that the only good hostess is the hostess capable of placing guest before self, but you can believe me it is true.

But whether or not she is vying for honors, custom obliges the woman who entertains at tea to offer such a variegated board that, what with the kitchen labor involved and the paraphernalia entailed in pouring and serving, the average self-help hostess will be given urgently to think before she undertakes a tea of any size.

A mixed afternoon party, where both tea and cocktails are served, seems to me a civilized compromise. Food at such a party needn't be nearly so elaborate. For one thing women long to keep alive in men's minds the fiction that they are ethereal creatures, capable of subsisting on little more than air; they'd sooner be caught dead than have men see them foraging up and down Everests of calories. And men want food that accompanies cocktails to be plain, absorbent, and identifiable. So at this kind of party the hostess can forget variety and concentrate on quality: simple food and plenty of it.

Little though I may like it, I am aware that the cocktail party, unalloyed, is with us to stay. I should have to be totally deaf to be ignorant of the fact that we live in a cocktail culture, whose unlovely symbol is the ring on the best mahogany, for this is forever being pointed out to me by sociologically minded friends who, no doubt, believe my antipathy to cocktail parties stems from personal bias. Not at all.

It is true that, except for an occasional glass of wine or beer,

I do not drink. But the reason I do not drink has nothing to do with disapproval of those who do. I do not drink simply because I have never needed to drink. I was born feeling gay, so why bother?

By all means let those who need the stimulation of cocktails take them, so long as they don't take too many — which is too often the case. To drink enough and no more is admirable, but to drink too much abominable. People are not gay when drunk, they have no imagination when drunk, they have no conversation when drunk. In short, they bore — and therein lies my grievance against cocktail parties. Or, rather, what cocktails parties have become.

Whoever coined the phrase "cocktail hour" should have lived longer. The term may still apply to the warm-up period before dinner in many households, but it bears about the same relation to the three- and four-hour drinking skirmishes now in style as an air rifle to the atomic bomb. "Come for cocktails," say the invitations, "six to eight." And the marathon is on. But not at six. People seem to have a morbid dread of arriving on time for a cocktail party. Perhaps they feel a certain constraint about being first at the bar. Or perhaps they are wiser than I give them credit for, and are simply forestalling the evil hour. In any case, no one is ever on time, either to arrive or to leave. Eight o'clock comes and goes unnoticed by all but the poor hostess, while the diehards carry on (I am talking here about the dedicated or elite-guard cocktail-party type, and they are legion), trusting to the small, gelid arrangements of old anchovies and cheese on damp bread which turn up from time to time to cushion the alcoholic assault on their insides. This, in the name of pleasure!

Perhaps we are, after all, a race of masochists. I can think of no other logical explanation for the persistence with which people go on giving cocktail parties, and the apparent joy people take in going to them. Personally, unless I am very sure of my hostess and therefore of the people I will meet in her house — or, of course, unless the occasion is one of professional demand — I do my best to avoid them. For I have come to the hard-earned conclusion that in nine cases out of ten the people who are invited to cocktail parties are the people your host has not thought worth inviting either to luncheon or to dinner — so why, I ask, should I bother with them?

The cocktail party host may or may not be knocking names off a list of people he "owes" in the least troublesome way he can, but the chances are good that he *is* troubling a fellow host. Ah, the dinners that have spoiled, the promising introductions botched, because some poor wretch at a cocktail party hasn't had the sense to say no to that fifth Martini! It is all very well to say of your guests, "They're great big grown-up people. If they don't know when to stop, whose fault is it?" Certainly no one should drink who doesn't know his capacity, but even a seasoned drinker makes mistakes and the commonest cause of his mistakes is that nothing is done at the average cocktail party to remind him that it is time to stop. This is a *pre-dinner* party, he tells himself, blandly ignoring his watch, and as long as this pre-dinner party goes on, whether it be until eight, nine, or ten o'clock, he feels he is observing the ground rules by staying with it. From cloudland, dinner looks a remote circumstance. So why not face him with it? To be sure, a cocktail party without food (I mean *real* food) is a relatively easy party to give, but *somebody* must take all those anchovies out of the cans and slice the cheese and butter the bread. Why not go a step further, and have ready a few simple supper dishes? No need to put yourself out on a limb by calling it dinner. Tell your guests simply that there will be cocktails and a simple buffet and let it be exactly that. But do in pity's name provide the poor creatures with something solid to eat. Alcoholism, we are told by compilers of ominous figures, is rapidly on the increase in America. Surely part of the blame must rest with the degeneration of what started out as reasonably civilized gatherings into drinking bouts, pure and simple.

All this by way of inveighing against. Now I must straddle the fence by conceding that there are sometimes valid reasons for cocktail parties. Politicians, business and professional people can't sensibly do more: when a congressman wants to be put on record by the press, when a cosmetics firm wants to introduce a new lipstick, when Marilyn Monroe wants to announce herself incorporated to the greater glory of Dostoevski, a cocktail party is the obvious means — the cheapest, shortest, and least arduous way of shaking hands with the greatest number of people in the shortest possible time.

These parties serve a definite purpose, and so, I believe, should the purely social cocktail party, if such there must be. It is beyond my powers of belief that the average woman could *enjoy* a mob milling about the premises solely for the purpose of receiving free drinks. As with a tea, if you must have a cocktail party let there be a reason. An out-of-town guest to be introduced, a prospective son-in-law put on display, or merely a new piece of furniture to be shown off — whatever it is, have a reason.

Then, too, make it a small party. Size is a virtue at a business cocktail party, but it is killing in the home. Assume, for instance, that you have planned a cocktail party to introduce a new personality to your friends. You invite, say, fifty guests. Each of the fifty is asked presumably because you believe he or she will enjoy meeting and talking to the guest of honor, and vice versa. But what chance, pray, has anyone to talk anything but idiocies when he is in competition with forty-nine others? Rather give five small parties of ten guests each, where decent conversation is possible and where your guest of honor will not be overwhelmed by numbers, and will have a chance to note and remember individual names and faces. This is simple kindness. Cocktail parties are stupefying enough without resort to mass anesthesia.

Dinner parties are, of course, the backbone of all entertaining. Considering that this is so, it is astonishing how many hostesses turn them into unqualified disasters. Food badly prepared and badly served is the surest way to guarantee an evening that flops, and later on I am going to discuss food and what to do about it at greater length.

But food alone does not make or break a dinner party. That is in the hands of the hostess and the atmosphere she creates for her guests. She is the pace setter. If she is relaxed and confident of pleasing, she will succeed. If she is tense and ill at ease, she will fail. Here is where suiting your party to your manner of living is important.

What if you can't singlehandedly manage a sit-down dinner for eight? Nowadays, with so many women doing without help, informality is accepted and even welcomed. What's wrong with a big bubbly pot of beans on the buffet (always provided they are good beans, of course), a salad, a loaf, and everybody to help himself — if that is the kind of party you are best equipped to give? Never entertain in a way that puts a strain on you. Never try to give dinner parties that are too large or too complicated for you to handle easily. On the other hand, if the buffet supper is your preference, beware of growing *too* casual. Everyone, I am sure, has experienced the oversubscribed small-apartment party where some poor devil must either stand huddled in a corner, or crouch, bone-sore, on the floor to eat his dinner, all in the name of "casual" entertaining. I'm all for casualness if it is also comfortable and pleasant, but don't let it run away with you.

By the same token, small seated dinners can turn into small seated nightmares if the hostess is unskilled in that form of entertaining. Choice of guests here is of the greatest importance, for if the hostess is unwise in those she brings together and is not herself conversationally deft she may find herself helpless in the hearing of talk that grows contrived and therefore deadly. Or again she may try to keep the mood so all-fired sedate that the guests are soon breathing glacial air.

To you who are young and just trying your wings at party-giving, I say look at yourself, look at your friends, look at your house, look at your budget, and design your parties to suit your needs and capacities. Don't be afraid to experiment. That is the only way you will learn what is best for you. And once you have learned (and I say this to old hands as well), don't be afraid to innovate. Stay within the framework that suits you, but don't formulize your parties to the point that your guests arrive wearily certain of what they are to eat, whom they will meet, and what they will talk about down to the last comma. Sameness is the dullest thing on earth. Give something new — if it is only a new face, a new game, a new way to glamorize macaroni.

My own preference in parties is not easy to choose, for I have yet to give a party of any kind that I didn't enjoy. But perhaps the parties that give me the greatest personal pleasure are the buffet suppers which I have given every Sunday night for the past four or five years during the fall and winter months when I am living in New York. These are the most informal parties imaginable. No one needs a special invitation. My friends know that they are wanted and welcome, and they come if they can — usually about twenty to thirty in all. My apartment at the Waldorf is too small to accommodate this number comfortably, so I take over one of the hotel's private suites. A buffet supper is set up to be served at nine o'clock, and all who come know they can count on a good game of cards — usually Canasta or bridge — good talk, and good food. Because the guest list fluctuates from week to week, and because the buffet is ample, varied, and unfailingly perfect, there is no stigma of sameness at these parties. The mood is gay and relaxed. Nobody dresses. Nobody cares. Least of all the hostess, who may have the best time of all!

To me this is the ideal way to give a party, and it is the kind that can easily be managed in anyone's home. Not every week, I hasten to say, but there is no reason why the same open-house principle can't apply at whatever time you choose to entertain. Simply let your friends know that they will be welcome on such and such a date, from such and such a time on, set up a few card tables, put on your most comfortable clothes, and relax with your guests. As to food, make it a movable feast, with plenty of good, simple food on the back of the stove — enough for all, including any who may drop in unexpectedly. I guarantee you'll have a successful, fondly remembered party.

Always remember that your first duty as a hostess is to your guests, and that that duty begins at the door. Arriving guests must be made to feel instantly welcome, and this you can only accomplish by having your welcome ready. If the first ring of the bell finds you in the kitchen frantically throwing together the dessert sauce, or in the bedroom just wriggling into your dress, or for any other reason among the missing, you will have contributed a decided damper to the evening.

Being late to your own party is inexcusable. One of the best-known hostesses in New York, a woman who entertains royally and, for the most part, well, is habitually late — often as much as three quarters of an hour — to her own parties. No one has yet been able to figure out why. Her house is fully and expertly staffed. She has had long experience as a hostess. There is absolutely no reason for her chronic lateness — which is also chronic rudeness — and yet it is now so taken for granted by her friends that they treat it as a joke. But it is no joke. It is, in fact, a bore. Guests take for granted that they have been invited to a party because their hostess likes them and looks forward to their company. It is deflating to say the least to find that, after all, she apparently cares so little that she cannot even take the trouble to receive you. Close friends may shrug it off as just another of poor Ruthie's vagaries. But less intimate friends who arrive on tick, subscribing to the old view that promptness is the politeness of kings, have every right to feel offended when their courteously timed entrances go ignored. The good hostess must have tact, and in entertaining as elsewhere, timing is an important part of tact.

First arrivals at your party, if they are not intimates, can create a little frost. *You* may be as relaxed as all get-out, but you can't be sure that newcomers to your circle are. Particularly when they arrive first into the pre-party hush are you likely to find yourself in need of an icebreaker. One way is to press one or two of your more carbonated friends into arriving early — people who chat easily and can be counted on to unbend the reserve that is the social armor of the shy or introvertish or just plain nervous. Or music of the right sort (and, please, not too loud) will create a pleasant party background until others arrive and conversation takes over. I am a great believer in the companionship of sound, and I have often observed how much more quickly guests are put at ease when they enter a room in which there is some sort of sociable-sounding noise going on in the background. I suppose I have in mind the burble of conversation that greets you when you enter a restaurant. It is warm, reassuring, it melts the feeling of insecurity and diminishes self-consciousness.

Another disarming, if small, device for making guests feel welcome is a guestbook. There must be something about affixing one's name to a more or less durable record that hints at immortality. At any rate, people seem to love doing it. Too, a guestbook is a handy log for the hostess as a reminder of who came when to dinner, besides leaving her with a tasteful collection of little messages by which to remember each.

Guestbook entries run naturally to pleasantry — they could scarcely do otherwise — but I recall one occasion when the sweetness-and-light dictum was dealt a walloping sock to the eye. This was in Hollywood back in the mid-thirties, and the doer of the deed was that pillar of the English theater, Mrs. Patrick Campbell.

Mrs. Campbell, after a long, futile courtship from Hollywood, had finally succumbed to the blandishments of Louis B. Mayer and consented to make a film there. The picture, her first, was called *Riptide* and starred Norma Shearer, then reigning player on the Metro-Goldwyn-Mayer lot.

Mrs. Campbell was past seventy at the time, and there were those who wondered how she'd lived so long, for she had by all counts unmatched and unchallenged claim to the wickedest tongue on two continents. Age didn't soften her. I knew Stella fairly well and saw her on and off through the years, and I sometimes suspect that she kept in training by gargling with lye. At all events, when she made her descent on Hollywood she was at the top of her form.

The guestbook incident took place at a luncheon given by Mayer for the *Riptide* company the day before the picture went into production, and it was preceded by one of those little social contretemps that give the most case-hardened hosts nightmares. Shearer, who had never met Mrs. Campbell, had already arrived at the Mayers' beach house when the great English star made her entrance. Shearer greeted her warmly. She felt sincerely that it was an honor and a privilege to have Mrs. Campbell in the picture with her, and she told her so.

Mrs. Campbell took the compliment graciously enough; but then, having evidently decided, as Gerald du Maurier once said of her in a like circumstance, "to make a meal of the little American actress," she turned her kindliest cannibal smile on Norma.

"And I, my dear Miss Shearer," she said in her wonderful throaty voice, "look forward so much to acting with *you* — you with your beautiful little *tiny*, ti-ny eyes!"

With this as an opener, it is small wonder the Mayers' party did not turn out to be the jolliest on record, but Mrs. Campbell was not in the least repentant. She had no use at all for people she was able to bully. She liked only those who stood up to her, and as the rest of the guests not unnaturally kept a wary distance from her for the balance of the afternoon, leaving her in solitary command of the arena, she was soon bored stiff.

Nor did she make any bones about it. For when Mayer offered her his guestbook to sign, she expressed her sentiments in one simple, derivative, and cruelly to the point line: "Quoth the raven — Stella Campbell."

Introductions, which should be one of the simplest duties for a hostess, often are not, partly because this chore necessarily falls on her at a time when her head may still be reeling from last-minute seeing-to, and partly because many women make it harder for themselves by going to ridiculous lengths to see that everybody has everybody else neatly sorted, tagged, and put in the proper slot.

I don't suppose the hostess lives who hasn't at one time or another experienced the panic of forgetting or confusing a name in the middle of an introduction — often as not the name of someone as close to her as her own mother. When you are giving a large party and everyone arrives at once and you have just remembered you forgot to order ice or just discovered the cook's been into the gin again, it isn't easy to keep a firm grip on the senses. There is nothing to do about a muddled introduction but laugh it off and start again. No one will be offended by a slip of the tongue or a slip of the memory, providing you carry it off as a joke and don't go to embarrassing lengths to try to cover up.

A far worse error, to my way of thinking, and one of the surest ways I know to throw guests off conversational balance, is to tag labels on each and every guest as introductions are made. Most people enjoy discovering others for themselves, and you may well be putting a hopeless crimp in the chance of two people finding they have something in common if you start them off with, "Mrs. Smith, may I present Mr. Jones, the celebrated uranium prospector," and to Mr. Jones, "Mrs. Smith paints the loveliest flowers on china." The chances are that Mr. Jones and Mrs. Smith will flee in alarm from a conversation pre-doomed by such mutually exclusive interests and never get around to discovering that they are, in fact, both addicted to whittling or Bette Davis or collecting old baseball scores. We all have something of the bloodhound in us. We all like to do our own tracking down. A new acquaintance is both a mystery and a challenge. Let your guests do their own sleuthing.

There are times, of course, when exceptions must be made. If, for example, you have invited to your party a truly distinguished personality whose face and name are not familiar to the rest of your guests, he should certainly be identified. If I, say, were to invite to one of my parties a newly appointed delegate to the United Nations it would be only courteous to see that the rest of my guests knew who he was. Come to that, it is only playing it safe to pin on labels where any political figures are concerned. All sorts of innocent blunders can be made in the name of political forthrightness. But the main thing is to make sure that respect will be accorded anyone whose position commands it.

Too, it is well to identify members of your family who are unknown to your friends. It is also discreet. No one wants suddenly to discover that that nice woman to whom he's just remarked on how well the hostess is looking, but how did she ever get tangled up with that dreary little man, is in fact the hostess's mother-in-law. For the same reason it is good sense to identify your husband's boss and business associates. No one is deliberately going to invite character assassins into his own parlor, but there's no sense taking chances.

But verbal identifications with each introduction are awkward. In cases where you feel it advisable to make sure names and occupations are understood it is best to do it beforehand. To illustrate: a few years ago in London, Rebecca West gave a dinner for me at the Athenæum Club. Knowing that I didn't know most of the other guests, a few days before the party she sent me a letter listing their names and a little synopsis explaining who each one was, what he did, etc. Since nothing pleases people more than their names being known, her guests were all delighted that I knew who they were. The dinner, of course, was a great success.

At a small party the simplest introduction is an announcement at large — each name mentioned clearly, and the newcomer's given once or more, as seems necessary. He may then be ushered to a place by whoever you think he'll find most congenial, or left to his own devices if he has friends in the company.

At a large party it is madness to attempt introductions all the way around. Present your newcomers to a few people chosen with a view to quick compatibility, after which they should be able to find their way around unassisted. The very fact that people are guests under the same roof is, or should be, sufficient bond to eliminate any tendency to stand-offishness. Let them alone. Let like find like: you may be sure they will.

Of course there will always be problem guests in need of the hostess's steadying hand. All the shy, difficult of approach people must be looked after and buoyed up, but this is a difficult order for a hostess at a large party. She cannot be expected to divert her whole attention from the rest of her guests for the sake of one timid soul. And it is invariably at large parties that the reluctant mixer becomes a problem. In a small group where general conversation is possible she (and it is almost certain to be a she) is less of a headache, for if she has the power of speech at all she will darned well have to use it; she may not ask questions, but she will certainly have to give answers. But in a large group she needs firm taking in charge.

Large, cheerful collections of people reduce her to jelly and she approaches them in a frame of mind not unlike the lamb's before slaughter.

When I give a large party, knowing that I cannot be all things to all guests at all times, I delegate deputy hosts to take care of these timid souls for me. Wives, of course, can count on husbands to take a share of the hosting duties, but at a very large party even two people cannot adequately carry the load. Then it is only sensible to ask a few close friends to help you in seeing that no one goes hungry or thirsty or bored. You cannot be in all places at once and no one expects you to be, but you must be sure at all times that no single guest is allowed to feel neglected.

Even at a small party it is often a good idea for a woman entertaining alone to ask a man to act as host. Among other things, he can see to the bar, for most women are careless or uncaring as bartenders. More especially, he can make other male guests his special province, leaving the hostess free to concentrate on the comfort of the ladies. This works both ways. I very often act as hostess for a man who is going it alone. Of course, a co-host is primarily useful as an extra pair of hands at a party where the guests are all intimates, but where there are to be any unknowns or unpredictables in the picture and you cannot feel sure of giving each his expected due, he is also a comfortable safeguard against unintentioned slights.

Not that I mean to suggest worrying guests witless. There is such a thing as the oversolicitous hostess, and I'll come to her. But equally irritating is the hostess who is so ardently laissez-faire in her attitude toward her guests that the poor guests may well begin to wonder why they were invited in the first place. As I have said before, I am all in favor of casualness at a party. In fact, without an agreeable amount of it any party is doomed. Yet actually it requires as much of a hostess's attention artfully to leave guests to their own amusements as it does to ride herd on them. One's eye must always be on the lookout for the empty glass, the empty plate, the sudden ominous quiet from the corner where the conversational wind has died. This can be accomplished with every air of casualness, but casualness is a far cry from indifference.

The oversolicitous hostess, on the other hand, is so bent on keeping her guests happy that she completely overdoes and ends by making them, in fact, miserable. This is the woman who hovers, nags, badgers, frets, interrupts, and dashes about pressing unwanted food and drink on you as though convinced she is providing you with your last square meal on earth. It is madness to worry at your guests like a dog at a bone; but many hostesses, particularly the inexperienced, are guilty of this. Their motives are kindly enough. They seek only to assure you that your every comfort and pleasure is their command. Unfortunately, in the course of making this point, they manage also to convey the suspicion that you are not altogether capable of independent thought. You must be led. You must be moved about from place to place like a pawn on a chessboard. You are not permitted to carry on the conversation of your choice for longer than is seemly in her watchful eye. At a given moment you are unceremoniously hiked off to talk to this one or that. It is a little like finding yourself in a slowly revolving cement mixer.

As a rule this need to bedevil and harass her guests seizes a hostess during the postlude to dinner, which is, in fact, the critical period at any party — the time when the talent of the hostess comes into full play. The start of a dinner party is, or should be, the least worrisome time. Guests arrive; they assemble. They greet one another or are introduced. Cocktails are served. There is a natural spontaneity and buoyancy at this moment when new friends and old meet and talk. At this stage the hostess can pretty well rely on her guests to carry the party themselves. Nor at dinner should she have much cause to worry, so long as she has one or two conversational crackers to toss into the air if need arises.

But after dinner, after the guests have wined and dined — ah, there the rub begins. Novelty has worn off, conversation perhaps dwindled, ennui settled like dust on satisfied stomachs and heads. Here is where the good hostess shows her stuff. If she is wise she will be content to keep her finger on the pulse of her party, holding up her sleeve a trick to be used only if the lethargy threatens to last. If she is not wise she will hear the death knell in the temporary lull and be galvanized into spasms of senseless activity.

When you give a dinner party you must make up your mind beforehand what you are going to do with the hours of famine that all too often follow the feast. Plan some diversion to carry the party into the evening — but do, in pity's name, be prepared to scuttle the best-laid plan if you find, when the time comes, that it must be forced on unwilling guests. If your party is flowing serenely after dinner and people are comfortably settled and at ease, obviously enjoying themselves, don't disturb them. If, for instance, it is the kind of dinner party to which the Duchess of Argyll invited me recently in England, where the guests were all people of wit and originality who set the spark spontaneously and spontaneously kept it aglow, then the evening will fly as that one did on the wings of words alone. (That one could hardly have failed, for Noel Coward, who is one of the wittiest men alive, was there, along with Mrs. John Ward and the ambassadors from France and Spain and others who are first-rate conversationalists.) It would be madness to interrupt such a gathering simply because you'd got it into your head that nothing would do but charades. When you force guests to play games or do anything else just because you've planned it, it is the end of an evening. If your guests are happy leave them to it. That's what they're there for. The time to nip in is when you see people being bored into the first stages of *rigor mortis.*

Games of all sorts are the most reliable stand-bys for the hostess with an unforeseeable evening on her hands. Dancing is another tried-and-true pastime, especially for the young. All you need for a dancing party is a good phonograph, a collection of records, floors that wear well, and tolerant neighbors.

An alternate form of amusement, and one that assumes as many forms as an amoeba and is sometimes as deadly, is the musical evening without dancing. Now I would be biting the hands that feed me if I were to take a foursquare stand against playing and singing at parties. I've built the niche I occupy in this world out of uncounted pianos, and well I know it. Everybody loves to sing — half the world, I am convinced, feels the concert stage is a poorer place for their absence from it — and at no time does this urge to give voice come out in fuller force than in the convivial climate of a party.

Music is the greatest unbender in the world, more so than anything that ever came out of a bottle, and music injected into a party at the right time, in the right place, and in the right way, is a sure cure for any stiffness that may have crept into the proceedings. Particularly is this so when people of importance are involved and dignity threatens to get the upper hand. One night a few winters ago I dined in Washington with the

Ambassador from Turkey, Feridun Erkin, and his wife. Madame Erkin, by the way, is a singer of extraordinary talent and enjoys the distinction of having been Leopold Stokowski's only pupil; in fact, it was at Stokowski's house in New York that I first met the Erkins. This night in Washington they had mustered the best of Capital society: Secretary of State and Mrs. John Foster Dulles were there; Secretary of the Treasury and Mrs. Humphrey; Senator and Mrs. Hickenlooper; our new Ambassador to Japan, Douglas MacArthur II, and his Wa-Wee; Chief of Air Operations General Twining and his wife; and several others. In short, enough big brass to freight the air so heavily with dignity that gaiety, had it been allowed to, might have died aborning. But after dinner Wa-Wee MacArthur and I took possession of the grand piano and, with Mrs. Dulles and Mrs. Humphrey, formed an impromptu barbershop quartet. As you may imagine, as we gave out with the old songs protocol flew out the window. Everybody had requests for favorites. Mrs. Dulles's both amused and touched me. She asked, rather wistfully, if I could play "Lover Come Back to Me."

That evening at the Erkins' has been repeated in like kind hundreds of times over in my career, so I speak as an authority when I say that a good piano — or, for that matter, a good accordion or fiddle or harmonica or musical saw or what will you — will save your party from the doldrums *if* — and it is a big one — IF your guests are in the mood either to listen willingly or to join in. If, for instance, I had plumped myself down at the Erkins' piano that night and played away to my heart's content and to no one else's — if, in short, I had found I was merely creating a noise and a detriment to conversation — I would have stopped like a shot.

Music, like everything else at a party, must be a shared enjoyment. You will not be running much risk of boring your guests if you have on hand a clever musician with a bagful of clever songs, or popular songs in which others can join, but at the first sign of disinterest, the first restless drifting away from the piano, pitch it down. If music does not pull people together then it belongs in the background. And I mean *background*. Never, never force music on unwilling ears.

This is all too often done. Unfortunately, we in America have turned into a race of noise maniacs. We love noise, the louder the better, and nowadays with the craze for such sonic improvements as Hi-Fi and FM amounting to a national disease, no eardrum is safe. True tonal reproduction of great music is a marvelous thing, but like a great many other marvels it suffers abuses. Who among you has not been forced to sit through an evening while an amplifier thunders and screeches canned music into your captive ears? Perhaps your host has just invested a month's wages in the latest and best of electronic equipment, the better to hear by. That is no reason to saddle a suffering friend with the need to invest a month of *his* wages in an ear specialist.

A group brought together for the express purpose of listening to good music is the only excuse for volume. In a gathering of different interests it will only dull the wits (if it doesn't entirely unseat them) and kill conversation. Perhaps, after all, that is what all this accent on noise is about. Certainly conversation as an art in our modern society is moribund, if not altogether dead. Perhaps we are simply using noise to conceal the fact that we have nothing to say.

Whatever the musical talent you provide in the way of entertainment, do in pity's name be sure it *is* talent. Better a fine recording than a second- or third-rate artist cluttering up the air. I like musical parties just fine if they're good. But they rarely are, because the people who give them don't have good artists. One of my pet dislikes, and one which I hereby nominate for speedy oblivion, is the so-called "musicale" where, nine times in ten, the stringed quartet or coloratura or harpsichordist are giving their all strictly from hunger. If they were truly fine performers they wouldn't need to rely on culturally minded patrons for their keep; they'd be playing to admission prices on a legitimate stage.

To give the devil his due, it is the perpetrators of these dreadful little affairs who deserve the blame. You are urged by some well-meaning friend to come to dine and afterwards to hear "the most extraordinary little soprano — quite remarkable, my dear," and if you are unwise you go and the extraordinary little soprano turns out to be a quite ordinary little pair of lungs whose art seems to hinge chiefly on practicing breath control. Moreover, you are expected to give full and respectful attention to this mediocrity — and woe betide the bored one who risks a fretful whisper! Your hostess is instantly shishing and shushing at you and you must collapse back into obedient attention, broken only by furtive peeks at your wrist watch.

When I have artists to entertain I have the tops. Of course, if you would have the best you must pay for it. Most good artists dislike party performances and consequently set fees that are generally prohibitive. All the same, if you can't afford to hire top entertainers you are better off with none.

Hiring artists to entertain at your parties is one thing. Inviting them on a purely social basis and then expecting them to exhibit their talent is unpardonable. Musical artists are peculiarly vulnerable to this sort of advantage-taking. No one, after all, would dream of asking Picasso to run up a little still-life, or Willie Maugham to dash off a little essay, but singers and musicians are all too often bidden to go through their paces like so many trained dogs. I make it a rule never to ask a distinguished artist to perform at my parties unless it has been specifically arranged for beforehand. Naturally, if such an artist elects voluntarily to sing or play I am enchanted, but that seldom happens.

At the risk of rousing the spleen of proud mamas and papas the world over, one further plea I must make in regard to home entertainment is the heartfelt one that you do, for heaven's sake, leave the children out of it. With few exceptions even the best of child entertainers are anathema to most of us, and the homebred variety are pure poison. As a matter of fact, showing off the children is generally a pretty painful procedure for the children themselves, unless their little egos are inflated out of all proportion to age and size. More than one tender id has limped into maturity the worse for parents who could not control the urge to showcase their young when company came.

Leave little Gwennie and Freddie to their simple childhood games or, better still, after a quick introduction around, to bed. I realize this sounds grumpy and unfeeling and that there are those who will complain, "You don't understand. You've never been a mother." Quite true. That does not mean I don't like children. I do. I fully agree with the sentiment of the Japanese poet, Kenko, who wrote that "too many children in a house, there can never be." But too many at the grownups' party — ah, that is something else again. Let them be seen. Let them be admired. Let them stay around long enough to pass the peanuts and be made over, and that is all. No songs. No dances. No stumbling recitations. No encouragement to take part in conversation to which they can't possibly contribute intelligently.

Further, I would extend this boycott of family talent to the grownups in the house as well. Father may be the finest baritone since Tibbett in the estimation of his loved ones, but the chances are good he ought to confine his talents to the shower. Happy Chandler, who is one of the nicest, sweetest people I know, is also unfortunately a tireless singer at parties. When Happy was in the Senate I used to run into him often at Washington parties. He and his wife and daughter would sing trio. The three of them, in fact, were so enamored of themselves singing trio, and so certain that everybody else was enamored of them singing trio, that they never stopped. They sang and sang and *sang*. They weren't bad, but they weren't good either. It got to be a little too much to have to go to parties and hear Happy and his folks forever singing.

Take it from me, family accomplishments are generally mediocre to everyone but the family. If people are really good they won't perform at all. A great pianist is impossible to get to the piano, but show a mediocre talent a piano and there's no holding him. Just keep in mind that when you judge the abilities of those you love you are adding a dimension of tribal pride to your thinking that others can't possibly share.

In the main I have been talking here about the married hostess who entertains in her own home. Now I want to say a word to the single women — and there are thousands of them — who, like myself, live in hotels or small apartments where it is not always comfortable or easy or in some cases even possible to entertain at luncheon or dinner as one might wish to. Women who work, in particular, are almost certain to be too busy or too tired at day's end to take the time required to plan and produce the perfect little dinner for six, even if small quarters provide adequate kitchen and dining facilities, which they often do not. My own kitchen at the Waldorf is tidy and compact and ideal for turning out a simple luncheon or dinner for two or three, but I would think twice before I tried to put it to use for any more complicated meal. (Not that I couldn't if I had to. I am, if I may be permitted another boast, a very good cook.)

The obvious answer to the problem is a restaurant. So here, now, a few dos and don'ts for the woman who entertains alone at a restaurant.

To begin with, it is advisable to choose one place and stick to it. Shop around, if you must. Have lunch at likely-looking prospects until you find one where you can be sure the food and service and, most important, the right-hand side of the menu are to your liking. Choose a quiet, elegant place, or as elegant as you can afford, where the atmosphere is at least a reasonable facsimile of a pleasant home setting — nothing big and brassy and nightclubby.

Early in your dealings with a new restaurant it is well to pay a personal call on the captain when you are planning a dinner party, to talk over ways and means. It will not only please him to have the benefit of your confidence, it will assure you of his personal interest in and attention to your party. With him you can choose the most suitable table, arrange for flowers, select wines and, if the party is to be large, decide on the menu. Order the meal beforehand only if there are to be more, say, than ten guests. In that case, you will be saving time and confusion for waiters and guests alike by planning the menu in advance. But if the party is small, let your guests order for themselves.

The stickiest problem for the woman who entertains in a restaurant is how, gracefully, to pay the check. Chivalry is not altogether dead. Men seem to suffer mortal discomfort at the sight of a woman ladling out bills in public to pay for their food and drink. It makes them feel ungallant and sheepish and that, in turn, gives women sympathetic fidgets. Here again, your personal touch-in with the captain will serve you. Either you may arrange with him to have the bill sent to you, or, if you plan to do any appreciable amount of entertaining at his restaurant and are not squeamish about adding to the first-of-the-month mail, you may open an account. Still another system which some restaurants encourage is to deposit a given sum of money with them against which you can draw, banker fashion. There are advantages to this, not the least being that your parties are paid for in advance — not a feeling I am acquainted with, but it has a comfortable sound. At all events, however you do it, be sure your bill is paid in private.

There is such a thing as giving *too* good a party, a condition you will recognize when the hour of polite departure has come and gone and you still have on your hands a roomful of people having a whale of a good time. Some people just plain don't know when to go home. Others may remind themselves to peek at the clock now and then — but then, the evening is *such* fun, and there are still volumes to be talked to So-and-so, and dear Maud, who is giving the party, looks fresh as a daisy, it would be a shame to break it up.

In such a case the dallier is certainly at fault for breaking the first rule of guestmanship, which is never to overstay a welcome. But dear Maud is also at fault for allowing her guests the impression that the place is theirs for as long as they care to make it. She is probably gritting her teeth to keep that smile in place and wondering bleakly if the sleeping six-year-old upstairs can be trusted to get his own breakfast come morning, or if the office will believe that twenty-four-hour virus story just once more.

There is absolutely no reason why a hostess should not take the bit between her own teeth when a party threatens to drag on beyond the limits of endurance and simply ask the hangers-on to go. She is foolish not to. She is only doing herself and her family a disservice by allowing the revels to continue and she is, moreover, doing her guests a disservice. Most of us lead busy lives. The chances are that a guest who has been dispatched home by his hostess will be grateful to her in the morning when he wakes with a hectic day to face and, thanks to the firm hand of his hostess, a clear head with which to face it.

Speeding lingerers can be done tactfully, the more so if the party is large. When I give a dance, for instance, and three o'clock comes I simply stop the music. This is usually signal enough that the ball is over. Another method at a large party, and one that should not be necessary but unfortunately often is, is to shut down the bar. Laggards, I find, are generally also the one-for-the-road set who do not, alas, always know how to count. Recently I heard of a resourceful hostess in Texas who brought a long-drawn-out cocktail party to a logical if risky close simply by turning off all the lights. That may work in Texas, but I think it would be a little dangerous in some of our less stately communities. (On the other hand perhaps it is more dangerous in Texas than anywhere else!)

At a small, informal party, where offstage signals aren't possible, the easiest and best way to break it up is by being frank. "Darlings," I might say, "you will simply have to forgive me. I am dead tired and I have to get to work early in the morning." No such legitimate excuse, if it is forthright and genuine, could or should be offensive to anyone, and if it is —

well then, let it be. A guest who cannot take honesty without rancor is a guest not worth having. At least, not the next time.

Worse perhaps than the dawdling guest is the dawdling hostess, the woman who sees you to the door and then seems determined to keep you there nervously shifting from one foot to the other and growing hotter and hotter inside your coat while she deplores your leaving, moans that the party will fall apart without you, assures you again and again what a delight it's been to have you, beseeches you to change your mind and stay a bit longer, makes plans for lunch on Tuesday, hopes you've *really* enjoyed yourself, and so on into the night. She means all this as flattery, of course. In her burbling, boisterous, overbearing way she is simply trying to let you know that you have put the breath of life into her party and that without you it may well die. She knows very well you will not be persuaded to stay. She regards her show of reluctance at losing you as her final duty to you as a hostess. You are meant to go off basking in the warmth of her admiration. Actually, all she manages to do is sweep you out on this rushing sea of clichés, with part of whatever pleasure you may have had during the evening drowned in the process.

When guests are ready to leave, let them leave. Let them know you've been happy in their company, bid them a fond good night, and end it. Don't clutter up your good-bys with persiflage. On the other hand, just be sure you *do* say good-by.

As bad as the hostess who is not on hand to bid her guests welcome is the hostess who can't be bothered to give each a personal farewell. The late Laurette Taylor found good-bys so odious that she refused to allow them at her parties. Not only would she not say good-by herself; she insisted that her guests make their exits as surreptitiously as possible. "There,

there!" she would cry across the room at sight of a parting exchange. "Stand not upon the order of your going — but for God's sake, go!" Laurette Taylor was an extraordinary personality, greatly loved by all who knew her, and so could get away with what in others less favored would be intolerable rudeness. Unless you choose to be known for your eccentricities rather than your charm, I would not suggest departing quite this far from rulebook behavior.

The good hostess must break rules, just as a good bridge player must sometimes break the rules of the game to take his tricks, but they must always, always, be broken within the limits of tact, good taste, discretion, and a sensitive awareness of the feelings of others. That, most of all. For the art of the hostess begins and ends in her capacity for keeping her antenna tuned to detect the first faint ripple of boredom or displeasure. How well she apprehends and considers the feelings of her guests — in the final analysis that is the quality on which the art of the good hostess depends. The bad hostess lacks it. The good hostess has it. The perfect hostess . . . ? Well, let's look at a few.

CHAPTER IV

The Perfect Hostess

— and Others

LET me introduce you to the man who killed Rasputin," Lady Emerald Cunard once announced to her guests at lunch. Not surprisingly, the Grand Duke Dmitri Pavlovich — who had indeed had a hand in dispatching the old menace — turned on· his heel and left.

Not, I grant you, an instance of behavior likely to make just anyone very, very popular as a hostess, yet such was the way of the woman who, shortly before the turn of the century, brought London society to its collective knee and kept it there for close to fifty years. Lady Cunard loved to gather her lions together, lash them with the whip of her tongue, and watch them fight to the blood. By pitting them one against another she sought to make her guests more interesting to herself, to each other, and, not at all incidentally, to exploit her own acid wit.

"Dear little Poppy," she would address an old friend. Then, turning to the others with a pleased smile, "She's been that for the past thirty-five years, haven't you, Poppy, darling?"

By such tactics Lady Cunard kept her guests in perpetual thrall to her, and because of the commanding position she occupied in the stringent social hierarchy of the day she got away with it. Few people with any hope of weathering London's social climate had the temerity to defy her. One of her few come-uppances was at the hands of one of the few opponents worthy of her — Lord Birkenhead, the great English lawyer and politician, and no mean barb-tosser himself. The occasion was a dinner given by Lady Cunard.

"Do you mind if I smoke?" Birkenhead asked, producing one of his Gargantuan cigars long before dinner was over.

"Do you mind if we eat?" Lady Cunard inquired silkily.

"Not if you do it quietly," retorted His Lordship.

But Lady Cunard's waspish and frequently cruel tongue did not lessen her effectiveness as a hostess. On the contrary, it was an intriguing part of her showmanship. Society, shocked and delighted by her antics, showed itself so endlessly willing to come back for more that Lady Cunard was kept riding the crest long after less provocative hostesses would have seen fit to bow to new and abler competition. Almost until the outbreak of war in 1939, bids to the great Cunard mansion at No. 7 Grosvenor Square were deemed tantamount to social benediction. The parties there were glittering — the musical soirees in particular, for Lady Cunard, in addition to her talents as a hostess, had great artistic taste and was a generous patron of some of the finest musical talent of the time.

Lady Cunard is a clear-cut case of the power possible to a unique and willful personality — a striking example of the hostess who, by sheer force of character, imposes and establishes herself on society. True, she had the backing of a great name and a great fortune, but the secret of her success as a hostess was her individuality as a woman. Any hostess who would run at the front of the pack must give something that is different, out of the ordinary. In Lady Cunard's case this something was provocativeness. She carried it to pretty scandalous lengths at times — perhaps taking her cue from old Rasputin himself, with his dictum of "Sin and obtain forgiveness." Certainly she often sinned against what we accept as normal standards of courtesy, but, unorthodox though her methods were, they worked. Society forgave her. For all her snobbish quiddity, her intemperate talk, when she died in 1948 those who had known her — friends and enemies alike — remembered best that she had given them that most valued of gifts: a sense of excitement. Any hostess who can do that is made, and never mind the rules. I don't recommend that you go about guying your guests into temper tantrums as Lady Cunard did — only that you keep in mind that in the long run provocativeness will stand you in better stead than all the statelier rules of deportment combined.

Lady Cunard was by all odds the most spectacular, but she was by no means the only American of her time to cut a figure in London society. From the turn of the century on, London's reigning hostesses were all Americans. There were Lady Paget, Lady Essex, Maxine Elliott. There was Lady Ribblesdale — formerly Mrs. John Jacob Astor; also Maybelle Cory — formerly Ziegfeld Follies. There was the Duchess of Marlborough, who had been Consuelo Vanderbilt and is now Mme. Jacques Balsan, and whose marriage in 1895 to the ninth Duke is generally credited with bringing on the gold rush of titled Europeans to our heiress-bound shores.

Mme. Balsan is a top-notch hostess and another of the rare ones who are liked for themselves alone: she needed neither title nor Vanderbilt money to win her social laurels. Nowadays she is at her best as hostess to a few, preferring small parties to large: no doubt she had her fill of the pomp-and-ceremony school of hospitality during her years as mistress of Blenheim Palace. Though we are no longer friends, owing to a political dispute I had with her husband in 1940, I have stayed with Mme. Balsan — at her villa at Eze, at St. George Matel in Normandy, at her beautiful houses at Palm Beach and on Long Island — so I am able to vouch for her attributes as a thoughtful and gracious hostess. To my mind her only notable lack is her failure to recognize the hypodermic value of an occasional celebrity at her parties. As a hostess of standing she could draw talent from any field she chooses, but she does not. On different occasions I introduced such notables as Fritz Kreisler, Charlie Chaplin, and Grace Moore, both to her house and to the profit of her parties, but the practice apparently didn't take hold. No hostess should ignore the stimulation value of including at least one person of note in a group — whether he be world famous or merely the town's best parcheesi player.

A great London hostess in the twenties was the irrepressible Laura Corrigan, who established a formidable handicap in the American Cinderella Derby by covering the ground from switchboard operator to rich widow in a record six months and promptly setting out to buy her way into European society. Except for her wealth — and it was prodigious — Laura's social armor was not promising. She was not beautiful, she was not educated or particularly clever — her innocent blunders of speech provided almost as much amusement, behind her back, as her parties — but she was honest, she had vitality, and she had a heart as big as her bank. Laura ran her parties like a particularly benevolent mistress of ceremonies on a well-backed giveaway show. Guests were showered with favors, and as her taste in these ran to gold and precious stones, practical-minded hypocrites found it easy to swallow their prejudices against Laura's lowly beginnings on the grounds that being her guest was the next best thing to being gainfully employed. Laura had good friends who liked her for herself, but there were many more,

I'm afraid, who toadied to her for what they could get out of it.

Yet for all her love of money show, Laura was not a money snob. She never forgot that she'd come by her millions more or less by default, and that others were not as rich as she. She went out of her way to see that guests were not obliged to dip into their own pockets for the least thing — even such incidentals as tipping: "The staff is paid extra when guests are staying with me," read signs posted in each of her guestrooms, "so they do not expect anything from you. Neither do I wish you to give it."

Laura's one snobbery was her passion for hobnobbing with royalty. As an American she was not unique in this, but she carried it to unusual extremes. Anything went — if it pleased a royal heart. For example, when games were played at her parties Laura considered the night lost if some royal participant did not make off with the richest prize, and if she had to finagle a bit to swing it — well, in Laura's book, royalty was its own excuse.

Occasionally in her zeal for cozying up to crowns she overstepped. Once, indeed, she was taken over the coals by no less a personage than the Lord Chamberlain, after she'd startled a party by persisting in calling a member of the royal family by her Christian name. But Laura took her rebuffs gamely. There was the time she planned a dinner party in honor of the late Prince George, Duke of Kent. All the invitations were out, when, on the day before the party, the Duke thought better of the idea and sent his regrets. Laura went to work, putting pressure on everyone she knew to provide a suitable royal substitute to fill the place of honor. She managed finally to commandeer King Alphonso of Spain and, with this slight change in cast, the party went off as scheduled. The hostess's explanation to her other guests? "Where a Prince refused," said Laura dryly, "a King obliged."

Probably the best-known of Lady Cunard's American contemporaries abroad — and a very different kind of woman as well as hostess — was Lady Mendl, who rose to riches neither by marrying money nor by inheriting it. She did it the hard way. She made it. As Elsie de Wolfe, Lady Mendl was the first of her sex to make a profession of interior decorating, and was the author in this capacity of ideas so revolutionary that she succeeded in changing the American taste in interiors almost overnight. It was Elsie who banished the overstuffed look from living rooms, spread the craze for chintz through houses from Maine to California (she was popularly known as "The Chintz Lady"), whitened and lightened walls and furniture, and introduced into millionaires' and luxury women's clubs the styles of Louis XIV, XV, and XVI for a profitable 10 per cent on the bills.

Entertaining for Elsie was both an art and a business. In her line one never knew: the guest of today might well be the client of tomorrow. Combining business with pleasure is seldom likely to benefit a party and for that reason has never been my way, but Elsie was clever enough never to let the mixture grow stodgy. Her parties were masterpieces, and I can say with all candor that this was in great part due to the fact that she imitated me, for Elsie admitted it herself. She came quickly to understand my guiding precept that the best you can offer your guests is the unexpected. Elsie never used the same formula twice. Her dinner parties — particularly those at her exquisite little eighteenth-century Villa Trianon at Versailles where she spent her later years — were famous equally for the novelty of the food, the glitter of the guests, and the volatile charm of the hostess, who moved through it all like the re-embodied spirit of Marie Antoinette airily treating her court to a *fête galante.*

But there was nothing airy about Elsie's preparations for a party. Where I might sometimes put my faith in luck and *le bon Dieu*, Elsie went at it like a small, alert IBM calculator that didn't quite trust the help; she trusted no one and nothing, not even her own memory. A great believer in getting it down on paper, every detail of her parties was noted and put on file, along with her business records. (Keeping up with all this paper work was no easy task, and in later years she never moved without her secretary, Hilda West, to whom she left all her money when she died. It was well earned. Elsie would start dictating in her luxurious boudoir-bathroom immediately after breakfast, and continue on and off well into the night.)

Menus and the guests that went with them were carefully catalogued, to be consulted before each new party and so avoid duplication, for while most important hostesses take the easy way of sticking to the same menu dinner after dinner, Elsie would as soon turn in a repeat performance as be caught jumping up and down on Escoffier's grave. Nor did her infinite capacity for taking pains end with the drawing up of guest lists and orders to the chef. Invariably the last minutes before the appointed hour of a party would find her, gowned and jeweled to kill, fingering tables for the least speck of dust, studying flowers for best effect from every viewpoint, checking chairs for proper placement within an inch, and last, subjecting dining room and kitchens to a scrutiny as finicking as a military inspection.

Just as my party-giving owed its original success to the elements of surprise and informality, so Elsie's success was originally founded on the excellence of her food. No hostess can ignore the necessity of providing good food, but with Elsie designing the perfect menu amounted to a fetish. She would go to any amount of trouble for the sake of learning the secret of a single dish. I can remember to this day the delight and sensation she produced among her guests one night when she introduced a recipe for cooking duck that she had found at the Walterspiel restaurant in Munich. Not content with the written recipe, she and I made a special trip to Munich so that Elsie might confer with the Walterspiel's chef — such was her perfectionism. She collected unusual recipes as she collected celebrities, knowing how well the two blend when served together.

After perfect food, Elsie's three cardinal rules for a dinner party were: cold room, hot plates, and low table decorations (no one at Elsie's table ever had to peer through something seasonal to see who was facing him!). These are rules worth chiseling into the kitchen walls to be remembered and copied. For copy all you can, I say. Imitation is often the sure way to success. For myself, I have learned little from others in the art of entertaining: for my kind of parties I have only myself to blame! But while originality has worked for me, I don't advise it for everyone. The best in art and literature has usually begun with borrowings, and so it is with the art of entertaining.

Lady Cunard was the last of London's hostesses in the grand manner — for that matter, almost the last anywhere. Today in Paris and Rome and Madrid there are still a few houses where shades of the old grandeur linger, but even where they exist they no longer serve notice on the community, as they once did, of their owners' vested right to social leadership. In Rome today, for example, society's arbiter and ranking hostess is the American-born Baroness Lo Monaco — who does, to be sure, live in a palace, but only in an apartment in a palace. Still it is a beautiful apartment, and La Moffa, as she is called, is one of the most beautiful characters I have ever known: gay, loving, an ardent Christian Scientist, incapable of saying an unkind word of anyone, the most generous woman alive, and a born hostess.

As I write this I have on the desk beside me a letter from La Moffa, full of her plans for welcome when I arrive in Rome with Millicent Hearst in a few weeks' time. This Roman interlude will be past history by the time this book is in print, but the letter is so characteristic of La Moffa's zeal for making people happy that I want to touch on it. She has spread the word of our coming throughout Rome: every day and night for the three weeks of our stay we will enjoy the Romans' special brand of hospitality. The Duchess di Sangro, writes La Moffa, is planning a dinner for us. La Moffa herself will be hostess to sixty at another dinner for us. The Aga Khan has arrived in Rome and asked her help in planning a party at which we will dance . . . So her letter goes, reading like a page from the *Almanach de Gotha*, or the *Arabian Nights*.

But if European society has been largely democratized, in England the process is complete. Postwar austerity brought stringent rationing and an increase in taxes that inevitably forced the conversion of many of the once great houses into office buildings or apartments. Trained servants took up trade and disappeared. Few people had the heart — or the means — for more than token entertaining.

Now, with the lifting of food and clothes rationing, the picture is more cheerful. Money isn't exactly rolling in the streets — taxes see to that — but postwar tensions have been largely dissipated and the air once more smells free. People are giving parties again with something of the old spirit, if not the old splash, and American hostesses have re-established themselves as among the best in London. They are doing themselves proud. More importantly, as propagators of good will, they are doing their country proud.

Anyone visiting abroad is in the peculiarly ambiguous position when he entertains of being both host and guest in his own home — host in the obvious sense, guest in the sense that he is where he is by kind leave of whatever government is making him welcome at the time. In his role as host he may express all the individuality he wants. In his role as guest it behooves him to leave as pleasing an impression on his temporary host as possible. Americans visiting abroad often forget this; particularly, it seems, Americans visiting England. Perhaps because we are richer and stronger and healthier as a nation — perhaps, too, because we are young by comparison and feel at a certain cultural disadvantage in the face of venerable British tradition — we are apt to act arrogant, showy-off, like so many unpromising children who've made good and feel impelled to call attention to the fact by stunting in front of the old folks. No one who has been exposed to the spectacle of the American tourist, *specie vulgaris*, shirted in something vaguely akin to a tropical landscape in riot and expensively hung about with cameras and binoculars and related equipment, roistering his way through a meal in a foreign restaurant with demands for faster service, rarer meat, stronger coffee — all this laced together with side glances at the natives (how come they eat that funny left-handed way?) — can fail to be grateful to the more typical group of transplants who represent the best of American character and culture. These people do a wonderful job in countering the antagonism left in all too many corners of the globe by Joe Vulgar and company — a minority that has given us, along with a reputation for highhandedness, a reputation for irreverence that is as destructive as it is undeserved.

A small example of this was the hue and cry that went up in the London press after a dance given for the Queen by former Ambassador and Mrs. Winthrop Aldrich. Some of the younger members of the Embassy staff, so went the report, had had the effrontery to cut in on Her Majesty. There wasn't a word of truth in it, of course, but it was undoubtedly accepted as fact by people conditioned by the rough-diamond element to "those boorish Americans," and is typical of the kind of molehill misunderstanding that uneasy times have been known to compound into mountains.

The Aldriches were, in fact, ideal captains for the American diplomatic and quasi-diplomatic team in London. Enormously popular themselves, they entertained beautifully at the new Embassy, which was Barbara Hutton's gift to our government. I went to a delightful party there when I was in London a few years ago. The house is set in a manicured park of several acres (which must cost a pretty penny to keep up) and is on the stately side, but under Harriet Aldrich's skillful eye and hand it had been made cozy and charming inside — ideal for the blend of personal-informal and official-formal entertaining the Aldriches were called on to do so often, and which they did so well.

Bad hostesses, as I have learned to my regret, far outnumber the good. Of course, as with everything else, the bad ones come in degrees of badness, the range being, loosely, from pretty bad to awful to downright abysmal. In this last category, my nomination for honors goes to two sisterhoods: women of rank, and so-called "good" women.

Women of rank, to be sure, can't be too harshly criticized for their failure to entertain well: obligation to duty pretty well thrusts failure upon them. While they have on the one hand the advantage of being able to hand-pick their guests from the top drawer (who, for example, would turn down an invitation from Mrs. Eisenhower or the Queen of England? Or, in a less lofty area, from the mayor's wife?), they have on the other the disadvantage of having to stand forever on dignity. For this reason they are seldom good hostesses. Too much dignity at a party of any sort is lethal. No one is going to have fun when he must be conscious every minute of observing the stodgier rules of social behavior. Conversation palls under fear of inadvertence. Everyone minds his manners to a degree that paralyzes. In these circumstances, the most interesting people in the world are bound to grow bored and, therefore, boring.

By the same token, women who put the accent on probity automatically put their parties to death. Excessive virtue may be its own reward (which I question), but in a hostess it is about as rewarding as a dose of laudanum. Although I can't claim to have done any research in the matter personally, my guess is that this is a trouble from which clergymen's wives must inevitably suffer: living under constant restraint, as they do, never yet made a good hostess.

Nowadays, of course, our views on what, in another day, constituted "badness" have come in for some strenuous revision. Modern women smoke and take cocktails and use make-up and generally carry on in ways once possible only to what our proper Victorian mamas and grandmamas called "loose" women. Less than fifty years ago in America, for instance, a woman who went on the stage was immediately branded no better than she should be, and barred by Best Society as a threat to the morals of the young and the sanctity of the home. Now, distinguished people of the theater are welcomed with open arms — indeed, they are courted — even by the old guard. Can you imagine a hostess who would not feel flattered to count Miss Ethel Barrymore among her guests?

All the same, there is still a good deal of Victorianism lurking about, and there is a diehard element of society that condemns as "bad" any who refuse to conform to what it accepts as convention — convention, here, interpreted in a string of sermonish negatives. "Nice" women, say the diehards, never go hatless; nice women never cross their legs in public; nice women are never heard to laugh aloud. Nice women dress to comply to the view that the clothes of a lady are clothes no one will either notice or remember. So the list goes on, ad well-bred nauseam. Heaven knows, I am all in favor of decorum, so long as it does not rubber-stamp individuality out of existence. What I deplore is the unfair bias that frequently stems from this kind of smug-mindedness; it judges before it weighs.

I have met, I believe, most of the important women in public life over the last fifty years, and I have found that, by and large, the higher her position in point of rank, the worse the hostess. Even when there is no need to stand on ceremony, they simply do not know how to unbend — or else feel that to do so would cause them to lose face.

A delightful exception in this category is Queen Frederika of Greece. The Queen is a wonderful hostess: friendly, solicitous, and remarkably free of the stickier observances of protocol — remarkable, in particular, when one considers that her great-grandmother was that doughtiest of unbenders, Victoria herself. Queen Frederika has probably more vivid charm than any other living sovereign. She is beautiful, she has great warmth of personality and humor, and she has with it all an energetic sense of duty and love for her country, her three children, and her husband, the handsome King Paul, that is hard to beat.

The first occasion I had to observe these two charming people close at hand was when I was in Athens in the fall of 1954 and had the good fortune to lunch with them alone. It was a delightful few hours, for the King, too, has the rare knack of putting aside the stately air of office when they entertain informally. The talk was good — better, I am compelled to admit, than the food. I suppose I had expected something typically Greek — as why not? — but there was nothing Greek about lunch at the Queen's table that day. It was plain, pleasant food in the English style: eggs Benedict first (for you menu-hounds); then a chicken dish with vegetables; salad, cheese, and a simple blanc mange for the sweet. All very good, but hardly inspired. I don't think the Queen gives much thought to food — but to say that is to quibble. She is one of the busiest women in the world, engaged in far more important matters than what's for lunch. And food notwithstanding, she is, by virtue of her singular personality and charm, a superb hostess.

But what makes me chalk up a particularly large red letter against that day is that out of our talk over lunch came the idea for what I consider the most fabulous party I have ever given — at least at this writing.

I had been in Greece for some days and I had fallen in love with both the country and her people. I had also seen with my own eyes proof of what I had previously known only by hearsay — that it is one of the poorest countries in the world.

Thinking of this: "What can I do to help Greece?" I asked the Queen.

"Bring us tourists," said the Queen — and the world's first floating publicity party was launched. (I say first, and it was, in fact, the first of its kind, size, and end result. The preceding year Queen Frederika and King Paul had been hosts on a similar cruise, but theirs was what might be called a family affair: only royal guests. Their modest idea was to call attention to Greek tourism. Mine was to shout it to the four winds.)

Well then, how to go about planning such a cruise? The logical first move seemed to be to hunt up a ship. To my surprise, it was not long coming. Stavros Niarchos, the great Greek shipowner and patriot, gave his immediate and enthusiastic support to the project and forthwith arranged to put at my disposal — entirely free of charge! — the steamship *Achilleus*, sister ship of the *Agamemnon*, which had carried the Queen's royal passengers the year before. I have been on the receiving end of many generous acts in my life, but this gift of a ship was beyond even my considerable imagination. It was also, I need hardly say, a gift I could not possibly repay in kind; I could, however, make some effort to repay in kindness. I made up my mind to do a switch on the old story of the gift-bearing Greeks. We would not go to their islands empty-handed.

The problem then was, what to take? I am well enough acquainted with the Greek character to know that adults are far too proud to accept favors for themselves. On the other hand I did not see how they could possibly refuse gifts to their children. Armed with this notion I appealed to Claude Philippe, and, as usual when the cause is worthy, he came through magnificently. A heartening number of American manufacturers responded to Philippe's request for donations, and the result was that when the *Achilleus* put to sea on a fine August day in 1955 she was loaded to the gunwales with shoes, overalls, blue jeans, sweaters, food, chocolate, and so on, which we left with the proper authorities at our various ports of call for distribution to the children of the Greek islands.

After ship and cargo, there remained the much knottier matter of working out a suitable guest list, for while it is one thing to gather a hundred or so of one's friends together in a ballroom for a few hours of partying, it is quite another to bottle up the same number for two weeks on shipboard with any feeling of confidence that knives aren't going to turn up in assorted backs before it's all over. Well, here again I was either displaying unusual prescience or playing in my usual luck: when the big

day came, one hundred and ten good friends sailed out of
Venice, and one hundred and eight good friends sailed back —
not a bad showing, all considered!

Actually, while compatibility was a major factor in determin-
ing whom to ask, it was not uppermost. This cruise was designed,
remember, with one end in view: to stimulate the widest possible public interest in Greek tourism. Obviously this could only
be achieved if the press rallied to the cause, and equally obviously the press was more likely to take an interest in the doings
aboard the *Achilleus* if her company were made up of people
with some claim to importance — social, professional or otherwise. Then, too — again with an eye to ensuring maximum
news coverage — it was important that it be an international
group. I wanted, in short, as motley a collection of names-that-
make-news in various spheres as ever joined forces to ballyhoo a
cause. I was not disappointed. At any time of day during the
voyage a stroller on deck might find himself pausing to chat with
such sundry personalities as the Met's great bass baritone, Cesare
Siepi; former French Premier Paul Reynaud and Madame Reynaud; Olivia de Havilland and her French journalist husband,
Pierre Galante; Perle Mesta; novelist Frederic Prokosch; the
Byron Foys; designer Valerian Rybar; the Duchess of West-
minster, and dozens more of like importance. In all, seven
countries in addition to the United States were represented:
England, France, Italy, Spain, Greece, Brazil, and Vene-
zuela.

As to my hope of hitting the editorial jackpot — I don't believe there was an important popular magazine or newspaper in
North America, South America, Britain or Free Europe (Iron
Curtain Europe, too, for all I know, although I doubt if *that*
would bear looking into) that did not carry the story of the
cruise, and a gratifying number of them supplemented text

with pictures. Ironically, the picture that seemed to win widest favor in the editorial eye could hardly be classified as tourist-bait. This one showed me looking jolly as all get-out, saltily attired in an admiral's jacket and cap which Jean Dessès had sent to me from Paris a few days before the sailing. I wore them, of course, as a joke, not dreaming that the uniform, with me in it, would get a bigger play in the press than all my glamour gals and guys and the glories of Greece combined. Well, no matter. If this elderly map did anything to help put Greece on the tourist map, it was all to the good.

To put the record straight, I was not paid a cent by the Greek Government or by any of its agencies to organize this cruise. Money didn't enter into it. My only motive was enthusiasm. I leaped at the idea partly because it was a chance for new adventure — which is the breath of life to me — partly because it seemed a golden opportunity to entertain some of my friends as they had never been entertained before, but most of all, perhaps, because large areas of my thinking suggest that I finished out my last incarnation as a defrocked missionary and am bucking for a return to grace in this one. No sanctimony, you understand: my methods are strictly secular. "Do good and have fun," has always been my byword, and in this case I felt that to lend a hand to the deserving people of Greece, and to do it in this way, amply filled that bill. Moreover, looked at professionally, as a sample of press-agentry the cruise was unique. Individuals, products, ideas have been publicized to the high heavens — I've sent up some pretty partisan rockets myself in the course of my career; but no one had ever before undertaken to publicize an entire country — not, at least, in my way.

This cruise, then — perhaps crusade is the better word — measured up on all counts to my canon of what a good party should be: it was novel, it was fun, and it did good. For all these reasons it gave me great personal satisfaction. From the start, my cup was full to the brim. At Athens it ran over.

On the morning after our arrival there, a reception was held at the Royal Yacht Club in order that my guests might be presented to the King and Queen of the Hellenes. The party took place on the wide terrace of the club, which is reached from the entrance by a stairway. When the time came, I stood at the head of the stairs to welcome Their Majesties.

The Queen clapped me on the shoulder. "Elsa," she said with approval, "you made it!"

As one hostess to another, what nicer compliment could you ask?

Official parties are noisome businesses the world over, in America as elsewhere. Political parties, in particular, in my book, come under the head of cruel and unusual punishments. I have hardly ever been to one that wasn't a disaster.

To begin with, since these horrors are put together with no thought but of what is expedient, the majority wind up with masses of people who don't like each other standing around in grim little knots doing their best to look polite about it. At dinner, assuming there are any in the company you would like to talk to, there is little chance you'll succeed, for seating is by the strictest protocol. Assume, say, that some foreign secretary and his wife are among the guests. They are given the places of honor at the head of the table, and other less important guests are placed in descending order right down the length of the table. Because I have no position, I am always placed at the end, which enables me to observe the diminishing tempo these parties invariably have. Dinner begins, to everyone's relief (at least it's a change of pace): andante. At the halfway mark, mediocre food and forced conversation have taken their toll: adagio.

From there on, it is steady diminuendo, down to full stop. To no one's surprise, everyone gets up early and leaves.

One of the few Washington hostesses I have known who was capable of putting life into a political party was the late Evalyn Walsh McLean. That was because she was not afraid to break the rules. Her lack of inhibitions sometimes took new statesmen aback, but they soon learned to appreciate the value of her judgment, particularly when it was brought to bear on her exceedingly un-protocolish way with a guest list.

Mrs. McLean was keenly interested in national affairs, she had sound political sense, and she kept her ear to the ground. When important issues were brewing, when controversies and political fires were starting up, Mrs. McLean knew where; and knew, more importantly, who was best equipped to put them out. These key people would then be summoned to lunch — a very informal lunch — where issues that might have taken weeks to thrash out in protocol-bound meeting rooms were likely to be settled before the soup cooled. Her value as a behind-the-scenes figure was enormous, and political Washington knew it. At various times, I have been present at Mrs. McLean's house, Friendship, with Presidents, Vice-Presidents, ambassadors, diplomats, generals, Cabinet members, Supreme Court justices, and Senators without end. By doing away with protocol, Mrs. Mc-Lean turned Friendship House into a sort of upholstered political clearinghouse, where these men could relax and talk at their ease. It was the only house in Washington where entertaining mixed with politics in an air of good taste.

I will say that, of late, the general aspect of the social scene in Washington has improved. It has dignity, which it didn't have before. I know I have denounced dignity as a pleasure-killer, and I still do, but I am talking here not about the kind of stern punctilio that turns so many official parties into exercises resembling close-order drills, but the dignity of manners and taste. Obviously, dignity in judicious amounts is necessary when entertaining is carried on in the name of government. Diplomats and foreign dignitaries must be suitably impressed, and high-office holders given their due in respect of rank. Now there has been a return to this kind of dignity with grace, thanks to the woman who is undisputed leader of the capital's new political society, Mrs. Alice Roosevelt Longworth.

Having stood for half a century as a model hostess and upholder of good taste in Washington society, only Mrs. Longworth could have hoped to succeed to the town's social leadership when the Republicans took over in 1952, and succeed she did. No one contended her right to preside as hostess at President Eisenhower's first Inaugural Ball — Washington's top social honor — and she has been setting the tone and pace of official entertaining for the lesser ladies of the capital ever since.

I first met Mrs. Longworth in San Francisco in 1905. This was the year her father, Theodore Roosevelt, was riding the crest of his presidency; the year before her marriage to Nicholas Longworth. She was called "Princess Alice" and she was so nice to me that I have adored her ever since. Today we are still close friends, though our paths seldom cross. She has never changed. She is always the same — wearing funny hats and an old-fashioned hair-do, both characteristics of this remarkable woman with a brilliant mind.

Washington's best-known and most spectacular party-giver is, of course, Perle Mesta, and while I am devoted to Perle personally, and appreciate her talents as a hostess, she has one serious fault: she's too kindhearted. She has never learned to say No. Anyone who wants to go to one of Perle's parties, and who qualifies even vaguely for an invitation, gets an invitation.

I have scolded her about this time and again, pointing out that it is patently impossible to give a good party unless you put a strict limit on your guest list and stick to it. Particularly when you are a woman in Perle's position, if you plan a party for one hundred, five hundred will want to come, and if you let them the party is doomed. But this, with all her experience, she has never learned. That solid gold heart gets the upper hand.

When Perle stays away from the Café Society merry-go-round and sticks to her own milieu, she entertains extremely well. She is at her best in Washington, where she knows everybody worth knowing, and her parties there are always interesting. In January of 1955, for example, I went down to Washington to attend a dinner Perle was giving in honor of the departing Ambassador from France, Henri Bonnet, and his wife, Helie. It was a good party, a tribute to Perle's ability to win friends and collect influential people. One hundred and seventy guests were seated at dinner. The arrangements were excellent and the guests glittering. I have rarely seen more ambassadors and top brass gathered under one roof. And she had placed them well. I had an excellent seat between Malcolm Muir, of *Newsweek* magazine, and the Comte de Granville, counselor of the French Embassy in Washington — an amiable blend of press and politics that produced good, lively talk and, in consequence, a thoroughly enjoyable time for me.

Name anybody in the capital and Perle will produce him like a rabbit from a hat. Once, in New York, I mentioned to her that I would like to meet our three Chiefs of Staff together. The next time I was in Washington I went to a small dinner at Perle's and there they were: General Twining of the Air Forces, General Taylor of the Army, Admiral Burke of the Navy. It is at small parties like this, where protocol is involved, that Perle is most adept. Small parties, as I have had woeful cause to learn, frequently present thornier problems of protocol than large, where, under cover of the crowd, minor breaches may be handled with comparative ease. But at a small party the least breach will glare, and if the party is of the conglomerate type, where high government officials mix with people from the theater and the press and business — well, you may not be asking for it, but there's a better than even chance you'll get it: someone who in one way or another unwittingly treads on eminent toes, perhaps (and this is a common occurrence) by claiming, or trying to claim, a disproportionate amount of the hostess's attention, leaving a more important guest to make do as he can. As a matter of fact, this is a form of harassment most hostesses have to cope with on occasion — as, for instance, when one of your guests is your husband's boss, or that rich maiden aunt who just might see her way to putting the children through college, and you suddenly find yourself helpless in the toils of a well-meaning old schoolmate, bent on giving you a sneeze-by-sneeze run-through of little Gracie's latest allergy. Such a situation takes all the tact and diplomacy a hostess can muster to handle gracefully.

The manner in which a woman entertains does, of course, depend to a large extent on where and how she lives, and, while any attempt to slice up the country into so many little geographical units and then to say that this area or that outdoes all the rest in hospitality would be utter nonsense, it is true that city hostesses have an edge on their country counterparts, in terms of resources if not resourcefulness. For while geography has nothing at all to do with a woman's ability to entertain well, it has a good deal to do with her ability to entertain differently. Granting the personality factor to be of first importance, the second is the degree of novelty she is able to inject into her parties, and here is where living handy to the fleshpots is a decided help.

In a city novelty is everywhere at hand. New people are forever turning up to animate guest lists. Specialty shops and catering services in vast profusion offer every known food and drink to the menu planner, and if she mistrusts her ability to pilot her party to success at home, she can always take it out to dine as exotically or as homelily as she chooses. Then, of course, theaters and concert halls, for every taste and every budget, abound; and for night owls there are supper clubs and bistros and bars into the night. All this expedience does not, be it noted again, automatically turn a city woman into a superior hostess; it simply puts her in a better position to provide, easily, the essential something new and different, and unless she is woefully lacking in imagination or entirely dead from the neck up, she will take advantage of it.

As a matter of fact, the woman who must draw entirely on her own imagination to make her parties standouts — and succeeds — is the truly perfect hostess. In a small community, the woman who manages consistently to entertain with originality and flair wins my loudest huzzahs any day. For one thing, guest turnover in a small town is not apt to be very great, for the local populace is likely to stand substantially pat over the years, and the hostess's guest list with it. Also, since small-town food dealers can't really be expected to risk the mortgage by stocking fresh delicacies for which there is little demand, she must make do with things canned or things frozen, which may save her time but will tax her creative talents still further as she seeks to restore to these denatured products something of their original flavor. For her, then, ingenuity is the mainspring of success, and more power to her.

Unfortunately, there are too few of her. I have met a few

such, but I have met many more across the country who are not. It isn't always that these women lack imagination; they are simply too lazy to use it. They are content to type-cast themselves and their parties and be done with it.

City women are by no means blameless on this score: I know many whose parties turn out time after time to be exercises in pure monotony. Still, the reasonably adept city hostess does not so easily fall prey to routine, partly because, as I have said, she has the means to individualize her parties so abundantly at hand, partly because she is constantly being exposed to new ideas in entertaining — some of which are bound to brush off — and partly because the social complexities of city life are such that, if she does not meet them head on, she will soon find herself sitting beside a very lonely fire indeed. For the city dweller, unless she is so almighty reclusive she cannot bother with the simplest amenities, is always in the way of making new friends, simply because she is always in the way of meeting new people, some of whom are bound by the law of averages to strike a congenial chord. And as her social horizons widen, her social activities increase, and so does — or should — her proficiency. Taking this line of reasoning to its logical end, then, it follows that the greatest number of good hostesses is to be found where hostesses grow the thickest, and that, of course, by per capita reckoning, is in the city of New York. Partisan drum-beating? Not at all. Visitors to New York have themselves given the city top-rating for hospitality with that old line about it's being a nice place to visit but I wouldn't want to live there — fighting words to a staunch New Yorker, but words that are, in fact, a nice tribute to our friendliness.

New Yorkers, I am well aware, have a reputation — not unearned — for a particularly insular form of civic pride which leads them to suppose that everything about the place is superior, and that provincialism begins where Manhattan Island leaves off. Well, I'm as ardent a booster of my adopted home town as the next one, but I could scarcely have traveled the country as I have and believe for one minute that it represents a solitary peak in the art of civilized living in America. Indeed, there are areas that have it all over New York in understanding and preserving the gracious and graceful way of life, notably parts of the South where the old families — the only true aristocracy we have — persist in paying more than lip-service to the social and cultural traditions bequeathed them by their forebears. Successive generations of Southerners have struggled to preserve the best of their heritage, and if Northerners sometimes choose to regard this doggedness as a particularly unenlightened form of ancestor worship, perhaps that is because we began long ago to sell our own traditions to the money lenders.

Decent pride of possession is one thing — ostentation quite another; and when the latter spills over into the area of entertaining it is deplorable. New York, perhaps because it is still haunted by the world's richest and gaudiest ghosts, is also the world's most money-conscious city, and it has its share of hostesses who entertain in precisely the same spirit in which they buy their cars: to impress, not with beauty for its own sake, but with how much it cost. You know the kind — you are scarcely in the door before you are being treated to a household inventory, complete with prices. A good hostess is one who takes her circumstances for granted, and entertains in a way that befits her income and normal way of life. She doesn't seek to dazzle, only to please, and because she sets her scene naturally, without contrivance, she succeeds. If she is rich — well and good: an aura of wealth is a very pleasant and reassuring thing. But if she is not so rich, and is frank about it, there will be no strain and her parties will be good.

Those New Yorkers who, in my opinion, rate Best Hostess status are not, I admit, women troubled with any very pressing financial worries: some are out-and-out rich; some are in what are known as "comfortable circumstances"; some work — and work hard — for incomes sufficient to the absorbent needs of pleasant living as they see it. All have this in common: their parties are in perfect accord with the differing patterns of their lives.

One name — Mrs. William Woodward, Sr. — must head my list of New York hostesses, for while she no longer entertains as of old, the position she has always held in New York society remains unchallenged. Elsie Woodward stood, and stands, as a lesson in the innate good taste and steadfastness of character born of breeding. The sorrows she has borne during the last years have proved her courage. William Woodward, the husband she loved so deeply, died three years ago. Soon after, she lost one of her sisters, Edith. (There had been three — triplets.) Then her only son, Bill — killed by the blast of a shotgun fired by his wife when she mistook him in the dark for a prowler. The dignity and fortitude with which Mrs. Woodward bore herself in the wave of unpleasant publicity that followed this tragedy was magnificent. Her philosophy that life must be lived, no matter what one has lost, is, I believe, what pulled her through. This and her love for her grandsons, who are now her whole life.

Recently she has moved to an apartment in the Waldorf from the big Woodward house in East 86th Street, which was the last in the city still staffed and run as the great houses used to be. It was a gracious, welcoming house, done in exquisite taste, and the dinner parties Mrs. Woodward gave there lived up in every way to the beauty of the setting. The parties were often large: "A buffet dinner for fifty or more friends and acquaintances may turn out to be more amusing than a set party," Elsie would explain, "especially if there is some amateur talent in the group."

For her set parties, Mrs. Woodward was long in the habit of serving guinea hen, a popular — too popular — favorite with hostesses the world over. Now I have nothing against guinea hens personally — long life to them — but there came a time, and one guinea hen too many, when I felt I must put my foot down.

I was dining with Mrs. Woodward. Came the guinea hen, and the rebellion was on. "I cannot," I said to her firmly, "look another guinea hen in the face."

Mrs. Woodward laughed, informed the kitchen of the mutiny, and I ate ham. What is more, my one-woman strike was not forgotten. Not long after I again had dinner with Mrs. Woodward. Every dish was different from those she had customarily served before!

Some of the best and most unusual food I have eaten in New York has been at parties at the Edgar Leonards'. Adelaide Leonard is one of the cleverest hostesses I know, and her tiny house in East 62nd Street is a little gourmet's paradise. None of the usual guinea hens or *poulets suprême* or racks of underdone lamb turn up here to make you wish you'd settled for a tray in bed at home. Mrs. Leonard understands food. More, she understands how tedious repetition can be to guests — especially when the guests are people who dine out often, as most New Yorkers do. Put yourself in my place. How would you like to find yourself on, say, Saturday, contemplating your third or fourth guinea hen of the week? Anyone who has ever been taken with the megrims at sight of a turkey mounted on the party table in the first days of the post-Thanksgiving to New Year season will know what I'm talking about.

Another of New York's experts is Mrs. Charles Blackwell, who gives wonderful little bridge dinners with food that is always original and good. Or the occasion might be a small theater party. On these evenings the Blackwells follow the sensible English custom of serving a light snack before leaving for the theater, and supper at home after. Curtain time is thus made without undue peril to the digestion, no one sits through the performance fighting sleep, and supper is enjoyed without someone, at regular intervals, nervously announcing the time.

Mrs. Artur Rubinstein is a great hostess, and a cook whose genius in the kitchen is in a class with her husband's on the concert stage. And that, from me, is praise. I have known Artur since 1912, and I have always recognized him as a pianist of unique ability. All the same, few of us adequately appraise the talents of our old friends, and I confess that I had never fully realized the extent of Rubinstein's genius until the night of his concert at Carnegie Hall early in 1955. His performance then left no doubt in my mind that he is the greatest pianist of our day.

After the concert that night, the Rubinsteins gave a small supper at their Park Avenue apartment. The buffet table groaned with goodies. There was a wonderful hot borsch, a mouth-watering dish called *Coulubiac*, various salads, and a divine chocolate cake. When I complimented Nella on the perfection of the food she told me proudly that she had prepared it all herself. She had been cooking from nine o'clock that morning until time to leave for the concert.

"Artur has his piano," said Nella; "I play my sonatas on my stove."

Another New York hostess I must mention is a relative newcomer to the social horizon, Mrs. Norman Winston, wife of the builder who is Mayor Wagner's greatest crony around town.

Rosita is an exquisite hostess, gay, engaging, frankly outspoken — this last a trait that belies the Cherokee blood she inherits from her mother. Actually, Mrs. Winston is only a part-time New Yorker, for the Winstons now live a large part of the year in France, where Norman is presently engaged in building an entire town for the government. The Winstons own one of the most beautiful houses in Paris, where Rosita entertains, on a grander scale than in New York, at supper dances for two hundred or more — and where, incidentally, she now gives me my birthday party on the 24th of May each year. But the Winstons' parties in New York are small, in keeping with the size of their Sutton Square house, where no more than twelve can be seated at dinner. The house itself is a connoisseur's delight, a perfect frame for Rosita's flawless taste in paintings and furnishings. I call it the Jewel Box. One of the special pleasures for me when I go there are the flowers, which Rosita arranges beautifully herself.

Most of the women I have mentioned here live in houses or apartments large enough to permit entertaining on a more or less sizable scale. Small-apartment dwellers — and in New York, as in all cities, they are the vast majority — who manage to carpenter and cajole a few square yards of floor space into rooms that are both functional and charming and in which they manage to entertain without pain either to their guests or to themselves are the true winners. One of the best of these in New York is Mrs. T. Reed Vreeland. Diana is a career gal, on the staff of *Harper's Bazaar,* and her apartment is tiny, yet I have been to dinner parties there that Epicurus would have applauded, not only for the excellence of the food and wines, but for the staging as well. Guests at the Vreelands' — never more than eight — are entertained from first to last in a living room that is a masterpiece of ingenious planning. No awkward plate-on-the-lap juggling here. Dinner is served at a round table in one corner of the room. Guests sit around it on upholstered banquettes. Sound, which can become strident and ugly in a small area, is muted by over-all carpeting and heavy curtains. It is all comfortable, easy, and nicely elegant: everyone dresses, because, says Diana, "To us a party is always a gala occasion."

Artists seldom make good hosts, although writers and painters do better on the whole than actors and musicians, who are almost always, as suits the requirements of these callings, so much the focuses of their own consciousness and energies that they do not readily adapt to the more self-effacing aspects of party-giving. The writing and painting world has, to be sure, its share of egocentrics, but these are solitary professions — which accounts, no doubt, for the higher rate of proficiency in their ranks: a party is the only way the poor things ever get to see their audiences.

In New York, the John Gunthers are wonderful hosts, obedient to the principle of mixed groups, and so are Dorothy Thompson and her painter husband, Max Kopf. The Kopfs are far from rich. They live and entertain simply and with great charm in their small, comfortable Turtle Bay house in East 48th Street. There are no servants, and the parties are better than if there were. For when Dorothy gives a party it is her own creation from first to last. It is Dorothy who greets you at the door, Dorothy who plans, cooks, and supervises the buffet — usually Austro-German in style: I remember particularly well a delicious chicken paprika, and apfelstrudel for the gods. Guests in the Kopf ménage are generally people connected with the arts or politics, and there is a sprinkling of the younger element brought in by Dorothy's son by her marriage to Sinclair Lewis. They are gay, easy, relaxed parties, with plenty of good food and drink —

more than enough — good talk, and Dorothy's radiant good cheer to keep them rolling.

The necessity of giving careful thought and time to food is, I suppose, one reason actresses so rarely make good hostesses. In a profession that assesses glamour largely in terms of tape-measure and scale, hearty appetites must be sternly put down, and the best way to accomplish that, of course, is simply not to think about food at all. The result is that many actresses find it easier on their powers of self-discipline not to entertain at all (I have never known either Bette Davis or Joan Crawford, for instance, to give what could properly be called a party) — or, if they do succumb to the social urge, nine out of ten simply turn the planning of the menu over to some minion who couldn't care less, with results as dismal as they are predictable. What you get isn't really food — it's artifacts. Everything comes stuffed with something: beet root stuffed with cherries is one of my gloomier recollections of culinary life in Hollywood. And they are simply mad about paprika: it's everywhere. Even the butter pats turn up looking bloodshot. Still, as I've said before, it's a rare Hollywood guest who is either sober enough or food-conscious enough to care about what he eats, or for that matter, even to recognize it.

I suppose actresses are, in some respects, more to be pitied than envied. The glamour gals, anyway. Not only must they deny themselves exciting food — and if it's exciting it's fattening, let not the joy-through-roughage buffs deceive you — they must also deny themselves a good deal of the social freedom the rest of us enjoy. When they're working their only relaxation is sleep, and when they're not working they can go about freely in public only at risk of being hounded to death by favor-seekers, or torn limb from limb by devoted fans. As a result they

are forced into lives so restricted that no normal social inter-
change is possible, and most of them wouldn't know how to
deal with it if it were.

The best actress-hostesses are — begging their pardons — the
more mature among them. Put another way, they are the women
who have achieved solid professional standing, and the security
(of mind as well as money) that goes with it. They are established. Their private lives are no longer wholly bound to the
keep of studio publicity departments. They can afford to relax
now and then long enough to forget about being stars and concentrate on being human.

The late Fanny Brice loved to entertain, gave wonderful
parties, cooked like a dream, and ate like a trencherman. Fanny,
to be sure, was no glamour girl; an extra pound or two on Baby
Snooks mattered not at all, and that was just as well. For
Fanny's great specialties were Jewish dishes on the high-calory
side: potato pancakes, herring in sour cream; and she could turn
a simple dish like scrambled eggs into pure ambrosia by
serving it piping hot and a-bubble with Roquefort cheese.

At the glamorous and still-going-strong level, Constance Ben-
nett is one of the best hostesses I have ever known, and so are
Claudette Colbert, Irene Dunne and Rosalind Russell. Loretta
Young is a wonderful hostess. Joan Fontaine is absolute tops.
Sonja Henie is a good hostess in a big, splashing way — she
prefers to entertain out, in restaurants or night clubs, rather
than at home. Marlene Dietrich is a very special hostess who
loves to cook — loves to eat what she cooks, moreover, although
that she is able to keep her appetite under control was amply
demonstrated to any who saw her recent act at Las Vegas.

Ethel Barrymore is a superb hostess, and for her this is no
latter-day accomplishment. Ethel is a born practitioner of the
belief that since you only live once you might as well make it

as pleasant as possible all around, for yourself and everybody concerned with you. Years ago I used to see a lot of Ethel when both she and Jack were playing in New York. The three of us would meet at Ethel's house after their respective theaters closed, for supper and to play poker. Jack usually did the cooking, for he liked to cook and was good at it. Ethel brought to these intimate occasions exactly the same charm and warmth of spirit that lesser ladies of the theater are wont to reserve for strangers when box office is off. Graciousness to Ethel is a simple specification of living. Would there were more of her! Too many of us are slipshod in our close personal relationships, forgetting when we play host to a few cronies that they deserve the self-same courtesies and attentions as a ballroomful of V.I.P.'s.

Remember that, the next time good old So-and-so drops in for morning coffee. Be a hostess to her. She didn't come to sit in as your personal sounding board, or to mind the baby, or to help sort the laundry. She is a guest — unexpected, perhaps, in which case if you haven't the time or the inclination to entertain her, tell her to go away. That's a lot less rude than treating her like a useful but not irreplaceable household appliance. The truly perfect hostess is never a random performer. One guest or a hundred — she aims to please.

CHAPTER V

Men as Hosts

SKILL in the care and feeding of guests has so long been considered woman's prerogative that men who show any marked degree of proficiency in the field are generally supposed to have mastered a feat not altogether natural to them, like those performing dogs you see who've learned to walk erect and count to five. Women, of course, are responsible for the popularity of this ungenerous theory. Nothing pleases us more than to feel ourselves in exclusive charge of a preserve in which men feel not only ill at ease, but inept as well. Unwelcome, too, for women do not take kindly to claim-jumping. The fact is, they're jealous. I think the closest I ever came to being walked out on by an audience was when I told a group of women at a luncheon the last thing they wanted or expected to hear: that men are, in fact, better hosts than women. Well, the bridling that greeted this heresy subsided in due course, my audience stayed to hear me out, and in the end they had to agree that I was right.

For it is true. Not of all men, heaven knows. I know many who couldn't plan and carry off a good party if they tried. But if a man is a good host at all he is usually a winner. One reason, I believe, is that while men recognize entertaining as a necessary and even vital adjunct to the business of living, it is never quite as necessary or vital to them as the business of *making* a living.

To the average, non-working woman, homemaking and all that goes with it — including entertaining — is a career in itself and she treats it in dead earnest. To a man, entertaining is a pleasant means of escape from the demands of getting on in the career that pays the bills. And he treats it thus. When he gives a party he means to relax, forget the worries of the day, have fun. This does not mean he goes at it carelessly. He plans well, because planning is anticipating and therefore part of his pleasure, and also because his professional training has put him in the habit of forearming by means of foresight. He doesn't always hit it 100 per cent, of course. The best laid plans . . . and so on. But here I think is where much of his superiority lies, for when some unlooked-for snag *does* arise he takes it in stride. He doesn't worry. Where a woman might give way to hand-wringing and loud distress when the roast burns or the wine refuses to bubble, a man will laugh it off. He is determined that nothing short of sudden death will mar his enjoyment of his all-too-brief escape from workaday pursuits, so he keeps his humor high and his guests do too.

Then, too, men are notoriously open-handed as hosts. Women love to scrimp. They delight in cutting corners where they can, possibly because, if statistics are to be believed, women hold the nation's purse strings and mean to go on holding them, and the heavier the purse the better. At any rate, nothing puts an unholier gleam in a woman's eye than striking a blow for the economy, and often as not the richer the woman the brighter the gleam. Nine out of ten plan their parties with one eye on the shopping list, the other on the till. Now I don't flatly decry this approach: thrift, I am sure, is an admirable asset in women and one that is valued by the men they marry. But excessive thrift has no place in the design of a party. When you buy food and drink at a saving you may be sure that it is because you are buying second-rate food and drink. The best is never to be had at bargain prices. Men know this and they won't compromise for less than the best — anyway, not when they give a party. As a matter of fact, I have known men whose everyday behavior in regard to money would make Ebenezer Scrooge look prodigal, yet who will spare no expense when they entertain. Food, wines, flowers, service — all must be of the finest. Naturally, such magnanimity is pleasing to guests. It flatters them. It boosts their egos. Being treated pricelessly, they begin to feel priceless, and they bask in it.

Finally, the good host gives off an air of such resolute confidence in himself and in the certain success of the business at hand that the least optimistic arrival at his party all at once feels himself assured of having a good time and, consequently, *has* a good time. Awfully few women are able to present as poised an exterior as men do at the outset of a party. Women flutter, they giggle, they deliver their greetings in little shrieks, or if they're the introvertish sort they withdraw into shells of such chilling reserve that even the words of welcome sound frostbitten. The sympathetic state of mind into which this initial unease throws guests usually wears off as the party comes together and the hostess begins to relax, but it is a sorry way to open the festivities, and men seldom do. Not that men always *feel* so blissfully cocksure, but here again professional training serves them. They have learned to camouflage uncertainty and self-doubt. After all, a man in business cannot very well approach a prospective client or a meeting with the boss without an air of conviction that his feet are on the ground and his head in an orderly condition to deal sensibly with matters relevant to profit and loss. Confidence is his indispensable stock in trade. He may have to struggle to acquire it, but if he means to get on in the world acquire it he will.

Men excuse ineptness in women; they even find it rather endearing, to judge by the number who marry scatterbrains. But men look for authority in each other, and never more so than when they sit down to do business — even when the business is carried on in the guise of entertaining, as it frequently is. Thus the art of entertaining well is of greatest importance to a man. Some men, in fact — notably salesmen — succeed more on the strength of their convivial talents than on business ability. Some, alas, fumble diligently along in their jobs totally ignorant of the importance to their careers of social competence. How often have I seen a young man playing host in a restaurant to an older man — an important client, perhaps, or a prospective boss — with all the aplomb of a water buffalo slogging its way out of a quagmire. From the first clumsy handshake it is apparent that Junior has foundered blind into a situation for which he is woefully unprepared. Conversation is plainly a chore for him; he veers between hearty inanities and embarrassed mumbling, uncertain of the point at which it will be polite and proper for him to abandon the weather and get on with the purpose of the meeting. (Barring a cue from Senior, wait until coffee is my advice. Serious discussion is not compatible with the digestive processes.)

Then there is the matter of ordering. Menus come and are studied while the waiter hovers impatiently. It comes suddenly to Junior that, as host at the table, it is up to him to take charge. At this juncture he begins to feel a glimmer of confidence. The menu is a plain statement of facts and relieves him for the moment of the need to concoct small talk. On solid conversational ground now, he speaks up manfully.

"What will you have, sir?"

"I don't know. What do you suggest?"

Gone is Junior's moment of confidence. The ball, tossed neatly back at him, has caught him unprepared. What should he suggest? His eye darts, not unnoticed, to the right side of the menu. He remembers vaguely having heard that to offer the most expensive dish smacks of pretension. On the other hand it might seem niggling if he doesn't. So he wavers. It doesn't occur to him to ask the waiter for advice. As a matter of fact, this is precisely what should have occurred to him several hours earlier. As I have said before, it is always wise when entertaining in a restaurant to let the restaurant in on your plans ahead of time, and if, as in this case, your guest is a comparative stranger — but one whose good opinion is important to you — it is plain folly not to. Had Junior been on his toes he'd have gotten to the restaurant early, studied the menu, consulted the captain or waiter, and so been able to come out with one or two firm suggestions on request.

Now knowing your way around a menu may sound a relatively minor matter, and in most circumstances it would be. But in the case of this befuddled young man, not being able to give a quick, informed answer to his guest's call for advice — indeed, the inadequacy of his whole performance — may well cost him the good impression he is so eager to make. Big men attach importance to small skills: I once knew an industrialist in the habit of judging the efficiency potential of new employees simply by the care — or lack of it — with which they pasted postage stamps on envelopes, reasoning that a bungler of small chores is pretty apt to be a bungler of large. Just so might this young man's apparent inability to bring off the relatively simple social chore of standing one for lunch result, so far as his career is concerned, in a thumbs-down verdict. In his personal life he would be said to lack social awareness; in his professional life he would be deemed a bad hand at public relations, than which, to a businessman, there is no blacker sin.

Now, in saying that a man's professional training betters his aptitude as a host, I do not mean to suggest that social success is automatically the by-product of professional success. Far from it. The average businessman draws a sharp line between entertaining purely for pleasure and entertaining purely for the delectation of the board of directors. A few manage to distinguish themselves in both camps. The majority — and for the most part I am talking here about the earnest, backbone-of-commerce types: bankers, brokers, industrialists, and the like — seldom let their imaginations stray far enough from the exigencies of remaining solvent to grasp the techniques of simple sociableness. They may persuade themselves what all-round good fellows they are, and fancy, when they give parties — or, as is more likely, when their wives give parties for them — that in offering a cordial welcome to each arriving guest they are amply fulfilling the duties of the good host. But of course they are not. Their hearts aren't really in it. They find the exchange of pleasantries all very charming and nice — and tedious. They yearn for the moment when they may settle down with cigars and brandy and a few like-minded cronies to talk ponderous fiscal talk and fret about the state of the nation. Businessmen to the core, they are good hosts only to other businessmen, and that is hardly sufficient to the cause of general merriment at a party. (There is only one other class of people I know who can match them for vocational ardor to the exclusion of all else — and to the detriment of their talents as hosts — and that is the sporty set. The baseball players, football players, basketball players, tennis players, swimmers, boxers, *et al.* that I have met were nice sturdy specimens and good men all; but they live, eat, and sleep sports; they think only sports; they talk only sports. They can regale one another for hours on end with stories of contests won or lost; listeners from more sedentary spheres are apt to find the endurance point a matter of minutes.)

So much for the bad.

Let us now praise the good, starting, by way of softening the indictment, with a businessman — Pierre David-Weill, head of the great French banking house of Lazard Frères, and a fine host. Pierre is a true gourmet — not a particularly remarkable quality in a Frenchman, perhaps, but in the gourmet's art there are levels of perfection, even among Frenchmen, and Pierre stands awesomely close to the top. I have had dinners at his house in New York that were unsurpassed in my experience. For one thing, Pierre is mindful of the old warning that God sends meat and the Devil cooks, and he takes care to staff his kitchen from the side of the angels. His chef is unquestionably the finest in New York. Curiously enough, in France — at his houses in Paris and on the Riviera where I have often dined — the food, while certainly good, seldom measures up to the perfection of what he serves in New York.

I have never met a diplomat who was not a good host. I hope I never shall. International diplomacy is a touchy business at best, and when a diplomat, in line of duty, is host to a party of representatives of other powers, friendly or otherwise, his least breach of conduct may well send some proud chauvinist off in a state of dudgeon that nothing short of a White Paper will appease. Ambassadors, ministers, in fact everybody connected with an embassy down to the least secretary (and this includes their wives) must be able to function as efficiently in a drawing room as in a conference room, or very soon find themselves manning unimportant desks back home and wondering how they got there.

I was greatly impressed by a party I attended not long ago in a private dining room at the United Nations. New York was celebrating City Center Day, and the UN powers that be took graceful note of the occasion by inviting some of the City Center staff and members of the board (I am one) to lunch. To begin with, the roster of our hosts was impressive in itself. There were Secretary-General Dag Hammarskjold, Ambassador Henry Cabot Lodge, Dr. van Kleffens, Dr. Ralph Bunche, and perhaps a dozen more of the UN's leading delegates and officials. Now these are all important men, among the most important in the world, and I knew I could look forward to a rewarding time with them. Just how relaxed and gay a time it would be remained to be seen. Our hosts, after all, would be coming to the luncheon table direct from a morning spent coping with matters of gravest international concern. After lunch they would return to them. Their guests, on the other hand, while not what I'd call a sig-nally light-minded group, represented the comparatively frivolous world of the theater. With me, on the promotive side of City Center operations, were Mrs. Lytle Hull; Newbold Morris, chair-man of the board of directors; and Jean Dalrymple, director of the theater company. On the performing side were our first lady of the stage, Helen Hayes; Betsy von Furstenburg; Jessica Tandy; Harold Lang; Franchot Tone; and others. Considering the size of the gulf that separates these two areas of interest — on the one side man's fate, on the other his pleasure — it would be natural to suppose that a certain lack of rapport might creep into the proceedings. As it turned out, the only observable lack of rapport was between me and my old friend, Dr. van Kleffens, who remarked during his welcoming address that Miss Maxwell looked not a day older than she had when he first met her at the opening session of the United Nations in San Francisco in 1945. My reply to that was that Dr. van Kleffens had at least succeeded in proving Dr. Einstein's theory of the relativity of time. "With you," I said, "the clock has gone backwards!"

It was a wonderful party — easy, informal, relaxed. To a man, our hosts were witty, charming, and marvelously adept at making us feel sincerely welcome, that we and our work really mattered to them. I could not help thinking that women, entertaining in similar circumstances, would have found it difficult to reconcile the preoccupying differences between themselves and their guests. Women whose lives and interests and thinking patterns are widely separated never seem able to bridge the gap gracefully as men do. The cat comes out in them, not in any opprobrious sense — I like cats — but in the wary, slow, circling-for-time way strange cats have of appraising each other. Can you imagine, for example — and I hasten to say that I do not mean to liken this doubtful combination to the ladies and gentlemen of the United Nations and City Center — but can you imagine the executive committee of the D. A. R. playing host to a delegation from the chorus line at Minsky's with any kind of success? Not likely, and not because of snobbishness or of any conscious wish on the hostesses' part to patronize, but simply because women tend to become so absorbed in their own little worlds that only time and proximity will let them feel entirely comfortable in any other. Men are far more adaptable — the more open-minded and intelligent among them, anyway. They know how to step outside themselves, to suit their mood and manner to the mood and manner of the company and the occasion. As I have said, our hosts at the United Nations that day were doubtless facing an afternoon of sober decision and debate. Yet we were not once made conscious of it. Their full attention and concern was for their guests. That is the gift of the truly good host.

After diplomats on my list of best hosts come bachelors. Which is logical. A married man may have entered the wedded state with more ability for and knowledge about entertaining well than his wife will acquire in her lifetime, but unless he is unusually persevering or she is unusually feminist in her views on the domestic rights and privileges of man and wife, she will take firm hold of the duty she considers hers — entertaining — and that will be that. But the bachelor ruling his own roost entertains as it pleases him to entertain, and if he has any native talent whatsoever he will usually develop into a top-flight host. For one thing, he is almost invariably more inventive than the average woman because he is almost invariably self-taught. He may have been born with a connoisseur's taste in food and drink, but he didn't learn the ins and outs of planning and preparing a party at his mother's knee as his sister did — or should have — so he learns as he goes, unhampered by convention and with gratifyingly refreshing results.

Also in his favor is the fact that, while he probably gives fewer parties than the average woman, he feels bound to make those he does give standouts. If he is at all presentable — which, as a hostess gauges a bachelor, is roughly equivalent to saying if he has only one head, a suit of clothes, and the power of speech — he is certain to be in steady demand as a guest. No hostess needs to be told that extra men — whether bachelors by persuasion or single by circumstance — are as rare in most communities as black pearls, so that any that are available are pretty well bound to find themselves regulars on one guest list after another. (The popular bachelor's life is, indeed, so endlessly gay one wonders how they stand it. Not all of them do, it seems. Statistics show that the insanity rate among bachelors is three times higher than it is among married men. As a hostess, I won't labor the point, except to say that there are hostesses who press their advantage unfairly. Some of the duds I have seen foisted on obliging extra men as dinner partners would be enough to drive anyone off the deep end.) Be that as it may, as the bachelor's invitations pile up so do his obligations, and he inclines as a rule to meet these with a few large parties during each season rather than a spate of little dinners for six or eight which most hostesses favor. And, as I have said, though he gives fewer parties, because he gives fewer parties, he sees to it that those he does give are in the nature of events.

In New York, Lauder Greenway — to start off with an exception to that generality about size — is a fine bachelor host who does not run to large parties, nor to parties at home. His specialty is the little dinner for ten or twelve at one of his clubs — generally the Metropolitan or the Brook. These dinners have a character very much their own. Music predominates, for Lauder is, among other things, Vice-Chairman of the Board of Directors of the Metropolitan Opera Association, and his guests for the most part are people from the musical world. And the parties themselves are generally preludes to a night at the opera. Furthermore, the food is invariably good — not a state of affairs habitual to club dining rooms, and I once satisfied my curiosity on the point after a particularly fine Greenway dinner by asking the maître d'hôtel who had ordered it. "Mr. Greenway, himself," was the reply. As I might have known.

Incidentally, I have said elsewhere that the sensible procedure when entertaining a smallish party in a club or restaurant is to let each guest order for himself. An exception is the pre-theater or concert party. In such a case, whether your guests be two, four, or ten, it is nonsense to squander time at the table while people ponder what they will eat. Always order beforehand. Set the hour early so that there is plenty of time to enjoy the meal, and be sure to let the restaurant know the precise moment at which you'll leave for the theater so that they can plan the service accordingly.

Another excellent theater-night host is Duke Fulco di

Verdura, jeweler to fashion and, in bachelor ranks, one of the best cooks I know. Verdura is of the Continental persuasion, that good theater stimulates good appetite and that the time to satisfy it is after. So his parties are generally planned for the late, hungry hours after the opera or the theater, when he takes over in the kitchen of his handsome apartment to concoct sublime Italian dishes. One that I am particularly fond of is spaghetti bathed in an exquisite sauce of mussels — perfect proof of to what ambrosial uses the humble *pasta* may be put, given a little imagination and the whim to indulge it.

Iva Patcévitch, publisher of *Vogue*, is a wonderful host. His house in East 70th Street is, as befits the house of a dealer in taste, stunningly done from top to bottom, and let no one doubt the importance of the *mise en scène* to good party-giving. Patcévitch likes to give Canasta parties, these on the large side, with a guest-list range of from twenty to fifty. To feed and deploy a group of this size smoothly, without fuss, with a minimum of last-minute who-plays-where-and-with-whom, and with all the necessary paraphernalia of the game ready and in order when the playing begins, is an intricate business and requires a practiced hand. Patcévitch does it with great skill. The moves from cocktails to dinner to the card tables are made easily, in an atmosphere of leisure, with none of the monitoring, social-director overtones that women so often adopt when they give this kind of party. No one is made to feel bound to an inflexible timetable. Dinner is served promptly, but because there are always going to be stragglers at a party of this size, it is always something that can stand waiting if need be, and even improve as it waits — a *bœuf Bourgignon* or the like.

One of the few New York businessmen who recognize the lunch hour for what it's worth is Count Lanfranco Rasponi, public relations expert and benefactor to artists: as a side interest, he owns and operates the Sagittarius Gallery, largely as a showcase for young painters. Rasponi often entertains at delightful small luncheon parties at the Colony. For dinner, he prefers to entertain at home, where he serves food that is simple, but as delicious as any to be found in New York. I never refuse his invitations.

As anyone who has ever met me, read me, or come within electronic range of my voice is likely to know, one of my wilder enthusiasms in people is my long-time friend and companion in a thousand memories, Cole Porter. As a matter of fact, I have used so many words over the years to describe my admiration for this gifted gentleman from Indiana turned *homme du monde* that it would be superfluous to add to them at any great length here. Certainly as an artist Cole needs no explaining: if there is an inhabitant of the civilized world who has not at one time or another sung, whistled, or danced to his music, he must either be still in the cradle or stone deaf. But at the personal level it bears repeating that Cole understands the art of good living as few men do. His taste is impeccable, and on the elegant side. He has, for instance, a fondness for wearing embroidered waistcoats and for period-piece canes — these a painful necessity, since he suffered a serious fall from a horse some years ago. (His collection is imposing. One belonged to Beau Brummel, another to Louis XV — two gentlemen not without some claim to elegance themselves.) More to the point in this context is Cole's innate elegance of mind. He is witty, urbane, kind, something of a gallant, and the most loyal of friends — all markings of a great gentleman and of a great host as well.

Nowadays Cole entertains on a comparatively modest scale — modest, anyway, in comparison to the big, colorful hooplas with which he and Linda Porter titivated international society back in the twenties. Since Linda's death a few years ago Cole has made his New York headquarters in a handsome ten-room apartment on the thirty-third floor of the Waldorf Towers, and in California, a house in the Brentwood section, where he keeps a fine chef all year round, just in case. But the New York apartment is officially home, and there he likes to entertain quietly, usually at luncheon. For dinner he is very apt to take his guests to the Pavillon, which he considers the finest restaurant in the world, as do I.

As to food, Cole is the nearest thing to Lucullus I know — a gourmet in the best cosmopolitan tradition, with a sturdy dash of plain Hoosier thrown in. He is most particular about what he eats, but far from insisting on food that is exotic beyond the purse and patience of ordinary folk, he prefers simple foods, perfectly prepared. Too many who claim to be gourmets are, in fact, nothing but food snobs. To these people a dish must be rare, intricate, and, above all, expensive before it is deemed worthy of their delicate palates. Cole knows, as all true gourmets know, that pretension has little to do with the joys of table. Lamb hash, for example, is a great favorite of his, but it must be *good* lamb hash, seasoned to perfection and on the wet side. Another simple favorite is the flaked fish-and-rice dish called kedgeree, and Indiana relatives keep him supplied with wonderful little sausages — yards of them arrive at regular intervals — which Cole likes to serve *en casserole* with flageolets, the little green kidney beans of France. Also from Indiana comes a divine fruit cake baked by one of his cousins that is like no other fruit cake I have ever tasted. Just what the ingredients are that give it its special magic I don't know. I do know that it has prunes in it, and figs, and no flour, and that Cole eats it in staggering amounts. Unfortunately, so do I!

If marriage is the undoing of some men as hosts I concede that it may also be their making. My friends Eric and Eleanor Loder, for example, have settled into a comfortable pattern of marriage: Eleanor looks after their business interests, Eric runs the house, and they are one of the happiest couples I know. Such is their devotion that in the twenty-five years of their marriage the Loders have been separated for only one night, when Eleanor had to make a flying trip to Canada on business. Eleanor first took the plunge into business some years ago after she discovered that the men responsible for handling her extensive holdings were negligent in their management. Somewhat to her own surprise, I think, she turned out to be a financial wizard, and is today a very rich woman. But if Eleanor is energetic in regard to business matters, in home matters she has inherited the Southern belle's traditional laziness. So it falls to Eric to wrestle with the chef, order the food, buy the wines. I must say it agrees with him. I have known Eric since 1912 and today, at seventy, he is still handsome, still young at heart, still gay.

Hamilton Fish Armstrong, publisher of *Foreign Affairs* magazine, gives wonderful parties in the charming little red-brick house in West 10th Street that has been in his family for several generations and where he was born. One of the best parties of the year is the supper party the Armstrongs always give each winter just before Christmas. Ham himself greets you at the door and ushers you in — urbane, affable, and with the born host's gift for apportioning himself among the company in equal amounts and with justice to all, for he is possessed of one of those protean minds that can adapt itself instantly to whatever shape the conversation of the moment happens to take — just so long as it is intelligent conversation. Like all first-rate minds, his cannot abide the second-rate in anything, least of all in people, and that is one of the reasons his parties are so good. The

At my 1955 Tiara Ball for Stavros Niarchos. From left to right: Italian Ambassador in Washington Manlio Brosio; Greek Ambassador in Washington George Melas; U.S. Ambassador to Italy Clare Boothe Luce; U.S. Ambassador to Great Britain, Winthrop Aldrich; E. M.; Spanish Ambassador in Washington José Motrico; Hervé Alphand, Ambassador to U.N.

My cooking party in Hollywood. Joan Fontaine and Clark Gable join forces briefly at the same chafing dish. Center: Claudette Colbert concentrates, Ronald Colman considers.

My Tiara Ball. Guest of honor Stavros Niarchos pours for the hostess.

The Maypole party. Mrs. Lytle Hull and Ray Bolger showing the form that won the waltz contest.

My white-tie party for Cole Porter. can't imagine why chatting with th guest of honor made me look s tearful.

"Fifi" Fell made a beautiful, if nervous, living Maypole at my Maypole party.

Mrs. William C. T. Gaynor, Claude C. Philippe, and I ponder the program for the 1954 April in Paris Ball.

thens. I greet King Paul and Queen rederika at the reception for my ruise guests. Photographers had been anned, but one of the company couldn't resist a behind-scenes shot.

Six-star Admiral Maxwell (rank, courtesy Jean Dessès) ready to set sail from Venice for the Greek islands aboard the S.S. Achilleus.

Some of the guests at the barnya party. The Waldorf's Jade Roo recovered nicely.

I call her "la prima donna del mondo": Maria Meneghini Callas and E. M., Paris, 1957.

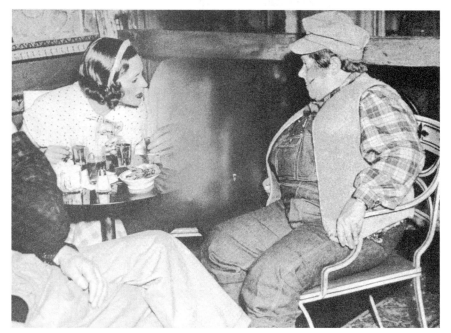

Dairymaid with diamonds, Mrs. Ogden Mills, at the barnyard party. Not being the dairymaid type, I went as a farmer. The thirsty ghost in the middle not identified.

Jerome Zerbe

as Sweet Sixteen; Clifton Webb as my schoolboy swain.

As Eartha Kitt's maid, complete with ruffles and Dali mustache, at a March of Dimes benefit.

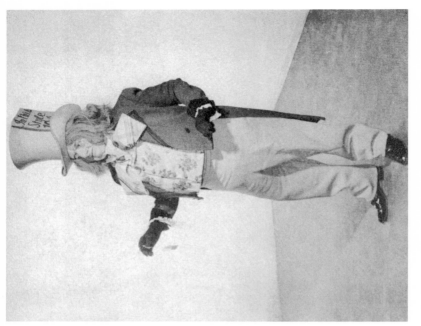

O'Doye — Paris

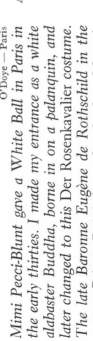

As the Mad Hatter on the television program, "Masquerade Party."

Mimi Pecci-Blunt gave a White Ball in Paris in the early thirties. I made my entrance as a white alabaster Buddha, borne in on a palanquin, and later changed to this Der Rosenkavalier costume. The late Baronne Eugène de Rothschild in the center; Prince Rainier's uncle, the late Marquis

Cav. E. Interguglielmi

he party was at the Duc di Verdura's lace at Palermo, where Nelson and dy Hamilton stayed. E. M.; Charles de Bestegui; Baroness Lo Monaco.

L. Beaugers

Paris, 1937. From left: Composer François Poulenc; Painter Norah Auric; the Marquis Sommi as Hitler; E. M. as Herriot.

he April in Paris Ball when Bea llie and I unexpectedly played nurse-aid to our elephants. The unjeweled epter Bea holds is a broom handle.

O'Doye — Paris

Niki de Gunzburg's Bal des Valses on the island in the Bois. From the left: the host; E. M.; Baronne "Baba" Lucinge; and Edouard Bourdet.

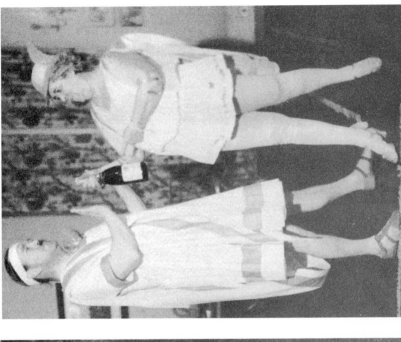

San Francisco financier William H. Crocker is the abstemious Greek to my Mercury.

I am at right as Marat, before the bath. Mrs. Henry Gray, as Charlotte Corday, getting ready for it.

guests are always interesting, informed, and informative people. I remember in one evening talking to such assorted intellects as Mrs. Irita Van Doren, editor of the *New York Herald Tribune Book Review*; Dorothy Thompson and Max Kopf; former Secretary of the Air Forces, Tom Finletter, and his wife, Gretchen (daughter of the late Walter Damrosch); Dr. and Mrs. Grayson Kirk; Lady John Marriott; and the John Barry Ryans, among others. I also remember leaving that party with a feeling of gratitude to my hosts for having fulfilled the ideal condition of party-giving. They had provided a few hours of complete escape from boobery. I went home with a mind cleared of the little lingering irritations left on it by the unavoidable mediocrities that clutter up most of our days. Willy-nilly, we are all forced now and then into the company of people who live, mentally, in fish ponds — rather sluggish fish ponds, at that. I know of no better remedy for the torpid aftereffects these people leave you with than a party like that one — where wit and wisdom were not only seen, they were most eloquently heard.

Cartoonists have battened for years on a situation that is, I suppose, more or less universal: that is the battle between the sexes over what constitutes a good time. In the cartoons this contrariety is generally framed as domestic comedy, with the wife in the case (cartoonists are nearly always men) invariably triumphant. Thus we are shown the husband struggling peevishly into dinner clothes, or being dragged from watching the fights on television with his cronies in order to make a fourth at bridge, or being made to suffer, not gladly, through a night at the opera. As a matter of fact, in real life too the wife usually does run the social show, and in most households the arrangement is probably perfectly satisfactory. She, after all, is the one on whom the major burden falls when there is entertaining to be done, and the deferent husband feels therefore that it is only cricket to let her have her head. For this he earns his wife's gratitude and, all else being equal, a reputation among their friends as an Ideal Husband — a label which, by the way, I have always considered questionable: the specimens I have met just seemed resigned, which is hardly man's ideal state. Nor do I believe women enjoy it. I can't imagine any woman really wanting to be married to a Milquetoast. Women, though they seldom admit it, like to be dominated. Of course, they owe it to their sex to try constantly for the upper hand, but their success when they get it can't be very rewarding; having always to be true and faithful to a true and faithful yes-man must be very boring at times. After all, what can be duller than a sure thing? Well, this is straying. The fact is that wives normally make it their business to take charge of the family's social doings, and interference from husbands is sternly discouraged. In this, many women are mistaken. A woman who marries a socially experienced man with pronounced preferences and knowledge about such things as what to serve for dinner and what diversions are to follow will, if she is sensible, let him have things his way. The concession needn't always be 100 per cent. Perhaps he prides himself only on a single specialty, in which case he should certainly be allowed to show it off. Sir Charles Mendl, for example, has a genius for planning the seating arrangements at a dinner party; Elsie wisely — indeed gladly — always left that task to him.

The point I am trying to make is that husbands and wives ought, when they entertain, to honor what each likes best to do, and what each does best.

In this respect, Palm Beach's Charles and Dorothy Munn are perfect examples. The Munns, as nearly as I can discover, have only two things in common: their marriage, which is a happy one, and money. Dorothy was a Spreckels of the sugar clan, and is — indulge me — one of the sweetest women alive; I call her "Sugar." Charles holds the patents for the pari-mutuel system of race-track betting, which is the next best thing to owning a producing gold mine, and is known fondly in horse-racing circles as "the Tote King." No, I take it back. There is a third meeting ground. Dorothy is a great outdoor girl, and is as ardent a racing fan as Charles; from this point on their interests diverge. Charles loves to entertain and is an excellent host. Dorothy is the most indifferent hostess I know. It isn't that she doesn't like to have people around. She does, but she ignores them. Charles loves to eat and knows food. Dorothy likes to eat as well as the next one, but she doesn't know the first thing about food. When I have stayed with them at their lovely Villa Amado it was Charles who ordered all the meals, and Charles again who performed the late-at-night kitchen ritual of scrambling eggs and making coffee while Dorothy looked on. Again, Charles likes to watch movies. Dorothy likes to play cards. So when they entertain, Charles shows movies to his cronies in one part of the house, Dorothy plays cards with hers in another, and everybody is happy. I know very well that this You-go-your-way, I'll-go-mine system isn't everybody's dish, nor for that matter could it be applied practicably to everybody's lives. At least not to the extent the Munns carry it. In Paris, for example, where they usually go each summer, they maintain apartments in different parts of the city — one for Dorothy, one for Charles. You can't do this sort of thing on the average budget, or with the kiddies around to worry about; but I'm not at all sure that fact isn't to be regretted. The Munns' eminently successful marriage gives evidence that periodically planned separation is a very good design for some marriages.

I have defended a handful of Hollywood hostesses against my own attack on that rich and largely unpalatable land, so it is now only fair to speak out for the handful of Hollywood's men to whom the art of entertaining means something more than what to expose on a reel of film. As a matter of fact, the small number of good Hollywood hosts is increasing. In the early days, as in any primitive civilization, survival was all that mattered to the movie-makers. They ate to keep their energies up for the fight with their competitors. Dinner parties as we know them didn't exist: there were brawls, and there were business conferences at which food was served, and that was about the extent of it. Inevitably, of course, as the picture business flourished, Hollywood began to take notice of itself as a new *Kulturkreis* and with this pleasing thought to live up to set about to establish a social order as rigidly stratified as any that then existed in other world capitals, but with one important difference. In Hollywood, money was the sole basis on which one's social position was fixed. The more money, the higher one stood, and while this is not in itself a necessarily censurable conception, it's bound to be a pretty futile one. Money and manners do not, alas, always go hand in hand. Nevertheless, the new Hollywood aristocracy did its best. As a starter they began to build houses suited to their station. They built castles and châteaux and haciendas and villas, they built mansions in every known style of architecture and some that defy recognition to this day. They brought marble from Italy with which to tile their bathrooms, then heightened the effect by installing solid gold plumbing fixtures — no doubt in a spirit of thrift; gold needs no polishing. They raided the market places of the world for treasures to fill their houses. They imported chefs from New York and London and Paris to run their kitchens, and they hired servants enough to keep DeMille in extras for years. Then, in these sumptuous surroundings, they gave parties. Here, unfortunately, any similarity between grand entertaining in Hollywood and grand entertaining in, say, London or Paris stopped. Guests flocked to the regular Saturday-night parties as they always had. They got drunk as they always had. They ignored the food as they always had. They might as well have been entertained in barns, as, indeed, one could only conclude they always had.

In the current crop of good Hollywood hosts, Arthur Hornblow, Jr., is a food connoisseur of the first order; his dinners are masterpieces. Ronald Colman and Clifton Webb are both charming hosts, as might be expected, and Clark Gable is another, as might not. Clark is essentially an outdoor man, which is not usually conducive to skill in the gentler homely arts, but he loves good food and is, as indicated earlier, a great cook.

Sam Goldwyn is a wonderful host, a great character, and a man who likes his work: his favorite way of entertaining guests after dinner is to show movies. Of course it is impossible to think of Sam without being reminded of his celebrated malapropisms. The latest to reach me came about during a visit to Hollywood by Field Marshal Viscount Montgomery. Montgomery had gone to dine with the Goldwyns, and at the appropriate moment Sam rose from the table, glass in hand.

"I should like you all to rise," said Sam with great dignity, "and join me in a toast to our honored guest, Lord Marshal Field Montgomery."

Sam isn't often topped, but in this instance he was. Out of the mild disconcertion that followed came the bland voice of Jack Warner. "Sam's got it wrong," said Jack. "What he *meant* to say was Lord Marshal Field Montgomery *Ward.*"

Jack Warner is deservedly famous as a wit and raconteur, and he is also, in my opinion, the best host in Hollywood. There are the usual reasons. Both Jack and his wife, Ann, understand the art of good living and indulge it. The food and drink at the Warners' is always excellent, the service efficient, the décor charming, the guests stimulating. But behind all these tangibles lies the essential warmth and generosity of spirit that mark the truly good host. To Jack an act of friendship is as involuntary as breathing. Last summer, for example, knowing that Dickie Gordon and I would be at our farm near Cannes before their arrival there, Jack insisted that we make ourselves at home in their villa, Aujourd'hui. So every day we packed a cold lunch, sat on the rocks in front of the villa, and splashed in the sea in isolated splendor. That is real generosity. To lend money or the like is one thing, but to lend your house is to lend a bit of yourself.

On another occasion, this time in New York, I developed a sudden longing to eat a good Mexican dinner. I hadn't been able to find a restaurant in town where the authentic dishes were served, but I remembered the Warners' fondness for Mexican food — they frequently serve it at their parties — and I wrote to them in Hollywood asking if they knew of one. My reply from them came in a rather unexpected, if typical, form: they sent me, by air express, a complete Mexican dinner which was delivered to me at the Waldorf, piping hot and good down to the last frijole.

Untitled, but no less noble in my view, are those three illimitably gifted Englishmen, Noel Coward, my old friend W. Somerset Maugham, and Cecil Beaton — brilliant, articulate, witty to a man — although not, curiously enough considering these assets, all good hosts. Anyway, not without qualification.

Heretofore I have used the words "entertaining" and "party-giving" as more or less synonymous, and so of course they may be, although there are instances in which the twain do not necessarily meet. Noel Coward and Somerset Maugham are two of the most entertaining men in the world, but they are not good party-givers. Cecil Beaton, on the other hand, is both entertaining *and* a good party-giver — ergo, a wonderful host. Cecil has an instinct for mixing the right people; it goes without saying that he knows how to provide them with the ultimate in background elegance (merely to enter his house in Pelham Gardens is to take on bloom), and he has the cosmopolite's taste for exciting food. A Beaton dinner is very apt to feature South American or Indian foods, accompanied by rice dishes with the appropriate hot sauces. I asked him once if there weren't any plain, everyday foods he liked. There were, said Cecil. "Breakfast foods — at any time *but* breakfast."

Noel Coward is one of my oldest and dearest friends, and a man whose wit, charm, and multiple talents have made him the most conspicuously prolific figure in the theater today. As a conversationalist he is beyond compare. There is no subject that does not strike the flint of his brilliance into giving off sparks of fiery wit. As a judge of food he is, if not expert, on his way to being: time was when Noel's disinterest in food amounted to disdain. Perhaps he has mellowed. In any case, he has now taken up cooking with characteristic enthusiasm, and will probably excel in that as he has in everything else. Still he is not a good host — at least not a good party-giver. Entertaining in that sense is not a part of his life; his very profession makes dinner parties while he is acting impossible. A supper party he may give to half a dozen old friends is not so much entertaining as old-home week. I have been his guest when he had a house at St. Margaret's Bay, and at his Goldenhurst Farm near the sea in Kent, and I was always happy to be there because Noel gives happiness to his friends. But that is just the point. Not essentially gregarious, he likes to be only with his closest friends and he is content to confine that circle to a very small circumference. He has little or no interest in people outside his professional orbit. If you are an artist, if you paint, or are a musician or writer you have a much better chance of enjoying yourself with Noel — or of Noel enjoying himself with you — than if you are a purely social adjunct of the everyday world. To his cronies — people like Gladys Caldthorpe, who designs all his sets, and the late writer Joyce Cary — he is a good host simply because he is his entertaining self. But I don't believe he could bring off a properly planned party to save him. I salute Noel on both cheeks as the perfect guest, but just as he'd hardly put me among the top ten actresses of the world — more likely tenth below bottom — so I wouldn't put him, and I don't think he'd expect me to, among the first flight of hosts.

Neither, when strictly observing the standards of perfection, can I put Somerset Maugham in that category. I have known Willie as writer, wit, wooer, and host for forty years and I adore him. I used to play waltzes for him till my nails scorched the keys while he whirled round and round with Syrie Wellcome, whom he later married. Now past eighty, he is unimpaired. In fine weather he swims every day, and his small compact figure is as erect as ever. I think he is the most polite man I have ever met. His manners are faultless, and given added grace by a natural, almost shy, charm, deep literary erudition, and a wicked sense of humor. More, he is a gourmet of the first order and serves delicious food. Yet he is not really a good host. For one thing, like Noel, he prefers few to many, but unlike Noel he makes no effort to cast the net of his hospitality over his many gifted friends. Strangely enough, he seems to prefer nonentities. As often as I have been his guest for lunch or dinner at his lovely Villa Mauresque at Cap Ferrat I have never met there anyone of outstanding social or artistic brilliance. I think perhaps I have an explanation for this. Maugham lives so much in his mind, he dwells so constantly in the companionship of books, he works so hard — if not so much now, he has during most of his life — that when he comes from his study he wants nothing more stimulating than a good game of bridge, or talk that is diverting because effortless.

I do not mean to write off the Messrs. Coward and Maugham as good hosts solely on the ground that they are averse to giving large parties. The fact is, they don't give parties at all. Call them rather get-togethers, which is something else again. A get-together just happens. A party, big or small, must have plan, harmony, pattern. As a matter of fact, though, I will take the get-together à la Coward and Maugham any day in preference to the most ambitious party that fails in these requirements. A large party takes an awful lot of doing. It is not enough to count on numberless guests to create their own momentum, or on some bizarre form of entertainment to keep it up. A large party relies for success on what the host alone can give it in the way of cohesive attraction. If it does not hold together, the host has failed.

To take a melancholy example: I went to an enormous party at Vallauris on the Riviera one day recently, fully expecting to have a wonderful time. Certainly the circumstances were auspicious. It was a Spanish party, and the hosts were Pablo Picasso, whose capacity for invention is undoubted, and the equally agile-minded French poet academician, Jean Cocteau. High point of the day was to be a stage-managed — i.e., faked — bullfight, for which purpose nine suitably menacing-looking bulls were added to the guest list, which was menacing enough in itself: one thousand bidden and accepted, not counting the bulls. By way of setting the mood, Picasso greeted the guests wearing a sombrero and plucking on a guitar. Cocteau wore a toreador's costume. Taken all in all, I did not see how such a colorfully conceived and mounted party could fail. Yet it did. By the time I arrived most of the company had assembled and was positively radiating boredom. As this is a state of mind to which I am unusually susceptible I soon fell in with it. It was hard to diagnose the precise trouble. Mainly, there seemed to be a sort of pervasive aimlessness in the air. No one seemed to know what to do, where to go, or to care much that they didn't. The hosts, for all their ornate efforts, had failed to provide the most important thing of all: a hub, a center, a focus of interest. Now a thousand people is, I grant, an unwieldy number to try to band together into one jolly, integrated crew. In fact, it can't be done. But a thousand people *can* be made to feel that they are joining in and enjoying a common experience — as, for instance, a theater audience will do — and in this Picasso and Cocteau failed. They promised a show, but they were without showmanship. Even the food, which, if exciting enough, can often be counted on to cover a multitude of sins, was inadequate and not very good. (I can't say I was surprised at this. Like most artists, neither Picasso nor Cocteau cares one whit about food. They eat when they feel like eating, never mind what.) Well, it was all just too bad. There was talent, there was scope, there was an incomparable setting, there was a dramatic idea, and the party was a flop. In the end it was left to the bulls to administer the *coup de grâce*. When the time came, *they* were too bored to fight.

It took an Englishman, Matthew Arnold, to declare France

"famed in all great arts, in none supreme." Hah! Presumably Mr. Arnold, although he traveled fairly extensively in France, had never been invited to dine at a Frenchman's home. In Arnold's time, as now, the French respected cookery as an art, and I do not believe there is a food expert in the world who will not concede their supremacy. The good French cook is a true artist, and, as true artists do, he sees beyond the immediate work in hand. The true artist's interest in his creation doesn't stop at filling the canvas. He knows that the finished work must be framed and displayed in a way that will set it off to best advantage; just so does the Frenchman concern himself with setting off the perfect meal. He knows that drab surroundings will detract from its charm, and so frames it with utmost care. He knows that dull company will dull all the senses, including taste, and so selects his guests as painstakingly as he selects the wines — for the maximum enhancement of his chef d'œuvre. All this being so, and Mr. Arnold to the contrary, it is obvious that this model Frenchman cannot fail to excel as a host.

The list of Frenchmen who belong in this distinguished category is long — too long to be done justice to here. One who is typical will do, and that is Baron Fred de Cabrol, who gives dinner parties that I consider masterpieces in miniature. The parties are invariably small; whether the Cabrols entertain in their large house on the Avenue Foch in Paris, or at their small country house, Trois Pommes, at Montfort l'Amaury, they make it a rule never to have more than twelve for dinner. Timing is an important factor in the serving of most foods, and at a large party, with people drinking cocktails and ruining their appetites with appetizers, it is next to impossible to get everyone to the table at the appointed time. So while the Cabrols may have as many as a hundred guests in after dinner, the limit for the table is strictly observed, and to good purpose.

One of the more beneficent aspects of the French passion for good cooking is that it is catching. No one with any degree of wit can stay long in France and fail to succumb to it. I have seen young American women arrive in Paris not knowing or caring how to boil water, only to find them two or three months later proudly showing off the latest lesson learned at the Cordon Bleu. And, since it is axiomatic that the convert is often more dedicated than the converter, foreign-born adherents to the French culinary persuasion not infrequently equal and sometimes even surpass their mentors. Thus two of the finest hosts in France hail originally from South America. One is Charles Bestegui. The other, Arturo Lopez-Willshaw.

Charles Bestegui has the most perfect taste, the most exquisite imagination of any man I know. Clare Boothe Luce has called this gentle and reserved man not one of the best hosts in France, but one of the best hosts in the world, and I agree. I have been entertained by Charles at small dinners and large, at banquets and at balls, and he has never failed to achieve an elegance so little seen these days that simply to share his hospitality is a bit like moving back into another century, to a time when taste and elegance mattered and a man who gave himself to the direct service of beauty could do so without risk of a public bullying. Charles is the eighteenth-century gentleman doing the best he can in the twentieth to pay his respects to that graceful and mannerly period, and doing his best, too, to resurrect and preserve a part of it. Recently he has bought the Château de Groussay at Montfort l'Amaury, a beautiful old château overlooking a lake, and an eighteenth-century *monument historique*. To it he has added two wings, one — with a backward nod to the seventeenth century — containing a Dutch room decorated in the style of that period, the other a perfect little theater of the eighteenth century, decorated in red silk and seating 250, with a center box reserved always for his friends, the Comte and Comtesse de Paris. Charles had his grand opening early this spring, while I was still in New York, alas, but later in the summer I will be among the audience watching a play or the ballet. No amateur theatricals these. Marcel Achard, one of France's foremost playwrights, has written a play to be performed there, the Comédie Française will do a play by Marivaux, and the Opéra Comique is also scheduled to appear. I don't know what more a host can offer than evenings like these — unless it is a taste for more: lengthiness is not a strong point with Charles. An early bird, his friends know that the curtain falls at midnight and that is when they must leave. And they do.

Arturo Lopez-Willshaw, whose father founded a tin empire in Chile, and who is now reputedly worth sixty million dollars, is as representative a citizen of the twentieth century as any man can be; nonetheless he pays homage to the virtues of the eighteenth, too. The Lopezes' house in Paris is Louis XVI throughout, a beautiful example of the period, to which Patricia Lopez adds the final note of opulence by keeping the rooms filled always with great clusters of wonderful flowers. Not the least of the Lopezes' accomplishments as hosts is their talent for giving large dinner parties perfectly. Quantity is a notoriously efficient thief of quality, and mass cooking is seldom all it should be, yet I have been to parties at the Lopezes' where a hundred guests were seated and where the food, the service, all the arrangements, were as perfect as if we had been no more than ten.

The word "considerate" doesn't come often to mind these days; there just don't seem to be many around who deserve it. The dictionary defines it as "observant of the rights and feelings of others; showing thoughtful kindness," and thus succinctly describes the Lopezes. They are considerate people. Possibly the most convincing proof of this is the loyalty of the people who work for them. Their two chefs, for example, have each been with them for sixteen years — the younger, having started as pastry chef at the startling age of fifteen, is now a fully qualified master chef and always goes along to take charge of the galley when they are aboard their beautiful yacht, the *Gaviota*. Then there is Patricia's observant regard for the individual tastes of their friends. Like most good hostesses who entertain often and in force, she keeps a file of menus and guests; unlike most hostesses, however, this record is not intended solely to avoid duplication. Its secondary purpose is to ensure duplication. Thus, when a guest shows a pronounced fondness for a particular dish, the fact is duly noted in the file and the next time he comes — unless it is to a large dinner when it is obviously impractical to cater to individual tastes — he is very likely to be served it again. Nor is the Lopez thoughtfulness reserved for the home. At a recent dinner at the Paul Dubonnets' in Paris, the food was exceptionally good, and we were all lavish in our praise to the hosts. Only Arturo thought to go into the kitchen afterward to personally present *his* compliments to the chef.

My last candidate for inclusion in this company of notable hosts is a man who, properly speaking, doesn't really qualify at all: Prince Aly Khan is less a working host than a star attraction at his own parties; but I include him nevertheless for the simple, time-honored, and most feminine of reasons — that I love him. I have known Aly for something over ten years now, and I admit that the friendship got under way handicapped by what was then my belief in the popular theory that he is a playboy, nothing more. Being shorn of that notion was a slow process, but a complete one. As I came to know him, I came also to know that

Aly's much-publicized romances have completely obscured the more significant facts of his life. Certainly he loves beautiful women. Certainly women find it easy to love him. That's bad? More enviable, I should say. What few people realize is that Aly is a hard-working businessman who has for many years successfully managed the multimillion-dollar horse-breeding business he owned jointly with his father, the Aga Khan, and that he was equally hard-working and conscientious in discharging his duties as the potential spiritual leader of the Ismaili. In naming Aly's son, Prince Karim, as his successor, the Aga Khan felt that a young, untried man, about whom there had been no publicity of any kind, would be the best choice. Karim is a serious young man, and I do not believe he will ever become as emotionally involved with women as his father and grandfather were. I believe Aly must have been very much hurt by his father's decision to bypass him. All the same, I was devoted to the Aga, and I am also devoted to the Begum Aga Khan, who proved her devotion to her husband until his death, and who has now become the first Moslem woman to be an acknowledged leader of the Ismaili, as her late husband wished.

I will say for Aly as a host that when he gives a party there is one predictable thing about it: that is that the end result is wholly unpredictable. For the art of giving the completely casual party, one that gathers itself together like leaves in the wind, that begins, remains, and ends on an entirely disorganized note, I hand him all honors. People seem to be coming and going all the time at his house in Paris, and at his Château de l'Horizon at Cannes. (As a householder, Aly may well hold a world record; he owns in the neighborhood of twenty houses, but these two in France are his bases.) Fortunately, he has a perfect staff which always manages to rise to the exigencies of guests arriving for lunch or dinner at the last minute, for he enjoys a crowd and invites everyone he meets on the spur of the moment. As if this weren't clamorous enough, he also likes a background of music; when he is at the Château de l'Horizon, bands play steadily from midday to midnight. Aly, in short, entertains, but he doesn't give parties. His parties give themselves, and if that's the way he wants it it's all right with me. If only the host is on hand, I'll go any time.

CHAPTER VI

The Pleasure of Your Company

"BRING anyone you like," Laura Corrigan used to say to casual friends when she first began launching herself as a hostess in London. Needless to say the friends obliged, and the result was that Laura's parties — awash though they consequently were with the titles she coveted, and thus perfect in her eyes — could not properly be called parties at all. Webster defines a party, in the social sense of the word, as "a select company" — and so it is, or should be. But select was scarcely the word for Laura's indiscriminately gathered, often lively, often amusing, but just as often incoherent company: there were times when her drawing room suggested nothing so much as an ultra-elegant station waiting room, in which the only discernible bond between the waitees was that they were all ticketed aboard the same gravy train.

For guests, of course, this all-comers-welcome system of invitation has its points. Not knowing who you're going to be thrown with, you go to the party in the expectation of surprise, and it may, if you're lucky, turn out to be a pleasant one. If not, you can always plead that nasty old migraine coming on again and leave — which, in the case of the hostess who has been foolish enough, or amiable enough, or ignorant enough, to admit total strangers to her house with no other recommendation than they happen to be friends of friends, is no more than she deserves. It is all very well for a guest to take chances on his company for the evening. For a hostess it is pure folly. No really good hostess will take a chance on inflicting misfits on her friends. Laura, it is true — in spite of, or perhaps because of, her vacuum-cleaner method of pulling in guests — made quite a name for herself as a hostess; but it was not, as I have said, a particularly enviable one: she was laughed at almost as much as she was sponged on. Laura's popularity was, I'm afraid, a plain case of money gilding the pill.

But not all the money in the world, not even when it is backed by great and unshakable social position, can save a party that is open to just anybody from turning into a calamity, if not a complete rout. My rating of a guest is high. I see no reason in giving a party to people you do not know or, knowing, care not at all to know better. When I draw up a guest list for a party I am — I have learned to be — less a hostess than a dictator. I, and I alone, decide who is to be invited, and in deciding I consider only two qualifications. One is that I know and like the person. The other, that he or she have something to contribute to the success of the party. No one is ever asked to a party of mine because of his position, however exalted. (Contrary to popular opinion, I know. Critics of my column have complained that "Elsa Maxwell never writes about Mrs. Brown or Mrs. Smith — only titles." It is true that I know and like quite a number of titled people. All the world loves a title, no country more than ours, and that is why I write about them. If I didn't nobody would read my column. All the same, there are many Mrs. Browns and Mrs. Smiths in my life whom I like, and whom I would rather entertain than the most imposing of crowned heads, if the head under the crown was not to my liking.) And, certainly, no one, however exalted, is ever admitted to a party of mine unless he or she has been expressly asked to be there. When, as sometimes happens, I am forced to deal with self-appointed candidates for my list — pesterers for invitations, would-be crashers and the like — the tyrant comes out in me full-fledged: Nero could not have turned thumbs down with less remorse.

I have never quite understood the mentality of the determined crasher: certainly the last place *I* would ever want to be is a party to which I hadn't been invited, and I cannot imagine how anyone with a modicum of pride could feel otherwise. Still, the breed exists — people who will resort to any device to be seen at a party they think they shouldn't miss, the object apparently being twofold: first, to be able to boast afterwards of having been there, and second, to take private revenge on the hostess who was weak-minded enough to tolerate the intrusion by going on to describe, with suitable embellishments, how ghastly it all was. Only once in my party-giving career have I let myself be pressed into admitting a crasher, and the result was every bit as tiresome as I'd feared. This was in Hollywood (come to think of it, perhaps that explains the lapse; perhaps I was slightly addled by the place). In any case, I was giving a party and I had heard through friends that a woman I knew only slightly — only well enough in fact to have registered three things about her: one, that she was extremely rich; two, that she looked like a bad Japanese print; and three, that I didn't much like her — that this woman, anyway, was determined to come to my party. I was equally determined that she should not. Imagine with what pleasure, then, I glanced down the line of arrivals on the night of the party and beheld none other than the bad print herself. I was standing, I remember, with Clifton Webb, his mother, Mabel, and Mrs. Darryl Zanuck, peaceable souls all, who, when they saw my hackles rise and heard me announce that the woman was not to be admitted, begged me not to embarrass her. It would be all right, they assured me. Besides, the party was large. She'd be swallowed up, go unnoticed, I'd see. Finally, reluctantly, I agreed to let her stay. I greeted her, I shook her hand, if not very cordially, and from then on I watched her. Little people always like to make a show of themselves, and this one was no exception. First, she spotted Clark Gable, plunked herself down in front of him, and set to work boring him. When he was finally able to escape she proceeded on, going from one guest to the next, boring all the way. The moment came when I could stand it no longer. There was a little bar off the main room, and when I saw it was empty I went in and beckoned to her, very sweetly, as if I had something charming and friendly to confide to her. In she tripped, and I let her have it.

"You," I said, "were not invited to this party, and you will have to go — quickly."

She looked astonished. "But what have I done?"

"Everything wrong," I said, a remark she chose to take, for some reason, as a reflection on her ancestry.

"I'll have you know," she spluttered, "that my background is every bit as good as yours!"

"Your background," I said, "may be infinitely better. I don't know and I don't care. I simply know that this is my party and that I am asking you to leave it."

She left.

Little as I liked the woman, I'll give her credit for one thing: she had skin a rhinoceros could envy. But she showed a certain humor when, the following day, she sent me three dozen roses, with a little note — thanking me for the party!

There have been no repeats of that disagreeable incident and there won't be. I enjoy the belief that, after all these years of standing my ground on the matter of crashers, my antipathy to the breed is generally known and respected. Every now and again, though, I am given a rude surprise. For example, on the night of my party for Cole the man at the door came to me early on to say that a titled Englishwoman, wife of a well-known British diplomat, had asked to be admitted with two of her friends. (Position, I should mention, is not necessarily synonymous with good taste. I know of one member of the British royal family who went to a Park Lane millionaire's party, uninvited, "just for fun." She was taken by a friend and didn't know her host from Adam. No doubt the host in this instance was flattered by the lady's presence, but that does not offset the fact that it was a most unseemly and tasteless thing for her to do.) But back to my lady . . . I sent out word that she could not come in, but the word proved insufficient. She persisted in badgering the man on the door until, after an uncomfortable hour of this, I took matters into my own hands and went out to her. The lady was indignant. She had, she said, called my apartment and been told it would be all right for her to come to the party.

"Then there has been a mistake," I told her. "It is not all right — it is all wrong. I'm sorry, but only my friends have been invited to this party, and you are not welcome."

"But what can I possibly say to my friends outside?"

"That," I said, "is up to you. I can only say that I don't know them, and I don't want to know them. I am sorry, Lady ——, but that is the way it is."

And that is, indeed, the way it is. Even when a close friend rings up to ask if he may bring someone I do not know to my party I say No. Of course, if he should ask to bring Sir Winston and Lady Churchill, or someone of equal distinction, then objection would melt. I am human. But by and large, once I have designed a guest list to my satisfaction, it stands as written.

Your guest list, after all, *is* your party, your blueprint for the ultimate grand design, and it is up to you to keep it under control. If you have done the job well you have — usually not without difficulty — worked out a plan that is in perfect balance. The minute you let friends or family persuade you to add to it here and there the balance will be gone; and nine times in ten, the success of your party with it.

Well, then, you are going to give a party, and you are going to start, of course, by deciding whom to invite. Consider, first, the capacity of your room. Never have more people than you can put comfortably into one room. Split your party into two rooms and you will at once sacrifice all intimacy.

The first names for the list will be easy enough. It is almost always the wish to see dear old So-and-so, or to bring people of common interest together, or to celebrate some special occasion, that prompts parties; and each of these conditions automatically carries the nucleus of a guest list with it. Then, too, most of us know a sprinkling of people who are what might be called party-proof: people who are attractive to meet, who are good mixers, good talkers, generally reliable guests in any company, and who can be safely called on to fill in as needed. With these two groups, then, you have the framework of your party. Now let us suppose you have planned a dinner for twenty and find yourself, after the first-thought names are checked off, still shy that number. You may need fill-ins of either or both sexes. You want to introduce new faces, new talent. So, address book in hand, you begin to sift through the possibilities. Now in entertaining a group of this size it is imperative to be choosy. At a very large party — at a dance for, say, two hundred — it is possible to get away with a cipher or two: if they don't find one another, which is unlikely, you can always arrange to pool them together; but when your party is small, let no one character be wanting. Settle for nothing but the best. Be a celebrity chaser, if you will; celebrities exist in all localities and all walks of life. You like gardening: all right, ask the man or woman with the best garden in town. Your guest of honor has a hobby: ask the fellow enthusiast who is gay and instructive about that hobby. Another guest likes good food: then ask someone who also appreciates food and talks well about it. Still another is a Sunday painter — those two artists in the village aren't rich or famous, but how good they are to listen to, with their stories of other painters. In your immediate environment, choose from the top of the heap.

Call it snobbery if you like. I call it being selective. You don't take just anything that comes along in other walks of life, so why do so when entertaining? Always select the best as you see it, and your reputation as a hostess will quickly bloom. One word of advice, though, on how, having settled for the best, to be sure of getting them there: never seem too eager. A carefully calculated, polite indifference in the invitation does the trick, especially if their positions are up in the stratosphere.

So much for the positive approach to your guest list. Now let us look at the negative — whom to avoid:

In the first place never, in planning a party, give way to pity or sentiment or sense of obligation — this last least of all. Yet it happens all the time — the hostess who, contemplating an incomplete guest list, asks herself the question that, answered and acted on, is likely to throw the whole party out of kilter. Whom, she wonders dismally, do we owe? Now no one ever puts this question to himself gladly. You don't consciously think of the word "owe" in connection with people you enjoy. Owed guests are duty guests, obligations, and the minute you try to fit one into your party — look out! Ask because you feel you must, and the party's a bust before you start. Just because you have reason to be grateful to someone doesn't mean you must feel obligated to wine and dine him. There are other ways of saying thanks. After all, you aren't likely to ask your butcher to dinner simply because he supplied you with a good steak, so why labor the point with others? A good hostess, aware of the pitfalls, never wittingly puts herself under obligation to anyone. When invitations come to her from people she has no wish to entertain in return she simply, politely, and, if possible, with tactful emphasis as a discouragement to future bids, turns them down. I, for one, make it a rule never to accept invitations to parties where I am reasonably sure of being bored: accepting would mean not only one dull evening, but two. I'd feel obligated to return the invitation, and I flatly refuse to put myself under obligation to people who bore me. (My record for refusals, I should say in passing, has been made in New York, where society is so close-knit that many hostesses vary their guest lists not at all from one dinner party to the next. Very boring.) There are exceptions, of course. I am sometimes bound by calling to accept invitations I'd like to refuse, but I keep them, believe me, to an irreducible minimum. Such obligations are, of course, unavoidable for most of us, and in the average household I know that it is occasionally necessary, for business reasons or simply to keep peace in the family, to be entertained by and, in return, entertain duds. But do try to spare your valued friends these occasions; and if this isn't possible, at least refrain from letting the fact be known that you consider your party predoomed. Never say to friends, "You'll probably be bored to death by these people, but please come anyway." That way, you will be ruling out whatever chance there might have been of their discovering some community of interest. If you feel you must alibi yourself try to be a little subtle about it. You can always say, "We're having some people I don't think you've met, but whom you might find interesting." Which is only the truth. If the duty guests don't interest the others as personalities, they may at least interest them as specimens.

As bad as asking obligations — far worse, to my mind, since it is also downright dishonest — is asking people you hope to put under obligation to you. For that there is no excuse whatever. If you do feel bound to confer some favor or other on people in a position to do you a good turn — a very human if regrettable compulsion — then for pity's sake choose some other means than the pretense of enjoying their company. Unless you're a very rare actress indeed you're going to show the strain of being nice to people on whom you have ulterior designs. I recently gave a piece of advice on this subject to a woman who doubtless did not act on it, but I consider it sound advice, worth remembering *and* using. I met her on the street one day, bags under her eyes, looking ready for the hospital. I asked if she were ill.

"Worse, much worse," she groaned. "I have to give a party for the Browns!"

"*Have* to give a party? I should think you'd be delighted. I *long* for a reason to give a party."

"You," she said feelingly, "don't *know* the Browns. The trouble is, Mrs. Brown's brother is considering my son for a job in his bank. It's a good opening for him — so, I'm giving a dinner for the Browns. Will you come?"

"Certainly not," I said. "And if I were you I'd call the whole thing off. Send Mrs. Brown a good book, tell her you know she'll enjoy it; then you can *both* stay home and have a lovely time."

There are only two kinds of ulterior-motive entertaining for which I can see a shred of excuse: one is entertaining in what may best be called the world of affairs. The other, débutante dance entertaining. In the first instance, curiosity on the part of a person of prominence to look over a young man or woman of promise in a field that concerns him is certainly justifiable. And, after all, the invitation need not be repeated. I remember, for instance, how tongues wagged when the young Laborite, Aneurin Bevan, first came to London, swallowed his all-consuming class prejudice and, wearing a gray suit and flaming red tie with everyone else in white ties and tails, went to dine with Lord Beaverbrook. Why did Lord Beaverbrook, whose acquaintance with the social amenities has always been slight to say the least, bother with this amiable and intelligent, but politically antagonistic young man? Presumably because Bevan's star was rumored to be rising and Beaverbrook wanted to observe the ascendant at first hand. Why did Bevan walk docilely into the opponent's camp? Out of curiosity no doubt, perhaps the attraction of good food and wine, but more I am sure to see what manner of man Beaverbrook was, with his wealth and power and position — all three of which Bevan, of course, would wish to destroy when he himself came to power. Yes, in the intricate business of empire building, social means are understandably used to serve ambitious ends — and that covers débutantes as well, who are something of empire builders themselves (or so their ambitious mamas hope). Obviously there is something to be said for giving the most auspicious possible boost to the marriageable young, however it's done — whether as in London, where the girls all climb on a conveyer belt at the beginning of the season, the mothers alternating with parties for them, or as in New York, where the belles are poured into one vast hopper for a single night's ball, and that's that. Either way, girl meets girl, thus presumably meets brother of girl, and the contest is on.

It sounds callous, but try, too, when you entertain, to keep your family out of it. Believe me, nobody wants to meet your relatives. Naturally if you can produce one who boasts some personal distinction other than the accident of birth that hung him on your family tree, then by all means include him. The trick here is to be sure you're being strictly objective. Not many people see their relatives as others see them: sentiment comes into it, or clan loyalty, or sense of duty — considerations with which your friends may sympathize, but don't expect them to like it. Family presences — particularly the elders among them — tend to give other guests an uneasy feeling of being under surveillance. No one is quicker than a great-aunt — or even, for that matter, a great-niece — at looking for faults in the company one keeps: knowing this, your friends will bend over backwards to do you the favor of leaving a good impression, becoming in the process all too self-consciously amiable and correct. Worse, they will let themselves be monopolized. From your own point of view, family will inevitably complicate your job as hostess in one of two ways — either (*a*) by so far forgetting their status as guests, subject to the usual rules of good guest behavior, that they simply settle into the best chairs and wait to be amused, or (*b*) by so far remembering their status as family that they will feel moved to pitch in with a familial hand: self-appointed stewards in your house, they go meddlesomely about making little suggestions, sincerely trying to be of help, but usually only managing to get in your way. They are, in short, neither fish nor fowl at your parties and they don't belong there. Try to bear in mind that while fate makes our relatives, there is nothing in the natural law that obliges us to make the friends of our choice share in that fate.

Avoid people with causes to boost or grievances to air. You will quickly find them buttonholing and trumpeting and boring all within reach.

Avoid the very shy, uncertain, introverted types. They may not mean to throw a damper on things — indeed they will be so pathetic in their eagerness not to do anything at all to attract notice that it will be impossible not to notice and be dampened by them. Then, too, there is another risk inherent in this type: a bit of the lion lurks in every mouse, and alcohol can usually be depended on to bring it out. A cocktail or two, and your bashful mute may very well turn — or fancy he's turning — into the life of the party, to everyone's distress including his own, come the next day.

Avoid always having the same people together, and by the the same token — and this is another point on which I lock horns with the rulebooks — avoid categorizing groups so that you wind up with a roomful of people all of the same age, or profession, or hobby. As the arbiters have it, at a party where there is to be dancing you must ask only young people who enjoy dancing. At a party where the guest of honor is elderly, ask only more of the elderly. At a party where there is to be music ask only people who are musical. Nonsense. Carry this dictum to its final absurdity and if you happened to be entertaining an eminent herpetologist you would ask only snakes.

Mixing — clever mixing — is the making of any party. I always make it a point, for instance, even in a predominantly eggheaded group, to have a smattering of beautiful women regardless of whether they are dumbbells or not (and most beautiful women are not very bright). But beautiful women are like beautiful flowers. You must have them, and if you are

a clever hostess you will place them as you do your flowers —
for best effect. Put them where they'll be shown off to advantage. Put a lovely young girl next to a man with a beard. Mix.
Juggle. Keep the pattern changing.

As for the limits of age, there are none. It is true, of course,
that when you give a dance you will want to put the emphasis
on young people who enjoy dancing — most older people prefer
good conversation — but that's no reason to leave the older
people out of it. If they don't want to dance (and there's a
waltz or two left in us septuagenarians yet, believe it or not)
they can talk just as well, and probably enjoy themselves
more, to the accompaniment of pleasant music and the spectacle of the young getting off a fast cha-cha, than they would
in the more sedate atmosphere of somebody's drawing room.
If nothing else they can have a high old time making shocked
comparisons between the dances of *their* day and the satur-
nalias that pass for dances now.

But if you underplay older people at a dance, at the average
party it matters not at all how you mix ages. After all, a good
many oldsters are among the most interesting people in the
world. They've seen more than the young, done more, read
more, heard more, traveled more — how could they fail, then,
to have more to give? Leaving out the tedious reminiscers —
and I have never thought this so much a failing of advanced
age as of character: bores now, they probably always were bores
— what young person would not want to meet a man as rich
in experience as, say, Dr. Schweitzer, Toscanini, Senator Ful-
bright? At the other end of the stick, what older person would
not find something to interest him in Marlon Brando, in the
Shah of Iran — a living and fascinating king — in the Aly
Khan? No, age differences should be no barrier in entertaining.
Only be sure to combine them in good proportion. Always

have more of one group than the other. That way the larger group will absorb the smaller; divide them evenly and you are very apt to find them dividing themselves into separate camps — to each his own.

Too, mix people of different political and religious persuasions, different incomes, different professions. It's surprising how much understanding can be awakened in people of conflicting views over a good dinner, and the controversial talk along the way will keep things lively.

Of course, in mixing as in everything else, taste and judgment enter in: it is as bad to mix imprudently as not to mix at all. Obviously it would be unfair to bring sworn enemies together, just for the fun of lighting the fuse, and it would be the height of rudeness to have people who for one reason or another might be offensive to others at the same party.

In planning a guest list for a large party ask as many people as you need to fill your room, at the outset, to the point of crowding. That way there will be no vacuums at the crucial, starting hour, when it is important to set the right mood. Later, when people start drifting off before the party's over — as they will at any large party — those who are left will have formed their own groups, and gaps here and there won't matter.

Also at large parties — particularly, of course, if there is to be dancing, when it is vital — it is well to have extra men. At small seated parties aim to have the sexes balance. (If there must be an imbalance have it, as hardly needs saying, in favor of men; spare women spell death.) But most men, while they enjoy a chat together at a party, will be bored witless to find themselves seated side by side at dinner.

At very small parties — dinners for, say, six or eight — don't have only married couples. Break it up. If possible, ask at least one man and one woman who are new to the others, and preferably new to each other. No ulterior motive, you understand — although it's always fun to launch a romance if you can — but a new man brings out the best in any woman, and vice versa; and the two together will keep the rest of the company on their toes.

How you invite guests depends, of course, on the kind of party you're giving. If it's to be a large party with dancing, printed invitations should go out at least three weeks to a month before the date. Note that I say printed rather than engraved, as the rulebooks insist is proper for any and all formal — dress — occasions. Certainly invitations for such things as weddings, débutante balls, formal receptions, and the like are customarily engraved; but these aren't really parties — they're social rituals; not my kind of entertaining at all, and I don't propose to go into the ways and means of them here. Look to Mrs. Post and her lesser sisters if it's the ceremonious you're after in your entertaining. For that matter, any good stationer will be happy to show you samples of appropriate forms for formal invitations from which you can take your choice: in this event be guided only by the first precept of good taste — simplicity.

But with these more or less prescribed exceptions, I can see no reason for adding to the expense of an already expensive party — and the cost of giving a dance, in particular, is dizzying — by going into debt to an engraver simply to oblige the whim of the rulebookers. And my quarrel is not with the expense alone. Engraved invitations are invariably set pieces, subject to all manner of rules as to format and wording. As a result they look stiff, they *are* stiff, and stiffness is hardly the most desirable note to strike in a bid to come and have fun. Printed invitations, on the other hand, can be as colorful and gay as you choose, can say what you choose to say in whatever way you choose to say it. Why not give them a personal touch? Invest in a bottle of India ink, do it yourself, and let your local printer take it from there.

In the area of small-scale entertaining there is one species of hostess for whom an engraved form of invitation makes sense, and that is the city woman who entertains often, at home, and with a degree of formality — and by often I mean a dinner party a week, sometimes more. For her, it is a saving of time and trouble to have cards engraved — approximately 4" × 5" in size — on which spaces are left blank to be filled in as needed, as:

> Mr. and Mrs. John Doe Smith
> request the pleasure of
> [Miss Elsa Maxwell's]
> company [for dinner] on
> [day and date]
> at [8:00] o'clock
> 123 East Main Street
>
> R.s.v.p.

If evening dress is called for, *Black tie* is written in on the lower right-hand corner.

These cards may also double as reminders to acceptances to whom the hostess has telephoned the invitation or otherwise delivered it in person. In that case, lest the invitee feel obliged to accept all over again, the R.s.v.p. is simply crossed out.

For small informal parties at home, telephoned invitations are easy and expedient, in that you will know where you stand on acceptances and regrets and so be able to check them off — revising the guest list, if need be — as you go. For larger parties at home, there's nothing wrong with doing your asking by telephone either — except the risk you run of involving yourself with chatty friends just dying to settle in for a good gossip: when you've a list of thirty or forty names to work through in the shortest possible time, an informal note or a note written on your personal card (the fold-over type) is a simple matter of self-protection.

If your party is to be away from home — at a club or restaurant or hotel where reservations must be made — it is always well to let your guests have the particulars of time and place in writing. Even if the party is small, and you've done your initial inviting by telephone or in person, a written reminder to acceptances will safeguard against the address or the hour having been misunderstood, or jotted down on the wrong date on the calendar, or, as can happen to the most orderly of us, not jotted down at all. Too, follow-ups should be sent, and for the same reasons, if your invitations have been given verbally and several weeks in advance . . . lest they forget. But this last contingency is not apt to arise often — not the way we do things here. Most Americans are in the habit of inviting friends on the spur of the moment for a party the next night or the next week — I do it myself when I'm in New York, where my friends are all of a good sixty seconds away by telephone; where, moreover, I'm usually pretty well acquainted with their datebooks. In Europe, however, where the social observances are considerably more measured and where the telephone is not held to be the center of all existence as it is to us, hostesses send out invitations for lunch or dinner — however small and informal the party is to be — about three weeks in advance, and engraved reminder cards about a week in advance. The usual form for the reminder is:

This is to remind you that
The Duke and Duchess of ——
expect you
on [day and date]
for [lunch or dinner]
at [   ] o'clock
[address]

Many American hostesses — at least those with heavy social schedules — use these reminder cards, but for the majority, who entertain only occasionally and then informally, a handwritten note, or, again, a note on a personal card, even a line or two on a "penny" postcard, is perfectly adequate. Indeed, for the great number of modern-day hostesses formal reminder cards would be downright pretentious — hardly suitable, let's say, for the casserole-and-salad-on-the-buffet kind of party, over which the hostess presides, when she's not in the kitchen, done up in her best dirndl.

But engraved, printed, written, telephoned, or simply mentioned in passing — however you do your inviting — *be explicit*. Nothing is more maddening than the casually offered, "We're having a few people in on Friday — our anniversary. Will you come? Eightish?" — this from someone you don't know particularly well, and whose way of entertaining you know not at all. That Friday now. Presumably the next — but is it? Could it be that you are expected to know on what particular Friday their anniversary falls? And "eightish." Dinner, of course — but, again, is it? There *are* people who dine at the incredible hours of six or — less incredibly — seven, and consider eight o'clock and on the shank of the evening. (On this point, America is the only country I know where any such confusion is possible: we seem to dine at all hours, from sundown on. In Spain, for instance, a guest understands that an invitation for 11 P.M. means dinner. In France it is 10:30, in Italy 9:30, in London 8:30. New Yorkers pretty generally favor 8:00, but in other parts of the country it is often earlier.) But to get on with the puzzle: what about dress? No clue in the invitation there. Full fig? Or the same old regulation black-with-pearls?

Unless your invitations are to intimates, people who know you well and whom you've entertained often, make sure they are unmistakably clear. As a hostess, your obligation to guests is to make things as comfortable for them as possible, and confusing them at the outset is no help at all. Never leave a guest-to-be in the smallest doubt as to the day, the date, and the hour when he is expected, nor for what purpose (dinner? a fourth at bridge? dancing? the theater?), nor how he should be dressed. Properly worded, for example, that befuddling bid above would have gone something like this: "Will you come for dinner, and bridge after, on Friday, the eighteenth? Eight o'clock — and we're not dressing." A bit more succinct, perhaps, than normal delivery would make it, but the bones of the event are there no matter how many little pleasantries you add to flesh them up.

Note, too, that nothing is said of an anniversary. Giving a shower or birthday party or other such for a mutual friend is one thing: guests are asked to bring gifts and no apologies needed. All right, too, to rally a few intimates — repeat, *intimates* — for the birthday of a member of your family with the understanding that some little thing in hand is expected of them. But to ask casual friends, to even suggest to them that they put themselves out of time and pocket to mark a celebration in which they cannot conceivably have more than a polite interest is unfair: most of us have more births and birthdays and weddings to cope with than we care to think about as it is.

Always be sure that a guest coming to your house for the first time has the address correct and in hand, and if it is a sometime guest, confirm it for him. If you are a suburban or country dweller and your guests are coming by car, give them not only the address but precise directions for finding the place — a landmarked map is a nice courtesy and a blessing to the driver. If they are coming by train, either send them a timetable on which you've checked a recommended train, or ask them to let you know the one it will be convenient for them to take. In either case, tell them if they'll be met at the station and by whom and if it isn't possible to meet them (and you would need a very valid excuse indeed for not doing so), write out the directions they will need to give a taxi man. Nothing can be more dismaying than to alight from a train onto a strange station platform with only the vaguest notion of where to go from there: pioneer blood is not strong in most of us.

And while we're in the country: what to wear to a party is always a burning question, especially to women, and a good hostess will always be sure her guests are spared possible embarrassment by giving them what data they need in this regard, never more necessarily than when she entertains on a country week end. Always advise prospective house guests what the social program for their stay is to be — day and night, outdoors and in — so that there is no chance of their arriving amply supplied with tweeds and bathing suits, but nothing to wear to that gala country club dance you neglected to mention.

I make it a rule to answer all invitations at once, knowing only too well how difficult it is for a hostess to complete plans for her party — more than difficult: impossible — while there is any doubt as to the number of guests she will have. When you are on the receiving end of an invitation it is simple good manners to write or telephone your reply on the same day it is received if possible — certainly not more than a day or two after. This is not only good manners — it is a good investment in your own social future. Hostesses, like elephants, have prodigious memories for the good turn.

In writing a note of acceptance, keep it brief. It is enough to say "Delighted — on the 10th at 8:00," or the like. Never mind the effusions about looking forward to with pleasure, etc. At this point all your hostess wants to know is *will you?* or *won't you?* Above all, don't pester her with questions (Will you mind awfully if I'm a bit late? Are the So-and-sos to be there?). She has enough to do without having to write unnecessary letters.

When you must send regrets to a hostess whose party you will be sincerely sorry to miss, let her know your reason for having to miss it and just how sincerely sorry you are. When you *want* to send regrets to a hostess whose parties you can cheerfully and forever do without, be polite about it but try, with tact, to close the door to future invitations. To take an example, there is a world of difference between such a refusal as, "I'm so sorry that a previous engagement will keep me from joining you on the eighteenth. Thank you anyway for thinking of me. Sincerely," and one that is openly and honestly regretful, as, "I'm sick at having to miss your party on the eighteenth, but that, of all days, falls on the week end I'm to be in Washington. Know you'll understand, and that you'll make a huge success of it as always. Love."

The first note is courteous enough, all in good form, yet it hardly sounds as if missing this party or future ones will weigh too heavily on your spirit, and if the hostess is at all perceptive there's a good chance you won't have to worry about refusing her twice. The second note, on the other hand, can leave no doubt as to your affection for the hostess and the value you put on holding a permanent place on her list. It has what I can only call the graceful plus — that small, decisive extra in our relationships that marks the difference between the good friendships — those that last and deepen with time — and the passing friendships that are missed, when they pass, scarcely at all. Never mind how the plus is expressed — a gratuitous word, a gratuitous gesture — it's the thought that counts. I am thinking, for instance, of a day recently when I came back from lunch to find two dozen beautiful long-stemmed red roses waiting for me, sent by the Irving Berlins along with a little note of regret at having to miss one of my parties. It was a charming thing to do, the plus gesture of people who take friendship as a trust, who know the art of pleasing others, who understand, in fact, the art of being good guests, even *in absentia.*

CHAPTER VII

The Perfect Guest — and Others

RATING yourself as a host is a relatively simple matter: if you give a good party you know it; if you give a bad party you know it, and since the reasons for success or failure are bound to be obvious to any reasonably perceptive mind you learn by these experiences, remedy what faults there may be, and so improve — it is hoped — as you go.

But how many people ever bother to take a good long critical look at themselves as *guests*? How many merely assume that all a host asks of them is the loan of their presence for an evening? How many, indeed, are sooner or later going to have to wake up one sad day wondering what ever happened to those nice Smiths or Browns down the way who give such charming parties, but who've somehow overlooked them of late? Could it be something they've done? It could be indeed. Good guests are too valuable to good hosts to be dropped lightly and without reason. The fault in such a case is necessarily with the guest.

So then — any among you who've ever turned up missing on somebody's guest list, listen well. This chapter is for you.

To begin with, fix in your mind the fact that the impression you make at a party is essentially the impression in microcosm that you make on the world, and that your success or failure as a guest is therefore a fair reflection of your success or failure as a human being. I am not talking about material success. Money and fame have no more to do with the art of being a good guest than with the art of being a good host. Indeed, the great big self-important world of success — particularly when the success is self-made — is a positive breeding ground for some of the worst guests in the world: filled with a sense of their own consequence, they make no effort to put themselves out for the sake of pleasing others. The late Paul Kruger, president of the Transvaal and a formidable figure in the political life of South Africa, was so little interested in people not immediately concerned with his political ambitions that when he went to purely social parties and found no other guests he deemed worthy of his time he simply clammed up. Once in London one of his hostesses, desperate to have the great man say *something* the others might one day recollect for their grandchildren, tried to draw him out. "I came to eat, not to talk," said Kruger, and did just that. Heaven forbid he should ever have been my guest. Not twice anyway. Unless a celebrity is also a congenial human being, I'll take a personable nonentity any day.

For success as a guest is strictly a matter of personality. Look at me. Certainly no one could have asked me to parties back in the early days because of my importance — of which there was none — or my beauty, of which there was, if anything, less. I was asked because I gave value as a guest. Hostesses liked me, liked my chatter, liked my piano playing. Well then, how can they like you? What have you got to offer as a guest? And if the answer to that is a candid "Not much" — if you are shy, uncertain, if you know yourself to be something less than magnetic as a personality, then do something about it. The truly colorful personality is largely a trick of nature — either you're born with it or you're not — but if yours is on the pale side there is nothing to keep you from toning it up. You can learn to develop an agreeable personality as you can anything else in life. You may not get to the top of the heap, but at least the effort you make will keep you off the bottom.

Stock in trade of the agreeable personality — that is, the good guest — is his ability as a conversationalist, an art that is, I fear, slated for oblivion in this country unless something is done to revive in us the habit of original thinking, a taste for the cultivation of fresh ideas, as opposed to our current mania for blank-eyed hearing and viewing and the cultivation in consequence of no taste whatever. Radios and television screens that are never dark are making us mentally rusty. Certainly there is much that is interesting and good to be seen on television, but the nourishment it affords the mind is limited at best and requires, moreover, no more mental exercise on the part of the viewer than an occasional decision for or against switching channels. Imagination, ideas, a knowledge and understanding of many things — these are the stuff of good conversation, and the truly adept conversationalist ranges a wide field in order to keep himself supplied with the materials of his trade. Listen to radio, look at television, by all means. But don't let your intellectual curiosity end there. You aren't going to get very far as a conversationalist if all you have to offer a company are the by now stale jokes you heard last night on somebody's comedy hour, or your considered opinion of the plot structure of a ten-year-old movie.

Broaden your frame of reference. Reach out for new ideas and let them stimulate you to some original ideas of your own. Read the latest books, and don't neglect those classics you've always meant to get around to, either. Know what is being written, what is being read, and read it. Keep up with newspapers and magazines. Know what is going on in the world of politics, of fashion, of the arts, and if it is only a superficial knowledge, merely enough to enable you to make reasonably intelligent sounds in almost any conversation touching on topics of the day — well, that's all right too. For the average woman, in fact, a smattering of learning is much to be preferred to a preponderance of intellect. "A woman," said Jane Austen — no fool — "if she have the misfortune of knowing anything, should conceal it as well as she can." An unfortunate truth perhaps, but a truth nonetheless, and not as contradictory to my injunction on keeping informed as it sounds. The ability to make good small talk is one thing, but a woman who parades an abundance of education is giving herself an awful handicap socially. I am all for women going to college, getting degrees, becoming veritable storehouses of weighty and profound fact — so long as they don't show it at the wrong times and in the wrong places. And a party is the wrong place. Women who know too much are not going to be popular with men, whose egos are fragile at best, or with other women who may not be as smart and won't relish the reminder. All this with the usual exceptions. Notably brilliant women are always a joy to listen to, even for men. Rebecca West, for instance, is one of the most delightful women in the world to meet and by all odds the most brilliant and captivating conversationalist I know. Marcia Davenport is another expert, and so are Clare Boothe Luce and Dorothy Thompson. But women like these are rare. The average woman — the noncareerist, the sensibly deferential wife, most of all the single woman in search of a man — will do well to remember that a little learning isn't half so dangerous as a whole lot put on view.

Wit has always been the peg on which the reputations of great conversationalists hang, but true wit isn't given to many of us, and if you haven't got it never mind. You'll be better off and a good deal more popular if you don't try to force it. A sense of humor, yes, but that is something else again. Humor is essentially the capacity for seeing things in a humorous and generally kindly light and involves no special intellectual prowess: I have known dogs who were positive comedians. Wit, on the other hand, is strictly a product of the intellect, is usually caustic, always spontaneous, and never (as humor often is) repetitious. The man with a sense of humor who gets a laugh from telling a certain type of joke today will probably go right on telling that type of joke and anticipating the same laugh for the rest of his life. The true wit, on the other hand, never repeats. The true wit rises to the target of the moment, releases his dart (suitably poisoned), and retires to wait for the next target to go up. He is quick, he is glib, he is original — and if he can't be original he is at least choosy about his sources. James Whistler and Oscar Wilde were both celebrated wits, though Wilde was not above claiming authorship now and then of lines he admired.

"By Jove, I wish I'd said that!" was Wilde's comment once after a particularly witty remark of Whistler's.

"Don't worry, Oscar," was Whistler's reply, "you will."

Thus wit — wonderfully quotable but seldom endearing. Someone has said that the well of true wit is truth itself, and so it is. But the truth as wits see it is rarely complimentary, and who wants to hear that kind of truth about himself? One thing, anyway, is certain — wit that evolves from a painful truth is not for amateurs. Unfortunately there are a lot of people around in society today who pride themselves on being wits but who are in fact nothing more than so many cliché experts with a penchant for the ready insult. No, don't try for wit. Settle for humor. You'll last longer.

Cultivate a memory for anecdote, for the odd and interesting fact, for entertaining gossip which can be trotted out when conversation lags. When you hear a good story, file it away in your head for the appropriate moment — only be sure that when the moment comes you know *how* to tell it. Never try to extemporize. Do as any good actor does: rehearse the bit in private before you try it on an audience, and if it makes it a better story to exaggerate a little in the telling, do so. Exaggeration is part and parcel of good storytelling. So, it bears repeating, is brevity. Keep your stories short and try not to tell them to the same people twice: it isn't easy to work up a good hearty laugh over a familiar punch line.

Learn to be as good a listener as a talker, for the good conversationalist is both, and he uses his talents as a listener to nourish his talents as a talker. Make it a matter of course to draw others out (there is more truth than humor to that old definition of a good conversationalist being someone who listens to *you*) and don't just assume an attitude of polite attention when others are speaking: *hear* them. Concentrate. Cut yourself off from outside distractions. Disraeli's wife, Lady Beaconsfield, attached so much importance to her ability to listen well that she made it a point always to eat a high tea before going out to dine, thus relieving herself of the temptation to let her attention stray from the talk to the food. In this way she missed no morsel of gossip that might be of use to her husband professionally or to herself socially: her chatty and exact accounts of where she had dined and what she had heard while dining made entertaining gossip for others later on.

Even if you are a ready and willing talker, just bubbling over with things to say, don't try to take over completely from more inhibited guests. Give them a chance, and if they don't seem able to take advantage of it, be prepared with a few topical assists. A provocative question on a subject that is slightly sensational, for instance, is a wonderful loosener of tongues. (Never ask really serious questions at a party. There's always the chance you'll get a really serious answer, and the death march will be on.) Three subjects that I have found to be sure-fire stops to the occasional silences that fall on parties are Sex, Love, and Who Hates Whom — and by that first-mentioned, let me assure the squeamish I mean nothing indelicate. The fact is that opinion on what constitutes sex appeal has as many heads as the hydra: ask a question about, say, what makes men want to leave home for Marilyn Monroe, or women for Clark Gable, or — closer to home — what is the particular allure of the local belle or beau in your town, and you will open the way to all sorts of lively and diverse theorizing.

In the second case — Love — well, it's been making the world go round for quite a spell now, so why not conversation? To take an example, in Rome not long ago I was a guest at a luncheon given by Mrs. Luce. All at once, and as may so often happen, conversation, like a clock running down, began to tick-tock into silence. I felt obliged to give it a shake.

"What is the difference," I asked in my best Maxwell Italian — which, if more Maxwell than Italian, is usually understood — "between *amour, amore,* and *love,* as the French, the Italians, and the English understand the word?" In an instant the tempo at the table swung to prestissimo, the party had come together again, and, best of all, had come together in discussion of a topic so universal that everyone had something to contribute to it and did: conversation was not only revived, it became general — which is always to be desired. The French, in my opinion the best party conversationalists in the world, are past masters at this, adept at keeping conversation generalized rather than letting it break up into so many little two-by-two colloquies as we not only do but are taught to consider proper: at seated dinners in America and in England, guests are expected to turn right, then left, at regular intervals, for all the world like good little soldiers carrying out a prescribed military maneuver. (Parenthetically, the timing of these turns is actually more a matter of instinct than of rule. The inexperienced are usually advised to watch the hostess and change sides when she does. This is as good advice in the matter as any, I suppose — though it leaves unsolved the dilemma of what to do when your hostess turns and your partner of the moment is deep into a story that will plainly take time to finish.)

But back to my foolproof subjects: in the third case, nothing seems to delight normally unbloodthirsty people more than a good rousing exposé of other people who are at each other's throats, complete with the reasons therefore, and, where possible, illustrative quotes from both sides: no one will deny that there is a good deal more entertainment value to be had from the waspish things people say about each other than from the pleasantries that pass between friends. Then too, when the feuders are known to others in the company — and sometimes even when they are not — there are bound to be those who will take sides for or against this one or that, and controversy, so long as it does not become bitter, is a wonderful spur to good conversation. So then, if there is a nice, eloquent backbiting feud going on in or near your range of acquaintanceship, make use of it. I guarantee it will get a slowed-up party very much on the move again.

Still another conversational gambit I have tried, though with not unqualified success, is what might be called the

Let's Get Personal opener — and my most recent experiment
with it may serve to illustrate the wisdom of keeping lead
questions at the level of general experience, or at least at the
level of people who aren't there. This was at a party in New
York at the Jock McLeans'. At dinner I was seated at a table
for six with Jock, Mrs. Gary Cooper, Mito Djorjadze, Thelma
Foy, and Shipwreck Kelly. Presently there came a lull in the
conversation. I turned to Thelma. What, I asked her, was
the greatest thrill she had ever had? To my astonishment,
Thelma, normally gardenia pale, turned pink as a peony. "I —
I can't tell," she stammered, and immediately burst into a
cascade of conversation to cover her confusion. Fascinated by
the effect on her of what seemed to me a perfectly innocent
question, I went around the table, asking each one the same
thing in turn. And would you believe it, not one of them
would say. As Thelma had done, they each refused to answer
and immediately turned the talk to something else. A question
I had thought would be the greatest kind of conversational
galvanizer turned out to be that all right — though not in
quite the way I'd expected. Everybody talked, and fast —
about everything *but* my choice of subject. In future perhaps
I had better stick to Sex, Love, and Who Hates Whom.

Never disrupt a conversation, however much you may dis-
agree with what is being said, by being argumentative on unimportant questions. If the subject under discussion is an
interesting and controversial one and you have something
valid to contribute to it, then by all means have your say. But
don't niggle about trivial matters, and don't flatly contradict
the accuracy of some little story another guest may be telling.
Also, if the story is meant to be funny, even though it may
strike you as something less than hilarious, laugh at it. Laugh
easily and long. There is nothing more flattering to a story-

teller than the real and honest laughter — or what he is pleased to think is the real and honest laughter — of his listeners.

When you meet an old friend at a party, someone you haven't seen in a long time, don't immediately engage your friend in a catch-up session of Do you remember when? and Whatever became of dear old So-and-so? in front of outsiders. There is nothing so brutal as leaving another guest out in the cold. If the temptation to bring each other up to date is too powerful to resist, or if you will have no other opportunity to do so in the foreseeable future, then do at least bring the outsider into it. In such a case I always make it a point to explain people and places and events as they come up, at the same time inviting the stranger to join in. "Now we are talking about So-and-so," I will say. "Do you know him?" Or, "Now we are talking about this-and-that. What do you think of it?"

Never try to hold the floor in a group or, in a twosome, to monopolize the conversation with some pet theme of your own. My old friend, the late Margot Asquith, was a vastly entertaining woman, a wonderful hostess — and a perfectly dreadful guest, simply because she could not bear dull or mediocre people: ever scintillating herself, others must scintillate around her, and if they did not measure up to her estimate of what was tolerable in the way of intelligence and wit (and her estimate was high) Margot invariably undertook to compensate for the lack all by herself. She was an exhibitionist, a sensationalist who adored having the limelight focused on her at all times. In equally lustrous company her love of attention might be met and matched, but all-star casts are rare. In the average group she was a deplorable guest, bent on disrupting the rhythm of any party in order to bring every eye and ear in her direction.

At a large mobile party it is of course possible to escape

conversational monopolists: if your hostess doesn't rescue you, you can usually manage to signal a passer-by into stepping in to break it up. But at a seated dinner if you have the bad luck to land alongside a monopolist you are helpless, for while *you* may be fully aware of your obligation to divide your time equally between right and left, the monopolist will in all likelihood be too far lost in admiration of the sound of his own voice to remember this bit of party *politesse*, so that short of showing him your back in the middle of a sentence — which, while tempting, would make *you* guilty of a rudeness — there is really nothing you can do but sit it out and hope for a speedy end to the tedium. This is an especially trying predicament if the person doing the talking happens also to be someone whose company you would normally enjoy. Then you feel bound to show an interest in what's being said, however dull you find it. This happened to me not long ago at a dinner in New York at the William Nicholses' — he is publisher of *This Week* magazine — although in relating the incident I must also confess that not only was my talkative dinner partner guilty of social error — so was I, and so was our host. I was seated between my friend, Francisco Urrutia, the Colombian Ambassador to the United States, on my left, and, on my right, Victor Kravchenko, whom I had not met before and whose identity, I'm afraid, did not at first register with me. The first guilt was mine. Señor Urrutia is a wonderfully entertaining man and we were soon happily and hard into a conversation so engaging that I lost track of time and duty and completely ignored Mr. Kravchenko. Whereupon Bill Nichols made the second mistake. Bill is a good host, and a watchful one, as a good host should be, but letting guests alone when they are plainly enjoying themselves is more important to good partygiving than minding their manners for them — usually stopping something pleasant and gay in the process — and that is what Bill did then. Suddenly he called down the table, "Elsa! Talk to Kravchenko!" Well, I'm a biddable sort. I turned at once to Kravchenko, still not knowing who he was, and I found him delightful. Earlier I have advised against hosts spelling out for guests just who the others are, what they do, what they are noted for if anything, because it is always much more fun for people to discover each other for themselves. This happened now. Kravchenko spoke of Russia. I asked him from what part of Russia he came. From the Ukraine, he said. I asked him what he did. He was in tin mines, he said. As we talked I began to connect the name Kravchenko with writing. Had he written a book? He had. And he told me about *I Chose Freedom* and something of his experiences behind the Iron Curtain that had led him finally to make that choice and then to write about it. Up to this point I had, as I have said, found him delightful. Then he made *his* mistake. He plunged into politics. Now Kravchenko is unquestionably a knowledgeable man in this field with much that is interesting and enlightening to say, but political speechifying, and overlong political speechifying at that, is about as fitting at a dinner party as a dirge at a wedding. Very soon, as Kravchenko talked, I found my attention wandering. I was getting bored, trying to feign an interest I didn't feel. It was not only that the talk was of politics — I'm as keen to be up on the subject as the next one — but that it went on too long. Any subject, even a good gossipy one, becomes dull if it is dwelt on too long. Remember that, if you would not be remembered as a bore.

But back for a minute to the matter of not identifying guests. The exception to this, again as noted earlier, is when a guest is someone of importance but one whose name and calling might not be familiar to the others. Such a one should always be identified by the host, and at a smallish party there is little doubt that he will do so. On the other hand — particularly if his party is large and there are celebrities present in quantity — he may not. For this reason it is always the better part of prudence for a guest going for the first time into a group of more or less prominent people to find out for himself just who is who as a simple precaution against that occupational hazard of all unwary party-goers — that of opening the mouth and putting the foot squarely into it. To take an example: certainly no sensible new bride would dream of going to a party given by, say, her husband's boss, at which she would be meeting other members of the firm and their wives for the first time, without committing the organizational hierarchy to memory beforehand: "And what do you do, Mr. Smith?" would scarcely be the most tactful question to ask a man, only to discover that she was addressing the Executive Vice-President in charge of her husband's future. In the same way, any guest ought always to know to whom he is talking at parties where he knows there are people, important or otherwise, whose good opinion of him is desirable, and if he can't be certain he will do well to keep his conversation to such innocuous subjects as the weather or the latest fad in tranquillizers until he's sure of his ground. Better still, in such a situation let the other take the lead: if it's one of the important ones he'll soon let you know it.

In sum, then, here are ten main points for the good conversationalist to remember:

1. Keep yourself informed on matters of current interest by reading the latest books, magazines, and the newspapers every day.

2. If you are a woman with the good luck to be very, very learned, don't have the bad sense to show it.

3. Be as amusing as it's in you to be, but keep your humor

kindly. Leave malice to the professional wits. You'll last longer.

4. Be a good listener.

5. Keep on mental file a handful of short and generally apropos anecdotes and/or provocative questions that may be used to fill in lulls or revitalize a dying conversation, but try not to use the same line twice in the same company.

6. Don't be argumentative about matters of no importance.

7. When someone tells a story that is plainly meant to be funny, laugh at it.

8. Don't carry on private conversations in front of strangers unless you can also contrive to bring them into it.

9. Don't try to monopolize the conversation of a group, or of a lone listener.

10. Don't ask personal questions of, or make personal observations to, people whose identities you're not sure of. The face you save may be your own.

Now as to good guest behavior in general:

First, if you can't go to a party in a mood to enjoy yourself and to make others enjoy you, if you are too tired to keep up your end of things or too distracted by some private worry to care, don't go. You won't be doing your hostess any favor by presenting her with a body in which the spirit very evidently lies pining to be elsewhere. Moods of this kind are, of course, unpredictable: all of us who lead busy lives, professional or private, gamble every morning of the year on our probable state of nerves come evening. All sorts of anxieties and pressures may blow up out of unexpected quarters during the course of a day to leave us feeling flogged at the end of it. And there is that party to face. Well, don't. When that happens to you, even if it is awkwardly late in the day (and barring the possibility that your appearance at the party is in the nature of a command performance, that you are the guest of honor or the like) go to the telephone, call your hostess, and call yourself off. Tell her the truth. Say frankly that you feel wretched, that you'd be a drag on everybody, that she and her party will be infinitely better off for your absence. After all, you wouldn't wittingly go to a party carrying with you the germ of a contagious disease: well, ennui is contagious too. Your hostess may not be overjoyed to have you fail her — for one thing it may throw her table off. But your presence under the circumstances would do that anyway. Send her flowers the next day, or a book you think she'll like, by way of a conciliatory gesture. She'll understand.

Be prompt in arriving at a party, but don't in pity's name be early. Better a few minutes late, though not more than ten or fifteen minutes late at the outside. Delay your arrival longer than that and you will only be adding to your hostess's worries, of which — if she is typical — she has ample already. If you find that for some unavoidable reason you are going to be detained longer than fifteen minutes, call and let your hostess know it, and make your message brief. Don't keep her glued to the phone while you explain the whys and wherefores of the delay. They can wait until you get there. And if she doesn't answer the phone herself don't have her called to it. Simply give the message to whoever does and waste no more time in getting there. (If I seem to be coming out foursquare against the telephone in these pages it is not to be misconstrued: my own telephone is my third hand. All the same, in insensitive hands it is probably the most cruelly used instrument since the invention of the thumbscrew.)

To men in particular — since they are most given to this

particular show of misplaced thoughtfulness to a hostess — say it with flowers by all means, but *don't* say it at the front door as you arrive for a party. Few men realize the thought and effort women put in to the arrangement of their flowers on party occasions — on any day of the week, come to that, but most especially for a party. Then they are chosen and placed with exactly the same regard for color, texture, and size as has been given every other ornament and piece of furniture in the house. They are an integral part of the décor, and they must fit. So the painstaking hostess lavishes the most loving care on seeing that her flowers are properly vased and arranged and placed — and what happens? Comes the smiling *galant*, flowers in hand, pleased as punch with himself and all blissfully unaware of the fact that while his hostess cannot fail to appreciate his thought of her, she is also very probably experiencing mild dismay at the disruption of her duties his nice gesture has caused. She can't just lay his flowers aside until later on when she has time to deal with them: unless they are to be allowed to wilt they must be seen to, and now. In the event there are servants in the house, well and good — though even at that, with a party in progress every member of the household is certain to be busy with more pressing matters than what to do with an unheralded bunch of flowers. More awkward still, if she is a self-help hostess going it alone *she* must abandon the door for the pantry in order to hunt up a vase — always assuming there's a spare — and get the things into water. And finally, and this to the house-proud hostess is the unkindest cut of all, lest the donor be offended his flowers must be put prominently on display in her already well-flowered room, in all likelihood throwing her whole carefully planned scheme off balance. Flowers are charming gifts and all women love to get them. But please, not, when you are going to a party, as gifts in hand. I like to send flowers to my friends before their parties — no later than noon on the day of the party — but I never do so without ringing them up a day or two before, telling them I plan to send flowers and asking what they want. Or, if you prefer, you can send them the next day.

On arrival, confine your greetings to your hostess to the customary salutations and let her take the lead from there, either — once coats and hats are disposed of — by introducing you around herself if her party is small, or by passing you on to another guest or group of guests if it is large. Don't try at once to claim her whole attention with a spate of irrelevant chatter. Your obligation to her at this point is to allow her the freedom she needs to get on with the business of welcoming new arrivals and of seeing that those already arrived are comfortably settled and served. As a matter of fact, at no time during a party should you demand an undue amount of your hostess's time. Always avoid drawing her into a conversation so long and so intricate that she is forced to ignore everybody else while it is going on. The chances are she won't be giving it her full attention anyway after the first five minutes or so; half her mind will be casting about for a polite means of escape back to her other guests.

Unless your hostess has expressly asked you to help her in her duties, don't. However close to her you may be, however much you've been encouraged to consider yourself a member of the family, don't go about giving orders to servants, or undertaking to see that glasses are kept filled, ash trays emptied and the like. Above all, leave the furniture alone. Women aren't so apt to offend in this way — even if we had the strength for it most of us know from personal experience how maddening it is to have a precisely arranged room willfully disarranged. But there are men, less symmetry-conscious than women, who think nothing of hitching or hauling a chair here and there to suit their convenience or, more probably, the convenience of a female guest who, not having asked for the service and therefore not feeling directly responsible for it, feels no compunction about taking advantage of it. No matter how much you may long to join a seated group at its own level, if there is no empty chair handy leave it that way. Sit on the floor if your legs won't support you. Or you can always stand in an attitude of such obvious discomfort that your hostess will eventually grasp your predicament and see to the furniture moving herself. If she fails in this, keep standing. It won't kill you.

About the only valid, active assistance you can give your hostess is the simple humanitarian act of rescuing lost souls. She can't be everywhere at once and at a large party there is always the possibility that a stranger in the group may be over-looked. When you see such — and they are easily identifiable by their expressions of determined affability and their habit of loitering just near enough to a conversation group to seem part of it, and just far enough away not to seem to intrude — take him in charge. If you find you've picked a dud, bear with it. Your hostess will rescue you in due course and she will love you forever.

At a large informal party of reasonably short duration, such as a cocktail party, the good guest not only keeps on his feet — he uses them. Parties of this kind are meant to move. Guests are expected to mingle, meeting and talking with as many others as possible. Especially at the start. Later on when the crowd thins out and the party has shaken down to a group pattern it is all right to settle in with cronies. But not at the start. Men,

I must say, are generally better behaved in this regard than women, who are fond of exercising what they believe to be the classic feminine right of holding court, or who feel it unbecomingly aggressive in one of their sex to seek out in place of being sought. Obviously no hostess either expects or wants a woman guest to go butterflying about, but neither does she expect or want a guest so unmindful of her part in the proceedings that she will, immediately on arrival, install herself in the first strategically situated chair she comes across, there to remain without budging till the bitter end. Sit if you will — admittedly women's prettier party shoes are not designed for stamina — but not in the same place throughout. Change your chair from time to time, and your company with it.

To warn supposedly sound-minded adults against drinking too much at a party should not be necessary, yet it needs to be said, because it happens; and more perhaps because, at parties, it is very apt to happen to people who customarily observe a strict alcoholic limit and know when they've had enough. Perhaps you think you know your capacity for the stuff, and perhaps you really do when you are at home and sit down to relax over a glass or two before dinner. But parties provide stimulations not normal to those quiet evenings at home. In the first place, when you go to a party you go already more or less exhilarated by the promise of a good time, and if the evening does in fact turn out to be bright and lively and gay your exhilaration is bound to increase. In this mood, then, you take that drink you don't need, and what happens? The excuse for alcohol is that it induces high spirits, but if the spirits are already high it is very apt to act as fuel to a small flame and produce an unexpected bonfire: I have seen people who are normally mild drinkers become so overstimulated by the kaleidoscope of noise and activity at a large party that the effect on them of what they believe to be a safe complement of drinks is doubled, and before they know it they are, if not woefully out of hand, at least making darned fools of themselves by talking too much, too loudly, and not infrequently with complete loss of discretion.

Then there is still another trap for the unwary drinker at a party — that is the ubiquitous pourer, the host or barman who seemingly cannot endure the sight of a glass on its way to being emptied. So he slips about filling half-empty glasses, preferably when the attention of whoever has charge of the glass is directed elsewhere. The result is that the unobservant drinker drinks on, content in the belief that he's still on his first when he is in fact, in point of volume, into his third or fourth. Some experienced party-goers with well-developed instincts for self-preservation have learned to guard against this practice by habitually holding a glass across its top, the hand cupping the bowl, thus preventing any unwanted replenishment while they aren't looking — a trick worth remembering, though one that wouldn't be necessary if the drinker would remember first to exercise his powers of restraint more, and his arm less. As a matter of fact, the best advice I can give to cocktail drinkers is that they make it a rule to drink *less* at parties than they would at home. Your family may be willing to put up with you if you overdo, but your friends aren't likely to for long.

When you go to dinner parties — eat. And by that I mean eat at least something, if not all, of whatever food is put before you whether you like it or not. This is only common courtesy in any circumstance — well, not quite any: such things as fried grasshoppers and a singularly revolting species of worm, among others, are being marketed these days under the guise of gourmet treats. Any hostess indelicate enough to serve this kind of thing deserves to have it not only left untouched, but flung forcibly from sight. Common courtesy, anyway, in normally hospitable circumstances — but most especially when your hostess has not only planned the menu herself but has done her own cooking as well and has very obviously taken pains over both. Then the very least you can do is to show your appreciation of her efforts by falling to with enthusiasm, real or feigned. To wave away a proffered dish, or to accept a helping of this or that and then leave it sitting untouched on your plate — tacit evidence of your distaste for something she's done in the hope of pleasing you — is out-and-out rudeness. A buffet dinner with a great spread of different dishes is, of course, something else again: then take what you will and leave what you won't. But when you accept an invitation to a seated dinner, or to a small one- or two-main-dish buffet dinner, you accept also the obligation to eat that dinner.

In the event you are on a special diet or subject to allergies from certain foods or for any other reason limited in what you can eat, tell your hostess so when she invites you. The chances are she will then arrange her menu to include foods you'll be able to eat, or she will at least, having been warned in advance, forgive you for passing up what you can't. If your diet regimen is rigid to the point of requiring special preparation of every morsel permitted you — such as an absolutely salt-free or fat-free or starch-free diet — then simply don't accept invitations to dine out. Explain your problem to your would-be hostess, override her offers, if she makes them, to have dishes prepared to your specifications (it won't be convenient however convincingly she tells you it will be), and ask if you may instead join the party after it has been fed.

Generally speaking, in short, it is the guest's duty to adapt himself to the hostess's fare, and not the other way around.

The single exception, the one circumstance in which the hostess should always design her menu to comply with a guest's requirements and in which a guest has every right to bypass forbidden foods if she does not, is when religious belief is involved. Of course this isn't always possible at very large parties: when you have, say, one hundred guests to feed you cannot, in most instances, be as scrupulous as you might wish to be about what this one or that can or cannot eat in good conscience. I say in most instances. Again there are exceptions, no matter how large the party. For example, when I was in San Francisco for the first United Nations Conference in 1945 I gave a dinner for a number of the delegates, including several from the Moslem countries. Obviously I could not expect these gentlemen to either break with their sacred traditions or go hungry. So for them I ordered the special dishes — all having to do with lamb, as I recall — permitted them under the dietary laws of their faith.

In a special case such as this, or again in the case of a small party where one or more of the guests are known to hold strong religious views in the matter of diet, it is up to the hostess to honor them. In all other cases, it is up to the guest to honor what is put before him — by eating it.

A common cause of embarrassment at formal dinners is the predicament of the guest who finds himself faced with a veritable xylophone of silver stretching out from either side of his place plate and is thereby faced also with the aching question, Which fork, O Lord, which spoon? Well, if you don't know don't let it worry you. A good many of the so-called Best People in society don't know either. Nor do they care. What could possibly be less important in this world of large issues than using the right fork? Still, if you worry about this kind of thing, the accepted procedure is to start on the first course with the fork or spoon at either of the outer edges (which side and whether it be fork or spoon obviously depending on what the first course is) and thereafter to work your way inward toward your plate. You can't make a mistake that way, and if you do come a cropper — by, say, picking up a soup spoon and finding yourself confronted with a plate of oysters — it's because the table wasn't properly set in the first place. In such a case, take the most logical-looking implement at hand. What people overlook in their fear of doing the wrong thing is that specific pieces of table silver are designed for the efficient eating of specific foods: obviously it makes sense, for example, to use a smaller fork for spearing fish or a salad than one would use for a sturdier dish such as roast beef. When in doubt, therefore, simply take the tool your reason tells you to. And if you're still afraid of appearing ignorant, keep an eye on your hostess and do as she does. In the event you are seated too far from the hostess to see her, look about for someone nearby who looks trustworthy in such little matters of refinement and follow his lead. Only don't, in this last case, count on always hitting it right. For what comfort there may be in the thought, everybody around you is very probably looking for a way out of the same dilemma, and you can't be too sure that the lead you choose to follow hasn't also chosen a lead to follow, but the wrong one. Once at a dinner party I absentmindedly picked up the wrong fork for oysters and was shortly amused to discover that everyone else at the table had done the same thing!

Know when to leave a party: to a hostess there is no more trying guest than the one who behaves as if each party may be his last and he means to make the most of it. Keep an eye on the clock (and it's an unwise hostess who doesn't have one prominently on view; not everyone wears a watch) and go when it tells you to.

Generally speaking, an invitation for luncheon at one o'clock — unless it is a card party or the like, with some kind of entertainment planned for after lunch — means guests should leave not later than three.

Invitations for tea and cocktail parties commonly specify the times guests are expected both to arrive and leave — four to seven, five to eight, etc. Observe them.

The hour of polite departure from a dinner party varies, depending on the kind of party it is. If it is a dinner party with dancing to follow, guests are welcome to stay for as long as the music lasts — until two or three in the morning, or until dawn if the hostess has gone all out and decided to make a night of it. The same is true if talent has been hired to entertain: stay as long as the talent and the hostess are willing to let the show go on, if you like. But small at-home dinners, without dancing or other after-dinner diversions planned, are something else again. Nowadays we do not observe the strict timetable that once bracketed the well-mannered dinner party in America. Forty years ago one arrived for an at-home dinner at seven and left at ten, and no nonsense. Our more casual modern customs have given rise to open-end evenings, but I should say that in most American households today a hostess has every right to expect guests to leave no later than midnight and preferably earlier. This during the week. A Friday or Saturday night party may go on longer, but not much. *You* may be able to spend all of Saturday or Sunday in bed, but your hosts may not, nor may they want to. Particularly if there are children in the house and no nursemaid to launch them of a morning, the late-staying guest gets no more than he deserves if he is sent on his way with a polite but firm good night.

At dinners where there is a guest of honor present it is polite practice to wait until he or she has left: indeed this is obligatory if the guest of honor is a person of rank, and it should be observed in all cases, within the limits of good sense. There are such things as guests of honor who don't realize their responsibilities as such and will stay and stay and *stay*. When this happens I can see no reason why lesser guests should be made to suffer. Go ahead and leave. They're the ill-mannered ones, not you.

In making your farewells tell your hostess simply and sincerely how much you've enjoyed her party — (never mind if you haven't; tell her so anyway) — but don't run on about it or attempt to conduct a post-mortem on the evening then and there. Say only what it is necessary to say and be gone. On the other hand, don't let that be the end of it. The rule-bookers, to be sure, assert that when a guest has said his thanks to his hostess in parting it is unnecessary to add to them by mail or telephone the next day. Well, perhaps it isn't actually necessary, but it's an awfully nice thing to do and a plus gesture all hostesses appreciate. Let's face it, there is no sweeter sound than praise, and when a woman has put her heart and soul, not to mention her elbow grease, into giving a party its success means a great deal to her and nothing will please her more than your unsolicited assurance that she has indeed succeeded. Call her the next day if you know her fairly well, or write her a note if you don't. And don't just generalize about how charming it all was. Single out some particular thing for your praise — a guest you particularly enjoyed talking or dancing with, a dish you particularly liked, something new and plainly prized about the house that you admired, or the like. Something that will, in short, add the pleasant conviction that you mean what you say. All this only, of course, if you really do. If the party has been a flop and you have in fact had a miserable time and your acquaintance with the hostess is one you'd just as soon not continue, then by all means do as the rulebooks advise: let your thanks end with a courteous exit line, and think no more about it. Otherwise, do the nice thing. Tell it to her twice.

So much, then, for the general dos and don'ts of good guestmanship. Sum them all up and you will see that the underlying principle is less a matter of strict obedience to a stodgy and prescribed set of rules than of simply putting into practice the words of that old aphorism — the one to the effect that doing as you would be done by is the surest way of pleasing. It is that simple. You wonder how *you* rate as a guest? Ask yourself this: When *you* give a party, what kind of a guest pleases *you*? What does this one do to earn a permanent place on your list, that one to be struck off? Tick off the qualities that put a guest of yours on the credit side — then go you and do likewise. In short, do as you would be done by. That essentially is the criterion to aim for in the art of being a good guest.

The perfect guest? As a matter of fact, there's no such thing. Or let me say rather that there is no such thing as the ready-made, all-purpose perfect personality to whom any hostess might confidently turn when in need of a spare guest for anything from a bridge foursome to a middling-sized dinner to a ball. Such a paragon doesn't exist. No, when a guest turns in what may be considered a perfect performance it is not of his own doing; it is due entirely to the skill of his hostess. He is perfect only insofar as his hostess makes him perfect, a product pure and simple of the company and environment in which she places him, and what may be one hostess's perfect guest may well be the next one's rotten apple.

Let me show you what I mean.

Here is a list of eleven of my friends who, with myself as hostess to even the number to twelve, would combine to make up my idea of the most perfect dinner party imaginable:

Women	*Men*
Duchess of Devonshire	Prince Aly Khan
Madame Callas	Mr. W. Somerset Maugham
Mrs. David Bruce	Duc di Verdura
Mrs. John Fell	Lord Astor
Mrs. Clare Boothe Luce	Mr. Noel Coward
Self	Mr. Cole Porter

Now why would this particular group (quite apart from my personal liking for each — always the first condition) create between them the perfect party? Here, in capsule, are the outstanding personal traits each has to offer.

First, I would ask the Duchess of Devonshire because she is the most beautiful young woman in London.

Maria Callas, because her beauty and musical genius make her one of the most glamorous women alive. Callas is completely alone in her field — as great a painter as Picasso, painting her operas in glowing and beautiful colors. She will take old, long-forgotten operas by Donizetti, Bellini, Gluck, and put into them such warmth and humanity that they become modern to the ear. She is without question the greatest creative artist in opera, the most fantastic talent, that I have ever known.

Mrs. Bruce, for the sparkling intelligence of her talk, honed to perfection by long association with diplomatic life.

Mrs. Fell, besides being as beautiful today as she was when I first knew her twenty-five years ago, radiates an artless charm that instantly enchants all she meets.

Mrs. Luce, because of her beauty, her spectacular success as writer, politician, diplomat, wife; chiefly because of her intelligence and wit.

As to the men:

Easily the sweetest on my list, Prince Aly Khan would be asked because he is also easily the most attractive man I know — and also perhaps because his hostess is slightly in love with him. Ever the best of reasons!

Willie Maugham, because his unparalleled gifts as writer, plus his great and intimate knowledge of the world as observant traveler, give him an aura of glamour no younger man could match.

Fulco di Verdura has a flawless social manner, and is besides one of the most erudite men I know. All history, both of Europe and of America, all poets, from Dante to Auden, are open books to him, as well as every artist, from Botticelli to Picasso and Peter Arno.

Lord Astor, when you break through the crust of his shyness, has the liveliness and charm of his mother — though without Nancy Astor's sometimes devastating acerbity.

Noel — well, Noel has no equal: always vivid, always original, ever a peerless wit.

Finally, Cole, on whom I could count for all that is best in a guest, but on one quality above all — his unfailing gaiety.

No, I would have no trouble whatever with this party. As hostess I would never have to bridge the gap of an awkward silence, for there would be no silence: conversation would fizz and flow like champagne from beginning to end. What makes me so certain of this? Because each of these people has in unique amount at least one — more than one, in fact, but one at least that stands out above the others — of the basic qualities contained in what I consider the Big Six in the catalogue of personal allure, these being (and I give them in the order in which they are represented on the guest list): Beauty, Glamour, Intelligence, Charm, Wit, Gaiety. (Among the women I have reserved this last category for the hostess: why not? In such a company I couldn't be anything *but* gay.) But the point to be made is that because each of these major personality factors acts as a complement to the other five, the end result is the perfect whole. Once they are brought together all that remains is for the hostess to juxtapose them in such a way that each brings out the best in the others. How would I seat this dream party? See page 184.

However, the fact that these particular people, each with his particular distinctiveness, would combine to make the perfect party does not mean that each would be, in other, less auspicious circumstances, the perfect guest. What, for example, if I were to ask to a party of this size not one but five outstanding beauties? No doubt the men would be enchanted, but the five beautiful women would be so busy competing with each other they'd turn the party into a private war of attrition. Again, what if I were to pit one glamorous personality against a roomful of indifferent Babbitts? A man of notable intelligence against a company of nitwits? A true wit against a little group of serious thinkers? And so on. In any of these cases my perfect guests would be perfect no more, for they would not be integrated with the whole; they would be bored and uncomfortable, they would show their discomfort, and their

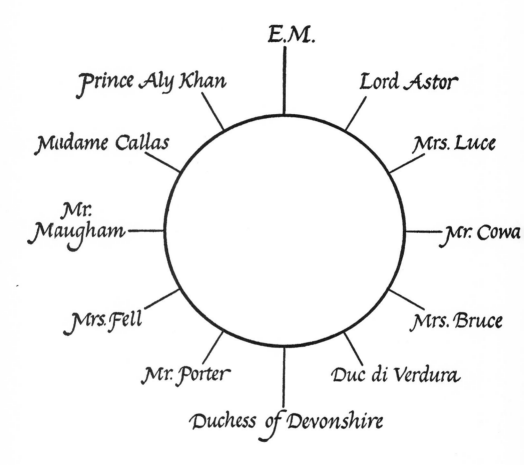

E.M.

Prince Aly Khan

Lord Astor

Madame Callas

Mrs. Luce

Mr. Maugham

Mr. Cowa

Mrs. Fell

Mrs. Bruce

Mr. Porter

Duc di Verdura

Duchess of Devonshire

discomfort would very soon sweep through the rest of the company like an impatient virus.

No, there is no such thing as the perfect guest, per se. Settle for being a good guest, and leave it to your hostess to provide from time to time the mounting and cast that will make you — if you are both lucky — the perfect one.

But if the perfect guest is pretty much the result of clever contriving on the part of the hostess, his opposite number, the bad guest, is to be had almost anywhere for the asking. Of course no one in his senses would give a party just to see how awful he could make it, but while I am in the party-planning mood, I want to confess to a morbid little game I sometimes indulge in, which is also, however, in the nature of occupational therapy. When things go against me, when plans hit snags, when I am having "one of those days," I console myself by dreaming up a situation beside which all else pales to insignificance. I invent a nightmare party. For example, the other day, a rainy one, I came home from a luncheon tired, feet damp, the suspicion of a cold coming on, and a party that was professionally important for me to attend staring me in the face. The prospects for a bang-up evening did not seem bright. Then I began to cheer myself by imagining an evening so infinitely less propitious that I was presently fully revived and looking forward with real zest to the one at hand. I fancied I was giving a dinner party, again for twelve. I give you the list of guests as I envisioned them on a seating plan, and without further comment, leaving it to you to use such familiarity as you may have with the personalities involved to imagine the degree of rapport possible between them. See page 186.

Well, psychologists tell us there is something of the sadist and something of the masochist in all of us, and I suspect this

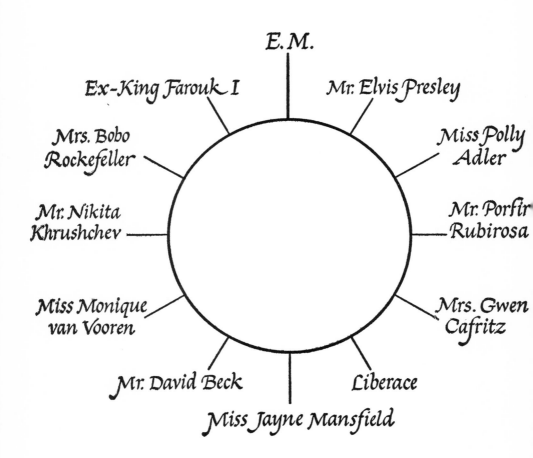

E. M.

Ex-King Farouk I

Mr. Elvis Presley

Mrs. Bobo
Rockefeller

Miss Polly
Adler

Mr. Nikita
Khrushchev

Mr. Porfir
Rubirosa

Miss Monique
van Vooren

Mrs. Gwen
Cafritz

Mr. David Beck

Liberace

Miss Jayne Mansfield

not-very-kind pastime is evidence of both ugly heads rearing themselves in my comfortably unprobed psyche. Still, it is a solacing, if unsporting, game to play now and then, and I can vouch for it as a cure for those pre-party blues, when all seems lost, the party and your good name as a hostess doomed, because of guests who for one reason or another cause you last-minute misgivings. Take heart. No party planned in good faith can be a complete failure. Perfect it may not be, but it won't be an unqualified, self-wrought catastrophe either. That's something.

CHAPTER VIII

These Can Kill a Party

ONE of the blessings I count is that I am not unusually gifted with second sight: I can think of no drearier existence than one in which I wakened every morning of my life facing a day that held no surprises. All the same as a hostess I am bound to say that there are times when a good reliable crystal ball would have its uses. Particularly in regard to the behavior potential of guests. For the fact is that no matter how carefully a hostess may have reviewed the personal qualifications of her guests, somewhere along the line — human nature being what is — she is going to find she has guessed wrong and is stuck with a bad one. At best, a bad one. At worst, a lethal one — one of those personalities so pervasively deadly it will kill a party cold in nothing flat. It isn't always that these people *mean* to be killjoys. Some, like bores, can't help themselves. Some are merely victims of circumstance. Some, on the other hand, not only know what they are doing when they set about to destroy a party, they seem to take the greatest possible pleasure in doing so. Well, there are all kinds, and ways to deal with each of them, and I will get to both canker and cure shortly.

First, however, let it not be thought that bad guests alone have it in them to kill a party. There are hostesses who can accomplish the same end with no outside help from anybody. I have known women who could plan a seemingly perfect party, people it with the most agreeable guests imaginable, then single-handedly kill it dead before it had half a chance to come to life.

There is, for one, the apologist — the hostess who is certain from the start that nothing is going to go right with her party and starts telling you so almost before you have your foot in the door. Lady Ribblesdale was one of these. With all in readiness for a party, with guests beginning to arrive, she would suddenly get it into her head that half the people she'd invited were washouts. "Mice men, mice men, nothing coming but mice men," she'd go around moaning dispiritingly to first arrivals. Generally she recovered her confidence as the party got under way, and the men who appeared either fitted the description not at all, or fitted it so well they went unnoticed. But the advanced-case apologist never gives up. On she goes through the evening abjectly calling attention to the fact, real or imagined, that the roast is overdone or the sauce badly seasoned, that the guest she'd counted on to *make* the party has treacherously failed her, that the florist has sent the wrong flowers, did you notice? — and so on through the whole sorry business, begging your pardon all the way. Then she sits back and wonders why no one seems to be enjoying himself.

In one respect at least the apologist has an edge on another type of party-killing hostess, the worrier, for while the apologist can easily convince herself that having begged your pardon she's gotten it and thereafter relax, the worrier never stops worrying, and neither as a result do her guests. Convinced from first to last that something is going to go wrong, she is a veritable wellspring of gloom whether it does or not. Worse, if the awful unexpected does happen she goes completely to pieces. A fuse suddenly blows, the lights go out. She panics. At the last minute there is a telephone call: the guest of honor is in bed with a temperature of 105°. She weeps. Too late she finds she has seated a woman at dinner next to a despised ex-husband. She scutters about in a frenzy of last-minute shifts in the seating plan, in all likelihood putting the whole table in a shambles. Everyone feels her distress and no one is happy.

Take my advice and never worry. Easy to say? Yes, but easy to do, too, if you who incline this way will learn to accept philosophically the fact that a thousand things *can* go wrong, they *do* go wrong, and that getting yourself into a taking when they do isn't going to help any. School yourself to make the best of accidents by learning to laugh at them, thereby encouraging your guests to laugh at them too. Make it amusing and you will make it of no consequence.

But with the exceptions as noted, it is the mischosen guest who commonly flummoxes the innocent hostess, and not the other way around. As I have said, it just plain isn't possible always to avoid a bad guest. Sometimes you will have to ask him as a matter of business or for family reasons. Sometimes he will simply fool you by doing a complete about-face on the behavior you have come to expect of him. Sometimes, in the case of a new acquaintance, he will teach you an abrupt lesson in the folly of trusting yourself as an instinctively sound judge of character. But however he gets to your party or whatever his crime once there, there is this about him: he is either tamable or expellable, and here are some tips on how:

Worst of the offending guests, because his offensiveness is negative and therefore difficult to define, is the show-me guest — he who arrives at your party, seats himself, folds his arms, presses his lips together, and deliberately defies you to amuse him. He is there, his attitude says plainly, only to see if you can do it. To him I show no quarter. When I give a party I always have someone stationed at the door — chiefly as a block to would-be crashers, but also to help out in situations such as this. Also when I give a party I always have a few of the latest books sent in. With these for props, I am ready for the show-me. I first send word to the door to have his (sometimes her, but rarely) coat ready. Then I beckon sweetly to the offender, and when he has followed me out of the party room I say to him, nicely but very firmly, "Darling, you are not happy here. Because you are not happy, I am not happy. So I think a good book and bed will be just the thing for you now." Before he can recover from his astonishment, his coat is put on, his hat or stick or gloves handed him, the book placed under his arm, and he finds himself on his way out, still not quite grasping what has happened to him. Brutal, yes. But so is he, and I recommend the treatment the next time you want to manage a discreet eviction.

Next on the list of bad guests come snobs, but let me first say that not all snobs are to be despised. Some snobs I approve of entirely — those who, in aspiring to the friendship of people they esteem, show a rather pathetic longing to be something, to make something better of themselves. I, for one, am the world's greatest snob when it comes to music and musicians. When a woman like Maria Callas comes to dine with me, when later I receive a charming note from her tucked into a sheaf of roses, when Nathan Milstein calls to tell me he will be delighted to come to one of my parties, I preen, I purr, I am beside myself with joy. Everybody has some kind of snobbism, and should have — when it is a snobbism that has to do with honest achievement, true creative ability. But the snobs I rail against, the snobs I will not endure at my parties or in my life, are, first, money snobs, and, second, purely social snobs.

Actually, of course, these are the snobs who should never be a problem at a party because they are so instantly recognizable for what they are they should never have been asked in the first place. Still, they do slip in now and then, even to parties of mine. The husband, perhaps, of a woman I like and admire, or the other way around. When this happens there is really nothing to do but welcome the creature and thereafter do what you can to prevent him from inflicting himself too painfully on others. The treatment here is fairly simple, for both money snobs and social snobs: that is a smart jab with a sharp pin to the most noticeably inflated area. In the case of a money snob, for instance, who has come to the point of advertising his bank account (a point reached by the true money snob usually within seconds of his arrival) change the subject at once to the one branch of the arts he is almost certain to know nothing about: literature. Money snobs like to pretend they know something about painting and sculpture, and indeed they often do: after all, it takes only a minute to look at a painting or a piece of sculpture and another minute to be told its value and so come to an immediate understanding of its artistic worth. But money snobs don't read books. In some cases I can call to mind, it is doubtful that they know how to read at all. And, while he may assume an attitude of superiority toward those poor — literally poor — souls who must rely for their riches on the imagination of other men's minds, the typical money snob's ignorance is, as a matter of fact, a source of humiliation to him. This, then, is your target of attack. Nip into his ego with a bookish question or two. It won't matter if you don't know what you're talking about: he won't either, remember. Tell him you've been going crazy not being able to remember the last lines of *Paradise Lost*. Can he help you out? Or that new book of Toynbee's you can't get out of your mind. How does he think it compares with the earlier work? If he has an answer, which is unlikely, all to the good. You will at least have got him off money. But the chances are he will have none, will be reluctant to stay in a conversation he doesn't understand, and will retire sensibly from the field.

Or (and while, in point of order, this should come first, I give it second simply because, being a measure of prevention against something you aren't always certain you will have to prevent, its usefulness is limited) there is the set-stage method. For this you need only a few early arrivals and an instinct for timing. Then, shortly before your money snob is due, turn the conversation onto money snobs in general. Mention one that you know — and if you don't know a flesh-and-blood specimen yourself, someone you've read about in the papers will do — and cite a few odious examples of his or her lapses of taste. Nearly everyone has crossed paths with money snobs at some time in their lives, so you will soon have a nice competitive conversation under way, with everyone comparing stories like mad. Into this atmosphere, then, walks *your* money snob. You greet him warmly. You bring him into the group. You make him feel part of it by briefing him on the topic at hand. "Darling," you say, "we were just talking about that dreadful So-and-so. Do you know him? The one who has all that money and does *nothing* but try to impress people with it. *Such* a bore!" That's all. He'll get the message.

Social snobs are also susceptible to the set-stage method, the only change needed being that you substitute name-droppers for money snobs as the topic of conversation they walk in on. When a social snob appears at your party without warning, however, the most dependable snubs are (1) pretending total ignorance of the names dropped — "Tom Jones, dear? No, I'm afraid I don't. Just who is he?" — and (2) pretending full but somewhat unsavory knowledge: "The Joneses? Of course, such nice people, and such a cross to bear — all that insanity in the family." The variations on these two themes are endless, and very workable.

Two species of bad guests I seldom if ever have at my parties are bores and carpers — bores because, well, because they bore, and carpers because they only come to find fault, full of the hope that your party will be a failure so that they may enjoy themselves later by telling others just how dreadful it was. Of carpers I honestly think I have none (and if I ever should find one present he will get the book-and-door treatment, but without the book), and of bores perhaps 10 per cent, which in a party of any size is not fatal. Still, even a minimum of bores at a party must be kept from inflicting their debilitating charms on other guests, and I long ago discovered what has proved to be the perfect solution to this problem. But first a statement of my case against bores in general. Recently in England I made a guest appearance with Malcolm Muggeridge, editor of *Punch*, on his weekly BBC television show, and in the course of the interview expressed my aversion to bores. It would seem that the bore situation is of universal interest. At any rate, the audience response to these remarks was so great that the *London Sunday Graphic* followed up by asking me to give them an interview on the subject. The body of the story that resulted was the following succinct summing-up:

What is a bore?
Maxwell definition: a vacuum cleaner of society, sucking up everything and giving nothing.

How do you spot one?
Bores are always anxious to be seen talking to you.

Bores will walk round and round the table after you so that you have to talk to them.

Bores are like barnacles. They fasten on to you and never let you go.

Bores have hobbies. They talk to you morning, noon and night about their hobbies.

Bores talk too much — or not at all. (One is as bad as the other.)

Are they dangerous?

Bores put you in a mental cemetery while you are still walking.

Bores will never admit that they bore. Under pressure people admit to murder, setting fire to the village church, or robbing a bank, but never to being bores.

How do you dodge 'em?

1. Cultivate a sense of self-preservation.

2. At a party seat all your bores at one table. Never sacrifice one good guest to them.

Says Miss Maxwell: I often think that one day for the sake of other people's happiness I will open a school for bores and try to tell them how not to be boring. And then the awful thought comes to me that I might be more boring to the bores than they would be to me.

As noted, my method of protecting others from bores is, at a large party, to seat them all together at one table. This not only serves the initial purpose of isolating them — it has a really electrifying effect on the bores themselves. Bores, like other dumb creatures of the field, instinctively recognize their own kind. They don't know why, they just do. A bore, therefore, put with a group of other bores, looks about him, correctly sizes up his companions, and — since, as I have said, it will never enter his head that he is one of them — will instantly decide that it is up to him to make the best of a bad situation by injecting a little life into things. Now when you have, say, ten people sitting together, each privately self-sworn to show the others what a rollicking good fellow he is, you are very soon going to have a rollicking good party going. I have found to my astonishment and delight that the bore table at my parties invariably turns out to be the merriest of all. Bursts of wild laughter erupt from them, their tongues seem never to be still, you find yourself craning your neck to hear what is causing all that gaiety. I don't know whether or not the practice of administering snake venom for the cure of snakebite is still considered effective, but I can guarantee that the principle applied to bores is a sure antidote against boredom.

The isolation method is possible of course only at large parties. At small parties, if you have for some reason been obliged to include a bore, your only recourse is to stay close to him, ready to move in as a buffer when you see him getting ready to do his worst to another guest. This may be a punishing assignment, but you're responsible for having him there and it is therefore up to you to protect the others from him. Relax your vigilance, let him get away from you, and someone is in for a bad time. Particularly if it is a talking bore — and they are in the majority, full of a really sublime confidence that every word they utter falls on fascinated ears. Should this happen, your best bet is a straight frontal attack. "All right, now, Bill," I will say. "That's enough of that. Stop right there." He'll stop. A little taken aback, perhaps, a little hurt, but he'll stop. Nothing has quite so stunning an effect on people as outspoken honesty.

The problem of what to do with excessive drinkers confounds most hostesses because they tend to regard inebriates as being in a mentally deranged state and therefore potentially dangerous. So they treat them with kid gloves, trying to coax them to the door with gentle words and a good many hollow little laughs, pampering all the way. Nonsense. Certainly, normally mild-mannered people have been known to turn violent in drink — nevertheless my advice to any host who has allowed such a situation to develop is to order the offender off the premises in no uncertain terms, and to be prepared to back up the order with a discreet show of bodily force if necessary. If you haven't one strong-armed man in the group to help, ask for a little team-work from a few of the spindlier ones. At any rate, get him out of the house, and I mean this for women who drink too much and become either sloppy or obstreperous as well as for men. I have no patience with them and neither should you. Only be sure in extreme cases that you not only get them out of *your* house, but that you also get them safely into their *own*. Call a cab and see them into it, or, if it is someone who has driven his own car, have someone else take him home. This much at least you owe to the excessive drinkers — for the fault, I am bound to say, is as much yours as theirs. You should never have allowed it to happen in the first place.

At my own parties I keep a careful eye on all my guests, particularly any suspected tipplers. Then if I see someone taking aboard more than he should, I put an end to it then and there. I simply do not allow a state of drunkenness to be reached by any guest at my parties, and neither should you. It is simple enough to stop. If the culprit is a man I take him aside and put it to him frankly. "Now, listen here," I will say, "lay off. You don't want to spoil the party, do you? You can have as much to drink as you can hold, so long as you can hold it. But no more. Is that understood?" It always is. If he doesn't stop entirely, he at least slows down to a safe speed.

If the culprit is a woman, my technique is both more direct and more painful. I simply go up behind her and give her pearls a twist. No, I am not kidding. I do. And it works like a charm. However, if garrotting is not your style, do as I do with a man. Simply tell her to stop, with the implication strong that if she does not she will have to leave. No one will flirt with the humiliation of being thrown out. She'll watch her step from there on. The main point is that it is up to you, the host or hostess, never to allow an ugly situation to develop because of too-liberal pouring, for which, after all, you and you alone are responsible.

Two other types who should be similarly rebuked at parties, if not barred altogether, are off-color-story tellers and what colloquialists have been pleased to dub "wolves" — though I have never for the life of me made sense of that particular sobriquet being hung on a species so closely resembling weasels. One thing I do know, however, is that a wolf — there doesn't seem to be a better word — is only as wolflike as a woman permits him to be, and that it therefore behooves a hostess who comes up against this particular unpleasantness to warn off not only the man, but the receptive lady in the case as well. Just be sure you do stop it. No really attractive man will be guilty of wolfishness. No really attractive man needs to be. It is always the creepy little fellow with the look of having spent his early years hoping vainly to make the team who fancies himself a Lothario, and since the sight of any man ogling a woman is not edifying at best, when this unattractive character goes into his act it is downright mortifying, an embarrassment to all who must witness it and, if there is a husband or a beau present — and there usually is — a straight-on invitation for a scene. Nowadays, I am pleased to say, this is a problem I never have to face at my parties because, after a few enlightening experiences with it in my early days, I have made it known I won't have it, and I don't: incipient wolves there may be at my parties, yes, but, in my presence, incipient they know enough to remain.

You must always, if you are to be a good hostess, have the courage to put your foot down on behavior that offends or in any way displeases you. Subtlety, hints, the slight reproving shake of the head, the message signaled mutely with the eye won't do the trick. Say it out, and say it in a way that will leave no doubt that you mean it. If you do this, and do it as often as the disagreeable necessity arises, you will soon *have* no more disagreeable necessities. This is the way I have learned to guard myself and my friends against bad drinkers, against irksomely amorous men, and certainly against those grubby individuals, off-color-story tellers. No one tells off-color stories at my parties because I have made it perfectly plain, and often, that I won't put up with it. But if some one of the uninitiated *were* to start such a story in my hearing, I know exactly what I would do, and I would advise you to do the same. Make no bones about it. Simply announce to the offender and, if need be, to all within hearing that he is to stop, and stop this minute. You may be sure word of your ultimatum will be talked about later, and lead in time to a reputation that will protect you from any chance of recurrence.

Gossip can scarcely be condemned as a party-killer: indeed good clever amusing gossip is the lifeblood of any party. But gossip of another sort — mean, corrosive, character-destroying gossip — should never be tolerated by a hostess, first, because if you allow it, you are in effect lending support to the spread of a story almost certain to be founded on fiction — "Have you heard," one of these birds of ill omen will ask, "that So-and-so is sleeping with So-and-so?" — How can they possibly *know?* — and, second, because deliberately malicious gossip, once it is in the open, will put a taint on the atmosphere of your party that will be almost impossible to erase. Heaven knows, I am no sweetness-and-light girl — I love a good gossip myself, so long as it is honest and fair — but plain scandalmongery leaves an unpleasant and, what is worse, lingering aftereffect. It is a little as if a snake had suddenly slithered across the floor. No one will be quite comfortable in the room again.

My father had a wonderful way of handling malicious gossips, and I have often followed his example, always with the looked-for result. (Parenthetically, my father's dislike of gossip was not typical of the sex. Men are and always have been greater gossips than women. Try eavesdropping on an all-male conversation group the next time you have a chance. You will find they are all tattling like mad — about each other's businesses, about each other's families, about who is being faithless to whom, etc. They relish it.) My father, in any case, would tolerate gossip only to a certain point. When one of my mother's friends came to call he would sit quietly by, listening to the two of them as they huddled over their coffee cups droning out the long litany of They Says — "They say that she . . ." "They say he *saw* her . . ." and on and on — until he could stand it no longer.

"You're speaking of So-and-so?" he'd ask suddenly, with the air of someone brought abruptly out of his own deep thoughts. "Funny you should mention her. I ran into her only last night and we were talking about you. She certainly thinks highly of you — went on at great length about what a fine woman you are."

"She *did?*" The answer was always the same, always incredulous.

"Yes," my father would say, "she spoke beautifully about you."

After the gossip had made her shamefaced exit my mother would turn to my father. "Did you really see Mrs. So-and-so last night?"

And of course he had not. "I never heard of the woman in my life before today," he would say.

As I say, I have used this method of counterattack with orchids many times in similar situations, and it has never failed me.

There is one problem guest for whom no hostess can be held accountable, and that is the guest who, all unbeknownst to her, arrives at her party to find himself face to face with someone for whom he harbors a grudge, latent or declared. For the sometimes embarrassing, sometimes funny, sometimes rowdy scenes that may result from this situation there is really no pat solution. You just need to keep your head and do whatever seems best in the particular circumstance. When and if an argument starts that threatens to become too heated I have found that the safest bet is to throw out some outrageous piece of fabricated news, guaranteed to arrest all ears. "Have you heard that So-and-so" — mentioning somebody's grandmother — "is going to have a baby?" Or, "Dreadful about the Empire State Building collapsing that way, isn't it?" you might say. It should be, anyway, something within the realm of possibility if not probability. Whatever it is, by the time your listeners realize your remark is a little wide of the truth, the crisis will have passed.

A battle fought in the open has at least the advantage of giving the hostess a chance to step in as referee. But when a grudge is nursed in silence there is nothing she can do — assuming she is aware of it at all — but leave it to the people involved to work it out in their own way. One of the cleverest maneuvers I have ever seen in a situation like this was at a dinner party in Rome, where Clare Boothe Luce suddenly, and very much to her surprise, found herself having to cope during dinner with a distinctly hostile fellow guest.

What had happened was this. Clare had only recently arrived to take over her ambassadorial duties and, as is the custom, the elite of Rome had paid its respects by calling at the Embassy to leave cards. Among the callers was the Infanta Beatrice, daughter of the ex-King of Spain, and wife of one of the most important men in Rome, Prince Alessandro Torlonia. About six weeks after Clare's arrival I went one afternoon to the Palazzo Torlonia to play backgammon with Alessandro. I asked him if he had met Mrs. Luce. I knew that Clare was not popular in Italy at that time. In the first place, she had made one or two unfortunate speeches: being new to diplomatic procedures, she had simply said what she'd been told to say. Later she learned better and wrote her own speeches. Then, too, she is beautiful, and to the Italian mind a beautiful woman belongs either in the kitchen, the drawing room, or in bed. Certainly not in politics. Anyway, with some notion of myself as a public relations agent I went on to Alessandro about Clare's great intelligence, her graciousness, her abilities. She would prove to be, I said, one of the best ambassadors America had ever sent to Italy.

All at once Torlonia exploded. "Don't talk to me about that woman!" he said. "My wife left a card at the Embassy with her own hand — *my wife!* A princess! Daughter of a king! And your Mrs. Luce didn't even have the courtesy to acknowledge it!"

I tried to soothe him. I explained that Mrs. Luce could hardly be blamed, that she could not so soon be expected to know who every caller was, that it was the fault of the Embassy staff for not telling her. But he would not be soothed. He insisted it was an unforgivable insult and one he would not forget.

On the following night I went to a dinner party given by my friend Countess Attolico. There were twenty ambassadors there that night, two at each of ten tables, and when I arrived I saw that Clare was acting as hostess at her table and saw, too, to my dismay — because I know Alessandro — that he had been placed at her left, with Count Zoppi, Undersecretary of State in the Foreign Office of De Gasperi's government, at her right.

There wasn't time to warn Clare. There was nothing to do but trust to her exquisite social sense. "Watch this," I told the others at my table. "Alessandro is a bad boy, and he'll do something outrageous, I know."

Clare talked first to Count Zoppi. After a while she turned to Torlonia to say a few words to him. Torlonia, with great deliberation, turned his back. Clare could not believe her eyes. Baffled, she turned back to Zoppi. Then, in her most charming manner, she tried Torlonia again. Again he gave her a broad show of back. Clare is not a woman who needs diagrams: this time she caught on. Without hesitation she leaned across Torlonia and launched into an animated conversation with the people on his other side. She didn't merely ignore Torlonia. She made such a show of cutting him out of the conversation that she was almost leaning in his lap, forcing him to sit there like a very chagrined lump of clay. Thus she saved her face. His snub could have reacted seriously against her, but she turned it into a personal victory for all to see.

There is a postscript. The following year, when I was again in Rome, Clare gave a party and asked me to come early to be there when the others arrived. I agreed, a little puzzled by the request, because I had never known her to give large parties and had assumed this would be one of her customary small gatherings, designed solely for good conversation. Well, I was wrong. They were all there that night, a hundred strong. All the people who had been most bitter about her the year before. She had won all of political Rome, and all of social Rome as well. I have no doubt that the great finesse with which she had bested so formidable an adversary as Torlonia had helped lay the groundwork.

These, then, are the people who can kill the best-planned party cold, if you let them. I hope I have succeeded in showing you how not to. And if some of the methods employed seem harsh — well, perhaps they are. Still, it has always been my belief that the least must be sacrificed to the greatest, and if you have to hurt or ruffle the feelings of one unruly guest to ensure the pleasure of the others, there is no alternative but to do so. You'll be a better hostess. What is more, you'll earn the everlasting respect of your guests — even the unruly ones.

go in the best of places and their chefs-d'œuvre with them. When your party is to be held at home, design the menu to fit the kitchen, the manner of service, above all the capabilities of the cook. Here again, don't stray too far from the conventional in your choice of foods. Better by far to have simple, familiar dishes excellently prepared than to attempt the different just for the sake of being different. A foreign flavor to a menu is all very well, and in America today there is a growing taste for foreign foods, but not when it is so foreign to the average palate as to be unpalatable.

Also, never serve food to guests that you have not served to yourself beforehand. If you are your own cook, kitchen-test new recipes yourself. If you have a cook in the kitchen and plan dishes that are new to her, put them on the family menu one night during the week preceding the party so that you may taste and judge and make such suggestions as need making in time for her to experiment at her leisure. You don't want a case of stage fright in the kitchen on the night of the party.

Cook or no cook, always — always, that is, unless you have that rare thing these days, a fully staffed kitchen — try to plan menus around dishes that may be prepared, or largely prepared, beforehand — dishes that will wait. This is especially true, of course, if you are your own cook. There is nothing more unsettling to a guest than the hostess who spends what should be that leisurely hour before dinner perched nervously on the edge of a chair, one eye on the clock, and poised to spring for the kitchen on an instant's notice. Build a recipe file of dishes that not only wait, but improve with waiting. All members of the stew family have this happy faculty, by whatever names they go: bœuf Bourgignon, bœuf Stroganoff, ragouts, goulashes, fish or meat curries and the like. Another advantage of these dishes is that, at an informal buffet supper, they may be eaten with a fork: no hazardous skirmishing with knives necessary.

Obviously not everything on your menu can be prepared beforehand. Some things will have to be left to the last — mixing the salad, buttering the rolls, a casserole popped into the oven, the coffee made, and so on. For the inexperienced cook-hostess, nagged by the worry of having to make everything come out on time, and together, a timetable of these things is a comfortable prop to rely on: this to be done at such and such an hour, that at such and such, and so on. Post it in the kitchen within easy consulting range — along with, incidentally, the menu, written out course by course and complete down to the last radish. How many hostesses, I wonder, have had the maddening experience after a party of coming upon some lovingly prepared little side dish resting forgotten and untouched in the icebox? With a detailed menu before you to consult before and during the serving this won't happen.

If you entertain often, and with normal overlapping of guests, keep a menu file so that you don't serve the same dishes to the same people too often. If you entertain seldom — perhaps not more than once or twice a year on any kind of scale — then the ban on sameness may be lifted: indeed, if there is a dish you do particularly well and that has proved itself at parties past then it is not only right but sensible to repeat: just as people go back often to restaurants to satisfy a hunger for the specialty of the house, so they may come to look forward to enjoying a specialty of yours. But again, this for the infrequent party-giver only. The specialty doesn't exist that your friends will want as a steady diet.

At all events, if you are doing it yourself, keep it simple, keep it to dishes you can make ahead of time — the day before if possible — and, whatever you do, have enough. Have more than enough, both of food and of drink Never allow yourself to get into that anguished state of mind an hour before your party begins brought on by sudden misgivings that there may not be enough.

Which brings us to the marketing list.

With the menu planned, and the number of people to be fed known, make a list of foods to be ordered. And be generous. Figure precisely what you will need of this or that per portion, per person, then add at least one-quarter to the total. In ordering meat, for example, it is customary to figure one pound of unboned meat per person. Spare your nerves and order one-and-a-quarter pound instead. Leftovers needn't be wasted in these safely refrigerated times. And if you should have to throw something out later, that is preferable by far to putting some hungry guest in the position of going back to the buffet table for seconds, only to find that if he takes them no one else will be able to.

When your marketing list is complete, check it over for anything that may be ordered in advance, and do so. Don't trust to luck that your butcher will have this or that particular cut of meat on hand on the day you want to cook it. Even if it is nothing out of the ordinary, early ordering will ensure your getting the quantity you need and the quality you want on the day you want it. Canned goods and such dry groceries as will keep should be laid in now, as well as wines and liquors. Leave till the last only dairy products, and market produce that must be bought garden-fresh to be at its best.

Food and drink settled, consider next the party *mise en scène* — lighting, flowers, decorations if any. Presumably you're not going to want special decorations for every party you give (though I could wish it were otherwise: a party, after all, however small, should always have a festive air about it, and gay nonessentials are the very essence of festivity) — but balls and special celebrations, such as patriotic and religious holidays, birthdays, anniversaries, showers, call for special treatment, and a great part of making them special is the imagination and resourcefulness with which you transform an everyday room into a room that reflects the spirit if not the letter of the occasion.

Decorations need not be expensive. A little cash, a lot of ideas, and the neighborhood five-and-dime are all you really need to turn your party room into anything from a snowy Christmas landscape to a Fourth of July picnic grounds. Of course, if you want to and can afford a decorator — and you should for a very large party in a very large room: it is one thing to trim one's own living room, quite another to turn to as carpenter, electrician, and painter, all of which skills are needed to do a satisfactory job on something of ballroom size; a decorator will hire technicians for these jobs, and supervise the work as well — if you want to and can afford a decorator, anyway, find one willing to listen to *your* ideas and carry them out. In other words, a good one — one who recognizes that the atmosphere he creates in a room for you must be as true a reflection of your taste in decorating as the guests who will presently occupy it are a reflection of your taste in people. Once he has your ideas he can then turn his talents to interpreting them in his own terms. In this, he should be given his head. After all, you're not paying him simply to do as he's told. In hiring a decorator you are availing yourself of the training and experience of an expert. Talk over your ideas with him, come to an understanding of the particular atmosphere you want to create, and leave the rest to him.

Be generous about your flowers, but not so generous that you have the place looking like the star's dressing room on opening night. On the other hand, don't skimp on them. One stiff bouquet brought in for the occasion is almost worse than none at all. Try to strike a happy medium, but if you err at all, err on the side of luxuriance. The kinds of flowers you have will, of course, pretty much depend, after personal preference, on the season — on the assumption, anyway, that the average housewife does not go in heavily for orchids or other such hothouse extravagances — and they should be gay and pretty, and decorative without looking institutional: some flowers, like gladiolas, while handsome in a garden, seem to have been designed by nature to adorn hotel lobbies. Aim for originality in the choice and arrangement of your flowers, as in anything else, but have them in keeping with the character and personality of your house. And always plan to have flowers delivered to you no later than noon on the day of the party, so that you will have ample time to arrange them as you wish. Never earlier than the day before. Even normally hardy leaves and flowers react unpredictably to changes in room temperatures, and tired, droopy-looking flowers are as bad as looking tired and droopy yourself.

Proper lighting is essential to a pleasant atmosphere, and by proper I mean light that flatters, that cheers without dazzling, that is intimate without inviting eyestrain. Too many of our modern methods of lighting are seemingly designed with a view to annihilating the human race. We will only be perpetuated, after all, so long as men are attracted to women and vice versa, but how there can be any hope for mutual attraction between the ghoulish faces that stand revealed by the contemporary idea of good lighting I cannot imagine. The general aim seems to be to do away with any and all pleasant illusion. This is accomplished in one of two ways: either the lights are cunningly concealed somewhere in the vicinity of the ceiling, casting a pale, indirect, ghastly green glow on the room and its occupants, or, crueler still, there is the relentlessly direct type — the spotlight that hangs immediately above your head, opaquely shaded to allow its full white glare to do its worst on you, for all the world like those naked bulbs the police — the movie police, anyway — shine in the face of a suspect in the hope of breaking his spirit. They know what they're doing. It's enough to break the most upright spirit. But direct or indirect, the result is the same. Make-up might as well not be used. Every line and pore and hollow is mercilessly disclosed and magnified, on young as on old.

To flatter, lights should be placed to cast a glow roughly at head level, a little above or a little below, but never so far above or below that facial features are cast into sharp relief. Anywhere from three to seven feet above the floor, give or take a little, and depending on whether it is a standing or table lamp, is a generally safe area. Also, lights should be soft, spread an even glow throughout the room, and on the warm side. Somewhere toward the end of *Lady Windermere's Fan*, Oscar Wilde acknowledged the value to women of warm light when he had one of his characters say, "I have never admitted that I am more than twenty-nine, or thirty at the most. Twenty-nine when there are pink shades, thirty when there are not." No question about it, warm rosy light is the kindest to all of us, men and women, and who would fly in the face of kindness?

In the room where you receive your guests have the lights bright enough to be cheerful without glaring. In the dining room softer lights are pleasant, candles pleasantest of all — just so there are enough of them to do the job. Men hate to eat in the half-dark, and women look washed out in it. In any case, study the lights in your rooms before you give a party, dimming any that are too strong, brightening any so low they cast any part of the room into shadow.

Houses, like faces, have a way of showing the normal wear-and-tear of time, and only a well-staffed house, or one managed by a woman in whom perfectionism amounts to mania, will go for very long without sagging or wrinkling or spotting a bit here and there. But when you entertain your house must look its best — clean, shining, nothing rundown, no untidy shelves or corners, no tarnished silver or clouded mirrors. Pleasant, pretty, well-ordered surroundings — elegant surroundings if you can afford elegance, a generally expensive commodity — are important to good entertaining.

The finest dinner in the world served in ugly or shabby or not-quite-clean surroundings would lose its appeal, and the room or rooms in which you entertain should always be made as pleasing to the eye as it is within the power of your skill and your pocketbook to make them. For that matter, not only when you entertain. At all times. You want to put a special shine on your house when you entertain, yes; to make things pleasanter for your friends, perhaps also to impress them a little. That's natural enough. But what about betweentimes? What about your family? How often do you think of treating them to the little extra touches that satisfy the soul along with the stomach? Paradise is lost, in my untried but observant eye, the day a wife finds it just too much trouble to pour the catsup into that pretty bowl and, instead, plunks the unlovely bottle on the table just as it came from the store. Nowadays, of course, the trend is all toward simplification in our living, and I've no very serious quarrel with that. But there is such a thing as oversimplification, and carelessness about small niceties is its natural child. Take eating in the kitchen, which more and more people are doing — I do myself when I am at the farm at Auribeau, and I love it. But eating in the kitchen, even the big streamlined, gadget-filled laboratories that pass for kitchens today, seems to give many women the idea that they are circumstantially relieved of any obligation beyond making the meal wholesome. How it is served or how attractive the table looks doesn't matter. If the meal is balanced, that is enough, and aesthetics be hanged. Well, the divorce rate is awfully high in this country. My hunch is that if a little of the slavish attention paid the creature comforts were to be diverted to a concern for the spiritual comforts, a lot of families would be happier. Eat in the kitchen by all means; but make it charming, make it romantic, make it gay. Make it a point of pride for your husband to pass on to the boys at the office the next day. Put a vase of flowers on the icebox. Put candles on the kitchen table and turn out the lights. And take off that apron. Never was a less romantic garment devised.

But let's get back to those lists. The house may well need special attention before your party, and the next program to plot is what's to be done and when. There will be, perhaps, that neglected spot on the carpet, upholstery in need of touching up here and there, something to be mended, something to be polished, something to be waxed, etc. Make a list of whatever household tasks need doing, and assign yourself one or more of them for each day preceding the party. Chores of this kind require a certain amount of physical exertion, and they should be well behind you on the day of the party. Not only is it important that you be relaxed when you greet your guests, your house must be too. Houses, again like faces, can have a nervous look to them. Never let guests walk into a room in which the flowers are still quivering in their vases from that last-minute flouncing, hastily thumped pillows sighing back into shape, the faint aura of furniture polish filling the air. With sensible planning your house should be ready to receive the most inquisitive eye on the morning of the party.

But having put your house in shining order for your party, don't expect it to stay that way once things get under way. Accidents will happen, and if you're going to worry about something being spilled on the now pristine carpet, or a cigarette burn on a burnished tabletop, then you shouldn't entertain. As a matter of fact I'm not at all sure the militantly house-proud woman shouldn't be restrained by law from ever entertaining at all. You all know her — the woman who glides about keeping a beady eye peeled for a wayward cigarette ash, a carelessly placed glass, with all the subtlety of an MP on patrol. Men in particular loathe this kind of vigilance, smacking as it does of the suspicion that the lady of the house fully expects the boorish in them to pop out the minute her back is turned. Back in the twenties, the playwright George Kelly spoke out for his sex in no uncertain terms against this kind of woman. The play, *Craig's Wife* — for those of you too young to remember either it or the motion-picture version in which Rosalind Russell later starred — concerned a woman whose passion for her household gods eventually drove everyone, including her husband, to abandon her, leaving her to find what comfort she might amid the spotless upholstery and bric-a-brac. Mrs. Craig was not, sad to say, a greatly overdrawn portrait. Many hostesses suffer, and their guests with them, from craigitis. I can sympathize, of course, with the perfectly natural desire to protect treasured belongings. Even though I have never been, and have no wish to be, a householder in my own right, I can understand that when time and energy and love and money have been poured over the floor plan of your dreams, it is only natural to want to guard it against unnecessary damage. I admire beauty and order and gleaming tabletops as well as the next woman, but not to the exclusion of all else — including my friends. There is little more discomfiting to a guest than the hand darting in with a timely ash tray, the agitated mopping up when a drink is accidentally spilled, the anguished wail when a spot of gravy splashes onto Grandma's best lace cloth. Face it. These things are going to happen, not with malice aforethought — unless you are drawing your guests from a school for vandals or out of trees — but because accidents do happen in the best-behaved companies and there is little you can do to prevent them. Take what precautions are necessary in the way of coasters and ash trays (and of these, the larger the better. Whoever first conceived of those midget affairs deserves to have all his furniture reduced to ashes) and trust to the good manners of your guests for the rest. Of course, if your teen-aged youngsters want to have the gang in, you will probably do well to take extraordinary measures. In that case, if they are to be let loose among the heirlooms, why not simply cover everything up? Plaster aluminum foil over precious wood surfaces. It will save the furniture, save your nerves, and look festive besides.

Always check the seating capacity of the party rooms against your guest list to be sure there will be a place for everyone. (The exception here is a cocktail party, which, if large and your room small, may require a reverse procedure — chairs being moved out to accommodate standees.) Borrow chairs from another part of the house or from a neighbor or rent them, if you haven't enough in the living room; and in the dining room never try to squeeze more people around the table than it will accommodate comfortably. No one is going to enjoy eating dinner, elbows pressed to sides. Plan to set up a small extra table, if need be, if it is only for an overflow of two. Even if you are serving a buffet, guests to sit where they will, be sure you have chairs to go around.

For a seated dinner, decide in advance how you will seat your guests, and if the party is to be for eight or more, put the seating arrangement on paper. Draw a diagram of the table, or tables, with placement of chairs indicated, and write in the names of who is to sit where. (I suggest you do this in pencil: if you are typical you will be making frequent changes.)

Start by putting in your own name as hostess, then place the host opposite you. (If you haven't a husband or other male member of the family to act as host, borrow somebody else's husband, or ask the man you know best.) Next, if there is a guest of honor, male, place him at your right. If there is a guest of honor, female, place her at the host's right. If there is no guest of honor — someone, that is, for whom the party is expressly given — choose as you see fit the woman who is to occupy the place of honor at the host's right. The rulebook dictate here is that the oldest woman present is given the place of honor, but unless you are entertaining a frankly grandmotherly old lady, I don't suggest you abide by it. Even if you are very young, the last thing a mature woman guest wants is a reminder that she no longer is. Or if, on the other hand, your women guests are all pretty much of an age — particularly of what is jocularly referred to as a "certain" age — no one is going to love you the better for putting the stamp of seniority on her. My own preference in deciding the guest to sit at the host's right is to choose the woman who is strange, or relatively strange, to the group. Singling her out for the place of honor flatters her, and gives her a sense of belonging in the group she almost certainly didn't have when she arrived. In any case, for whatever reason, when you have selected the woman to sit at the host's right, put her husband, if she has one, at your right. If she is unmarried or, anyway, unescorted, apply the same standard: put at your right the man who is a relative newcomer to the group.

With the guests to occupy the places of honor thus established, decide next what woman is to sit at the host's left, then the man to sit at *your* left. After that, if no protocol is involved, seat them as you will. I suggest, however, that if you move in pretty much the same social circle most of the time you make it a habit to note, when *you* are a guest at a dinner held not far in advance of your party, how your hostess has seated any who are also on your guest list. You don't want to put the same people together again too soon. Also, insofar as it's possible, take into account the personalities and likely degree of congeniality between guests you seat together. I know of no grimmer moment than the one of entering a dining room, spotting the man you'd rather be killed than sit next to, and discovering all at once that this is indeed to be your fate. You've come looking forward to a nice dinner party, and this happens! It is death. As a hostess you can't always be expected to know the personal likes and dislikes of all your guests, but when they are people you know reasonably well you can at least make an educated guess.

When you are having a very large party, such as a dance, and you have several or many tables, seat the most important woman at each in the place of the hostess, and the most important man opposite her as host. Not, preferably, the lady's husband. I am a great believer in separating at parties people who face each other across their own tables at home night after night.

Protocol must be observed, of course, if you are entertaining royalty. In such a case, the highest-ranking man present is customarily given the hostess's place at the head of the table, and the hostess sits at his right. The host keeps his place, with the place of honor at his right going either to the ranking gentleman's wife or to the woman of the highest rank. After that, guests are placed in descending order of importance.

At very large parties where protocol enters in, seating guests at round tables for eight or ten is a good idea, because nobody can tell who's sitting at the head and who at the foot. Personally, I prefer a round table for dinner at all times, though I am aware that in most modern houses, dining rooms (those that are left, anyway: the dining room as we once knew it seems to be giving way to a little extra footage, with table, in the living room) — that most dining rooms, anyway, are proportioned to house rectangular tables. But there is an intimacy to be had at a round table, a sort of charmed-circle feeling, that is pleasant, besides being conducive to general conversation.

But round or oval or rectangular, the place the hostess occupies at the table will be considered the head, and the host's the foot, and this being so the direction conversation takes will be determined by these two positions. For this reason it is always well to tell the host who you, as hostess, will talk with first, the man on your right or on your left, so that he may gauge himself accordingly. At a table for ten, for example, if you turn first to your right, and the host turns first to *his* right, someone along either side is going to be left to talk to himself. The same thing will happen at a table for twelve if you start at your right, the host at his left. Here again, of course, a preconceived plan may go awry. Your second choice in conversants may innocently blunder in on you first, and the wise host will keep an eye cocked in your direction before he makes his first move.

Check the linen, glassware, silver and china you plan to have on the table, to be sure all is as it should be, and also look over the serving dishes that will be used for each course for possible tarnish or chips. No one needs to be told that the party table should be as appealing to the eye as possible, but here again don't just settle for the conventional. Try to add an out-of-the-ordinary touch to the setting or service that will put the stamp of individuality on you as a hostess. One of the nice individual touches the Duchess of Windsor gives her parties, for example, is to serve long narrow loaves of French bread in baskets just the size of the loaf. Another is the way she serves butter, in small round deep china jars, one to each guest.

The Duchess is unquestionably one of the most important hostesses in Paris, and she is an exemplary one. She knows food. She knows wines. Her flowers are always wonderfully arranged — she now grows her own orchids — and she has a remarkable faculty for remembering individual tastes. "I think you like your coffee without sugar," she will say to a guest; or, "I think you'll enjoy this tea — it's the Chinese blend you like so much." This is a commendable trait in any hostess and all to the Duchess's credit. Too, she understands how to place her guests correctly. With her natural spirits and humor she is hard to equal as a hostess. I don't say this in regard to large parties such as the ones I give, but her dinners are always perfect, both at her house in Paris and at the Mill at Gif. I always salute a good party-giver, and both Their Royal Highnesses are very good at their special kind of entertaining.

Many hostesses who entertain on a large scale, formally and often, make a practice of putting menu cards on their tables so that guests will know what is coming and not overdo on the first course if the next one or two are especially to their liking. Menus are by no means necessary to the party table in the average household, even a household with servants, and they would be positively idiotic on the table of the hostess who does her own cooking and serving. Still when they can be used in good taste they add a nice touch of elegance to the table. The customary form is a single card, approximately 3″ × 5″, or 4″ × 6″ in size, with either the monogram or crest of the host centered at the top. The menu is then written in below under the heading LUNCHEON or DINNER, and the date added at the bottom, for the benefit of the guest who may want to carry the card off as a memento. The better clubs, hotels, and restaurants keep their own blank menu forms on hand for private parties, and will fill them in for you when you entertain out.

Always be sure ample provision is made for guests' coats and hats, even if you have to turn out a closet of your own things to do so. Nobody wants to see his best coat jammed into an overflowing closet from which it will presently emerge one large wrinkle. If your house or apartment is small, and closet space limited, at least make enough room to handle the men's coats and see that adequate shelf space is cleared to accommodate their hats. Women guests should be given the use of a bedroom or dressing room where they not only may put their coats but also may retire to primp. Ideally men, too, should have the use of a room to themselves, but if that can't be managed they will have to be content with hair-combing and tie-straightening in the bathroom.

One more precaution I urge is on you who keep pets you dote on: take a good long objective look at the darlings before a party and consider honestly how lovable they will seem to your guests. Do they beg? Do they bark? Do they bite? Are they so endlessly friendly that any old lap seems made for them? And if the answer to even one of these four questions is Yes, don't let them loose at your party. A well-trained, mannerly dog or cat is always a pleasure to have around; but animals who demand attention by jumping, pawing, drooling, cuddling hairily into laps, should be firmly banished. If you haven't a back yard or spare room or cellar where they may be isolated, board them out with understanding neighbors, or with a vet. In any case, don't expose your guests to their undoubted charms. There is an even greater charm to passing the time at a party unharried by the attentions of small, furry animals.

If your party plans include cards or other games, be sure you have ready and at hand all the necessary paraphernalia: score pads; sharpened pencils; full clean decks of cards (count them: cards have a way of disappearing); poker chips, if that is your game, etc. I also recommend having rulebooks available to players. The written word of authority is the only sure way to put a stop to disputes that might otherwise go on into the night. Also, when you plan cards, decide in advance what guests you want to have play together, and if there are to be several tables write down the names of the players to be grouped and put a list at each table. Never let there be that post-dinner, pre-game confusion and delay of deciding who is to play with whom.

My own preference in games is bridge. After that, poker. Canasta I go along with, though not very gladly. But bridge — well, Somerset Maugham has called it "the most entertaining game that the art of man has devised," and that is my sentiment exactly. I feel genuinely sorry for people who don't play it, for they are missing, if they only knew it, one of the most diverting amusements in life. I love to play it and I am not at all bad at it, given a good partner. As a matter of fact, I'm not at all bad at any card game, a fact I put down to a piece of advice given me years ago. "Always play for more than you can afford to lose," Winston Churchill once told me during a session of six-card bezique at Maxine Elliott's. "That is the only way to learn." And it's true. A beginner at bridge will learn to play better if he plays for higher stakes than he cares to lose, and also if he plays with better players than he is. Of course, good players who find themselves saddled with a beginner may not be too happy, but they are certain to cheer up (all except the beginner's partner, that is) when they find the beginner prepared to lose in order to learn.

But in bridge, mixing the bad with the good is a circumstance that should be left strictly to chance. It is the most class-conscious game in the world, and good and bad players should never deliberately be put together. The bad players will only be unhappy, and the good players will at the least be bored and at the most outraged to the point of mayhem. If you are in any doubt about the game of a prospective guest, do a little private sleuthing among his friends. Anything's fair in the interests of providing a good game for all players.

Also, keep husbands and wives apart. More divorces must surely begin at the bridge table than any place else. It is seldom you find a couple who play with equal skill, and the better of the two isn't going to feel constrained to conceal his displeasure with a partner at bridge who is also his partner in marriage. A husband, say, trapped at a table with a wife who is an inept player will almost invariably be outspoken in his criticism of her, to everyone's discomfort, or, if he is one of the rare ones, capable of extraordinary self-control, he will nonetheless show his pain by virtue of a face that hangs to his knees and the resolve plainly written on it to have this out with her the minute they're alone. It is an even more disastrous combination than a good violinist married to a woman who fancies herself a singer.

As a matter of fact, not only do I advise against letting husbands and wives play together, I also recommend that you keep them as far apart physically as possible. A wife, let us say, playing dummy at a table next to the one where her husband is deep into the struggle to make a difficult slam contract will inevitably feel a powerful urge to kibitz. So she hangs over the back of his chair, breathing — with various critical inflections — down his neck. The harassed man stands it as long as he can, finally erupts, demands heatedly that she leave him alone, and the scene all too often ends in a good, name-calling family fight. Put them at opposite sides of the room, I say, where they won't be able to see or hear how the other's game is going, and where the distance will act as a deterrent to wandering.

Duplicate bridge is fun — IF you have players who are evenly matched, or at least in the same league. This is bridge played as a contest, after all, and there is no fair competition possible when you pit amateurs at any game against pros. Actually, since the whole idea of duplicate bridge is to demonstrate skill, it should be reserved for good players only. You can't always collect a roomful of champions, but given a majority of experts, the average good player will rise to the challenge. Not long ago, for instance, I dared to pick up a gauntlet tossed me by John Crawford — whom I believe to be the world's finest cardplayer — and accepted an invitation to be his partner in a small unofficial duplicate bridge tournament at the Regency Club in New York. On the final tally we scored third, and so giddy was I at having held my own in that climate of expertise that I accused John of having made two bad doubles! Yes, we are still good friends. The point is that, right or wrong about those doubles, with a partner like Crawford to support, I played my best game, with every ounce of concentration and skill that was in me.

From the hostess's point of view there is no easier form of entertaining than a card party. After all, all the guests ask for are chairs, a table, and a deck or two. They do not need to be entertained; they entertain themselves. Conversation is barred, unless you are playing that abomination of abominations — chatty bridge. In any case, it is the best way I know to pass the hours between dinner and bedtime at an at-home party, and some avid cardplaying hostesses I know in New York have launched a new kind of dinner-with-cards party, one in which dinner is kept secondary to the game. Guests are invited to come early, around six o'clock, to play bridge or Canasta while cocktails are served. A simple buffet dinner interrupts the playing at about 8:00 or 8:30, after which the guests are allowed to get back to the serious business of the evening. This is a good plan, especially on week nights for working people who must rise early, as it allows plenty of playing time (well, not quite plenty; card addicts can never have enough), without dragging on deep into the night.

Parlor and word games will never take the place of cards as solid diversion, but they are often fun and an excellent means of buoying up a sagging party, or of unbending a stiff one. So long as they *are* fun. I can see no point at all in playing games that make you feel you're back in the schoolroom. What difference can it possibly make to your greater happiness in life that you don't know the exact angle of the list of the leaning tower of Pisa, or the name of the highest peak in the Andes? I like games that hinge on wit and mental agility — on intelligence, too, but not on the kind of intelligence that rests its case on a talent for hoarding little-known facts. Twenty Questions, for example, bores me to the nearest exit when the object to be guessed is so esoteric or obscure as to be lost to

anyone but a practicing encyclopedist. Besides, games like
Twenty Questions have the disadvantage, at a party, of being
largely one-man performances, the guesser holding the floor
for the run of the game, with the rest of the company, between
Yeses and Nos, put in the position of being mere interested
spectators. The best party games are those in which all players
participate equally. For example, there is a variation on Twenty
Questions that I like — first because, being limited to ten clues,
it goes faster; and second because the clue-giver alone knows
the answer. All the others collaborate in the guessing, which
makes for good lively general conjecture and talk. That
is What (or Who) Am I? And to illustrate, here is a set of
questions I posed at a recent party which had everyone guessing like mad until Austine Hearst finally got the answer. Can
you?

I said:

1. I am a piece of rock.
2. I am very old.
3. I have played an important role in the history of
languages.
4. I am valuable, because I brought light into abysmal
darkness.
5. I was stolen.
6. I am in England.
7. The country of my origin would like me back, but I
am not able to go.
8. Historians quarrel over me, but they have to abide
by me.
9. I am not a jewel to be worn around the neck.
10. I am prized because I am the only one of my kind in
the world. What am I?

Got it? (To see how well you did, turn to the last page of
this chapter.)

One final word on parlor games, whatever your fancy: don't force them on even one unwilling head. Here the minority, unfairly perhaps but necessarily, rules. One slightly sulky or balky player will spoil the fun for all the rest, and as there is clearly nothing to be gained by engaging in a pastime no one is going to wholeheartedly enjoy it is better simply to drop the whole idea and make a mental note not to invite the spoilsport next time you're in the mood for games.

Let us assume now that the day of the party has arrived. All is in order, all preparations made. But how prepared are you personally? Relaxed? Unworried? Nothing more pressing to do before the party begins than bathe and dress at your leisure? That is how it should be.

Always plan to keep the day of the party to yourself. Don't make lunch dates, or any other outside appointments, including the hairdresser. Have your hair and nails done the day before. Know what dress you are going to wear, and be sure that it is pressed, spotless, zippers working, all buttons in place, and that the accessories to go with it are in similarly perfect condition. Also, in the matter of dress, don't plan to wear anything designed to turn the eye of every woman at your party green with envy. Be as chic as you will, but keep to the conservative side. Your role, remember, is to please your guests, and you won't be pleasing the women much by appearing in something that will make them feel dowdy by comparison.

Schedule your afternoon, if it is humanly possible, to include a nap — a really beneficial nap, nightgowned, in bed, shades drawn.

Be dressed and ready for your guests at least half an hour before they are due. If your nerves are still a bit edgy, you can use this time to advantage by soothing them with a final, reassuring survey of the premises. Or, if you wish, by a still more direct method.

In the course of assembling the material for this book I asked a few top hostesses among my friends to let me in on their particular secrets of success. Nedda (Mrs. Josh) Logan confessed that while she is usually torn between anxiety and hope almost to the last, just before the party she overcomes her qualms, first, by ascertaining that no detail has been overlooked, that the flowers are perfect, the food and drink ample. Then, said Nedda, "I take a couple of very good drinks before the party starts, and the rest of the evening I seem to be carried along with the excitement of giving it." Nedda is also considerate of her guests' possible unease on arriving: "I ask the bartender to give everyone a very strong drink for their first. I feel this starts the party going."

Well, tranquillize as you will. One task only remains to be done in this final hour before the party, and that is to air the rooms thoroughly. Always receive your guests in a cool, freshly ventilated room, one from which all stuffiness and cooking odors have been cleared.

This done, sit down and relax. If you have prepared well there is nothing more you can do. Except enjoy your party.

(Answer to puzzle on p. 228: The Rosetta Stone)

CHAPTER X

The Art of Good Eating

B RILLAT-SAVARIN once remarked that a woman who couldn't make soup should not be allowed to marry — a sensible proposition, but one to which I would add that unless it is very good soup she shouldn't be allowed to entertain either. For a hostess, mere competence in regard to food is not enough — yet many women who do their own cooking and pride themselves on being good cooks are, in fact, no more than competent. Day in and day out they produce meals patterned to the dubious ideal of "plain home cooking" — a phrase too often descriptive in my opinion of plain dull cooking. It is not that these practicing cooks lack talent; rather that they are indifferent to experiment: taught to cook a certain dish in a certain way they go right on cooking it that way all their lives. With women who have cooks, ignorance of food is perhaps a shade more understandable but it is no more forgivable. Most cooks will match their standards to those of their employers. If a woman is indifferent to food, and unless she has an unusually dedicated and persevering chef in the kitchen, she — and her guests — will be served indifferent food. The really good hostess knows not only the basics of cookery, she adds an aesthetic dimension to the preparation and manner of serving her food that makes the simplest dish a delight.

As a matter of fact, a simple dish done to perfection is the true test of any cook's skill. The French have always had a special talent for this, though it was not until Escoffier made his influence felt, late in the nineteenth century, that simplicity at a Frenchman's table was considered a virtue anywhere outside the home. Before that time the criterion for *cuisiniers* in fashionable French restaurants was size. Banquet dishes were literally monumental: Antonin Carême, France's most famous chef in the early years of the century, even went to the length of studying architecture in order to improve his hand at mounting foods layer on layer. The result was, of course, that the food itself suffered. For one thing, it was almost impossible to keep dishes at proper serving temperatures. For another, the food was so done up diners could never be quite certain what they were biting into.

Escoffier, at the start of his career in Paris in the sixties, saw immediately the folly of this rococo and wasteful use of food. He was then not quite twenty, fresh from the family farm in a small village near Cannes where he had learned the art of traditional provincial French cookery in his grandmother's kitchen, and had acquired his lifelong professional creed: simplicity and honesty. He was also a thoroughgoing perfectionist, as was the man who was to make him famous. Some twenty years after Escoffier entered his trade, César Ritz hired him to take over the management of the kitchens at the Grand Hotel in Monte Carlo, with full leave to put his innovational theories to practice. This was the start of the new era in food. Escoffier and Ritz worked together for more than thirty years. Between them in that time they refined the tastes and eating habits of two continents, and sent the renown of classic French cooking around the world. Escoffier was at the Carlton in London, at the peak of his fame, when I first met him — a small, slender, erect figure, every inch the "King of Cooks and the Cook of Kings."

The French like to attribute the superiority of their cooking to unique conditions of soil and climate which, they believe, combine to make their produce superior to any in the world. I am inclined to think it more a matter of national character. The French are a thrifty people with a horror of waste and a consequent respect for even the humblest foods. Set a good French cook to preparing a simple omelet, for instance, and he will go about it as painstakingly as if he'd been appointed to immortalize the last egg on earth. The pan — always a special pan, used only for omelets — must be brought to the exact right temperature, the butter must be the sweetest and freshest available, the pepper freshly ground, the eggs mixed, poured, and timed just so; finally, the serving dish made piping hot.

It is this infinite capacity for taking pains, however modest the dish, that distinguishes the really good cook. I do not mean to write off Americans as totally bereft of this quality — many of them have it — but it stands to reason that the easier things are made for us, the lazier we are apt to become, and when foods arrive in the kitchen, as they do in ours, with half or all of the work of preparing them already done, the cook's pride in creativity is lessened, and with it some of the sense of responsibility for the condition in which the foods arrive at the table. After all, no one is going to worry too much about burning the toast when a new loaf can be had for pennies in a matter of minutes. On the other hand, a woman who has baked her own bread will be at pains to see that every last slice is toasted and served to perfection.

To serve good food you must be willing to go to the little extra trouble that marks the difference between one who cares about food and one who doesn't. Having dishes at the correct temperatures, for instance, is a small thing but one many cooks overlook. Serving cold foods on thoroughly chilled plates, hot foods on hot (not forgetting the coffee cups, which should always be pre-heated) makes all the difference in the appeal of the dish. Care in serving is, indeed, almost as important to the enjoyment of a meal as the food itself. Perhaps more so, since surveys have shown that the rich generally outlive the poor, one of the explanations offered being that the refinements of service common to the tables of the rich make for better digestion and consequently better health and longer life. This needn't be so. Rich or poor, anyone can afford the little extra trouble it takes to make food as appealing to the eye as to the taste.

The recipes on the following pages are a unique collection, gathered from some of the best and most famous hosts and hostesses in the world — all of them expert cooks who know food from the market place to the table. I can't claim to have sampled all these recipes; but I have sampled the hospitality of all the contributing cook hosts, and I can vouch for their dependability as guides to your increased knowledge of gourmet cooking; better, gourmet eating.

Dorothy Fellowes-Gordon

The best weeks of my summers are spent each year at Dickie Gordon's small, lovely old farm at Auribeau, not far from Cannes. Dickie is my oldest friend, and by all odds the best cook I know — an impartial claim, borne out by the eagerness with which our Riviera friends look forward to her dinners for days beforehand. "What are we going to have to eat on Thursday?" they will start asking hungrily on Monday. Dickie understands the value of surprise; her invariable answer is, "I won't tell." A special treat to me at Auribeau are the vegetables, all grown by Dickie on the farm. One in particular that I love is a kind of lettuce called *salatina*, the most delicate green I have ever tasted. Dickie discovered it in Venice — the only place in the world it could be grown, she was told. Nevertheless, she bought seed, planted it at Auribeau, and it throve.

Here, then, are some of Dickie's favorite recipes — and mine:

CHEESE CANAPÉS

Mix equal amounts of grated Parmesan and grated Swiss cheese, and add enough softened butter to make a good paste. Spread generously on Melba toast rounds. Put in hot oven until sizzling and brown on top.

OMELET À LA CRÈME
(4 servings)

Break 3 eggs into mixing bowl, and add an equal amount of heavy cream. Season lightly with salt and pepper. Mix, but don't beat. Refrigerate for 3 hours, or overnight. Add 1 cup of either shredded crab or lobster meat, or *fines herbes* (finely mixed herbs, such as parsley, chervil, tarragon, chives, etc.). Or omelet may be left plain. Heat 1 tablespoon butter in a skillet. When the butter sizzles without browning, the pan is at the correct temperature. Pour in egg mixture. Stir quickly with a fork, and cook for about 5 minutes, giving the pan an occasional shake. Fold, and serve at once. If you want to add to the richness, pour hot cream over the omelet before serving.

CREAMED SHELLFISH
(4 servings)

Drop 1½ cups of uncooked rice into lots of boiling water.

Cook until done — about 30 minutes. Drain, and put in a slow oven to dry. Make 2 cups of medium white sauce, have it hot, and drop into it 2 cups of raw, shelled shellfish — lobster, shrimp, or crab, or a mixture of the three. Cook for 5 minutes, or until the fish is just cooked through. Add 1 teaspoon of curry paste or powder, and a little onion juice. Serve on the rice.

ONION TART
(*4 to 6 servings*)

Sauté 1½ cups of finely chopped onion in butter until golden and soft. Beat 2 eggs, and add to them 1 cup of cream, well seasoned with salt and pepper. Prepare 2 cups of prepared biscuit mix according to directions on the package, roll out dough to ½″ thickness, and line a pie pan with it. Spread the onions on the dough, pour egg and cream mixture over onions, and bake in a 325° oven for 20 minutes.

SOUR CREAM BREAD

Sift together 3 cups of flour, 3 heaping teaspoons baking powder, and a pinch of salt. Mix in 1 cup sour cream. The dough should be the consistency of biscuit dough. Bake in loaf pan in 375° oven for 30 minutes.

CURRY
(*8 to 10 servings*)

Sauté 3 finely chopped onions in butter. Add 1 large apple, chopped; 1 eggplant, chopped; 1 green pepper, finely chopped. Into large saucepan or Dutch oven put 3 pounds of meat cut into 2″ cubes — either leg of mutton, lamb, or chicken. Add 1 teaspoon salt, and about 3 tablespoons curry paste or powder

— preferably paste. Cover with water. Put the grated meat of 1 coconut into a pan, cover with milk, and cook slowly for 15 minutes. Squeeze out and add to meat. Add sautéed vegetables to meat. Simmer for 2 hours, or until meat is tender, tasting occasionally to correct seasoning. Add more salt and curry as desired. Shortly before meat is done, add 1 large tomato, cut up; ⅓ cup dried raisins; and a little chopped, preserved ginger. Serve the curry with hot, dry rice, and any or all of the following side dishes: chopped cucumber, fresh chopped pineapple, roughly chopped peanuts, shredded coconut, chutney (several different kinds, if possible), crisply fried bacon broken into bits. (This curry is better, if anything, cooked the day before it is to be served.)

BULGARIAN CREAM
(6 servings)

Put 2 cups of meringues broken into smallish pieces into a serving dish. Make 2 cups of chocolate sauce by melting a rich, sweet chocolate together with a little milk; it should be a thick sauce. When sauce is cool pour it over the meringues. Top with 1 cup heavy cream, whipped and flavored with vanilla.

Mrs. George A. Garrett

One of the best hostesses in Washington is Ethel Garrett, whose husband was our Ambassador to Ireland. As all Washington hostesses in official circles suffer from perennial guest-list inflation, sixteen is usually the Garretts' minimum for dinner — a typical menu for which might be hot consommé first, served in soup plates with large tapioca and sherry added; filets of black English sole with white wine sauce; pheasant in casserole, and French-cut green beans; lime ice with strawberries, and small chocolate frosted cupcakes.

PHEASANT IN CASSEROLE
(*4 to 6 servings*)

Cut the breasts of 2 pheasants into serving pieces and sauté. Line bottom of casserole with strips of bacon, on top of which put cabbage cut in slices. Place pheasant breasts on this, cover with another layer of cabbage, and top with more bacon. Cook in 350° oven for 1½ hours. Pour in ½ bottle of red wine, and let simmer for 30 minutes more. Remove top layer of bacon and cabbage, and serve.

Perle Mesta

Perle's menus for small dinners are never more than four courses — often hot consommé first; then perhaps breast of duck with orange slices, string beans with ground almonds, wild rice, and banana fritters; endive salad with French dressing, and a ham mousse; pistachio soufflé, coffee. She never serves ice cream for dessert on the grounds that it isn't very exciting to serve people what can be had at any corner drugstore. Two of her favorite recipes are stuffed eggplant, and cream puffs with peppermint filling.

STUFFED EGGPLANT
(*2 large servings*)

Cut 1 large eggplant in half, put into cold water, bring to a boil, and simmer about ½ hour, or until tender. Take from water and cool. When quite cool, scoop out the soft meat,

leaving skins unbroken. Set skins aside. Chop the soft eggplant fine and season well with salt and pepper. Wet and
squeeze out 1½ cups of bread. Finely chop, separately, 1 onion
and 1 tomato, reserving tomato juice. Mince together 1 clove
of garlic, 1 bay leaf, a sprig of parsley, and a little thyme. Heat
2 tablespoons of shortening in a skillet and brown the onion
in it slightly. Add the chopped tomato, with its juices, and let
cook 4 or 5 minutes. Then add the minced herbs and garlic,
and the chopped eggplant. Add the bread and mix all well.
Season again to taste, and cook for 5 minutes longer. Remove
from stove and fill the shells with the mixture. Sprinkle tops
lightly with bread crumbs, dot with butter, and bake in 375°
oven 30 to 40 minutes, or until nicely browned on top.

CREAM PUFFS WITH PEPPERMINT FILLING
(12 servings)

In top of double boiler put ½ cup heavy cream, and ½ pound
of crushed peppermint stick candy. Cook over low heat until
candy dissolves. Soften ½ tablespoon gelatin in 1 tablespoon
cold water. Add to peppermint mixture. Cook a little longer.
Remove from stove and chill until partially set. Whip 1½ cups
heavy cream and fold in. Use to fill 12 cream-puff shells. Hot
chocolate sauce may be poured over just before serving, if
desired.

Margaret Case

Margaret often likes to start off a luncheon menu with a fish
and cheese soufflé, this followed by curried chicken, field
salad, then a macédoine of fresh fruits and chocolate cake.
For a spring menu, cold Senegalese soup might be the first

course, lamb chops the main course, hot asparagus with cold vinaigrette dressing, and, again, fruit — this time in a delicious brandy cream sauce.

FISH–CHEESE SOUFFLÉ
(4 *servings*)

Roll 4 filets of sole, fasten with toothpicks, and parboil. Put in bottom of greased, glass soufflé dish. In top of double boiler melt 2 tablespoons butter. Blend in 1 tablespoon flour. When well blended add 1 cup cream. Season with salt and cayenne. When this has thickened, add ¾ pound grated Swiss cheese. Stir until cheese has melted. Remove from fire and stir in beaten yolks of 3 eggs. Allow to cool slightly, then fold in the stiffly beaten whites of 3 eggs. Pour the soufflé mixture over the fish. Bake in a 375° oven for 30 minutes. This soufflé rises, though not as much as the usual soufflé. The quantity of cheese is important, and the use of cream instead of milk.

CREAM SENEGALESE SOUP
(6 *servings*)

Make a curry sauce as follows: in butter, brown 2 peeled and cut-up apples, 2 cut-up stalks of celery, and 2 cut-up onions. Add 2 or 3 tablespoons of curry powder, and simmer for 5 minutes. Add 2 tablespoons of flour and simmer for 5 minutes more. Add about 2 quarts of chicken or beef stock. Cook for 30 minutes. Strain and chill. When cold, add the following: 2 cups of light cream, some finely chopped chicken (about 1 cup), and salt to taste. Top with whipped cream, if desired. The soup may also be served hot. When served cold, garnish with chopped chives.

FRUIT IN BRANDY CREAM
(6 to 8 servings)

This recipe is good with cooked peaches, brandied peaches, fresh strawberries, or raspberries. If peaches are used cut them in quarters or slices, put in bowl with ½ cup of *crème de cacao* and refrigerate until cold. For the sauce use 2 cups of heavy cream for 3 or 4 cups of fruit. (If ordinary cream is used it should be kept in the icebox for 48 hours before using.) Have the cream, the bowl, and the egg beater cold. Beat the cream 1 minute. Add 1 teaspoon of Whippo, and sugar to taste. Then beat until as thick as possible. At the very last moment before serving, add ½ cup of brandy and fold in the fruit. There are many variations on this idea. At the Colony in New York, for example, Cointreau, or port wine and orange juice, is used to soak the fruit, and powdered macaroons added to the cream just before serving.

Mrs. William Woodward, Sr.

Elsie's mild criticism of most cooks is that they don't know how to make proper salad dressings, or how to cook a Virginia ham. Ham is usually on the menu for her buffet dinners, together with other cold meats, all carefully sliced. There will also be a hot chafing dish of either chicken à la king or lobster Newburg, several kinds of salads, fruit and cheese, and an easy-to-serve dessert, such as apple pie or *cœur à la crème*.

BOILED SALAD DRESSING
(Makes about 1¼ cup)

In saucepan mix together 1 teaspoon mustard, ½ teaspoon

salt, 1 teaspoon cornstarch, 1 teaspoon sugar. Beat in 2 egg yolks thoroughly. Add ½ cup vinegar. Cook over low flame until dressing begins to thicken. Then stir in ½ cup milk. Keep stirring until dressing is thick. Remove from flame. Cool.

UNCOOKED SALAD DRESSING

(*Makes about 2¼ cups*)

Make a base of 2 cups of olive oil and just enough vinegar to give the dressing a tang. To this add 1 pinch cayenne pepper, 1 tablespoon French mustard, 2 tablespoons finely chopped chives, 1 tablespoon finely chopped dill, 1 teaspoon sugar, and salt to taste. Beat until mixture is fairly thick.

SOAKING AND COOKING VIRGINIA HAMS

Soak ham in cold water from 36 to 48 hours, changing the water every 12 hours. Wash and scrape ham thoroughly, and place it, skin side down, in a boiler full of boiling water. (Sometimes a few bay leaves and a little thyme in the water in which the ham is cooked add a little flavor.) Let the temperature of the water fall slightly, and simmer 30 minutes for each pound of the ham's weight. Do not, on any account, allow water to boil again. When the ham is cooked remove the boiler from the fire, but do not take the ham out of the water until cool. (I let mine stay in the water overnight.) Peel off the skin carefully, cover the ham liberally with sugar, and bake in a slow oven until brown — from 20 to 30 minutes. Baste frequently with wine while baking.

CŒUR À LA CRÈME

(*4 servings*)

Blend thoroughly 2 small cream cheeses and 1 cup of sour

cream. Wrap in cheesecloth and hang in icebox for several hours, or overnight, so that moisture drips out. Then place, still in cheesecloth, in heart-shaped basket mold. Return to icebox for several hours. When ready to serve, turn onto serving platter, garnish with fruit (strawberries or raspberries) and, just before serving, pour sour cream over the top.

Clare Boothe Luce

The chef at the Villa Taverna in Rome was an Italian, Rocco, and when the Luces dined alone they preferred to eat the Italian dishes he did to perfection. The cuisine for official luncheons and dinners, however, complied with diplomatic custom and was invariably French. Rocco was versatile, and two of his best efforts were two of Clare's favorite recipes — Caesar salad, and a heavenly dessert, Cumberland House orange pancakes.

CAESAR SALAD
(4 large servings)

Sprinkle salt generously over inside of wooden bowl. Rub with cut clove of garlic. Break into bowl 3 heads of washed and dried Romaine in fair-sized lengths — about 2 inches. Have ready a small bowl in which are 5 filets of anchovies, finely chopped. Add these to greens with 4 tablespoons garlic-flavored oil, and mix well. Add a few drops of Worcestershire sauce. Add coarsely ground pepper to suit. Sprinkle over the whole 3 tablespoons of grated Parmesan cheese. Break over this a 2-minute coddled egg. Squeeze juice of 2 lemons over the egg. Now toss salad *lightly* but thoroughly, using wooden fork and spoon. Have bowl of hot croutons ready as last addition.

To make these, take 2 slices of sandwich bread, remove crust, cut each slice into 16 cubes. Fry golden in oil well scented with garlic. Drop into salad. Mix again and serve.

CUMBERLAND HOUSE ORANGE PANCAKES
(*4 to 6 servings*)

Cream ¼ pound sweet butter with ½ cup confectioners' sugar. Gradually beat in the juice and grated rind of 2 oranges. Turn this orange hard sauce into a glass jar and let it harden in refrigerator. Beat 3 egg yolks lightly, and add a pinch of salt and 1 cup milk. Stir in gradually ¾ cup sifted flour, and continue to stir until batter is smooth. Finally fold in 3 egg whites, stiffly beaten. In heavy iron skillet heat a generous amount of sweet butter over a low fire. When butter foams, pour in ½ cup pancake batter. When the pancake sets, loosen it carefully with a turner and keep it afloat in the butter until the underside is golden. Turn the pancake, add more butter, and keep pancake loose by shaking the skillet constantly until the pancake is crisp and brown on both sides. (Keep fire low or the butter will burn.) Repeat until all batter is used. Drain the pancakes on absorbent paper, then fold each quickly around 1 tablespoonful of the cold orange hard sauce. Top each pancake with another tablespoon of hard sauce, and serve them on a piping hot fireproof dish — so hot the butter sizzles. A dash of Cointreau added at the table enhances the flavor.

Mrs. Edgar Leonard
TROUT
(*4 servings*)

Put juice of 1 lemon in ice-cold water. Dip trout into this, then dry with cloth rubbed with garlic. Salt and pepper the trout inside and dust lightly with flour outside. Sauté trout in butter, shaking pan to prevent sticking. Cook about 3 minutes on each side. Remove trout from pan and keep warm. Add more butter to pan and sauté 1 medium onion, thinly sliced, until onion is transparent but not brown. Add 1 tablespoon lemon juice, salt and pepper, 1 tablespoon tarragon vinegar, 4 or 5 tablespoons white wine, 1 tablespoon finely chopped fresh herbs. Pour sauce over the trout. When this dish is served with the right white wine, you will imagine you are in Paris.

COTTAGE CHEESE PANCAKES

(6 to 8 servings)

Beat together 4 whole eggs, ½ teaspoon salt, 1 dessertspoon sugar. Add to mixture 1 cup cottage cheese, 1 cup sour cream, ½ cup sifted flour. Bake on hot griddle, and serve with butter and maple sirup.

Mrs. Charles Blackwell

One of Katherine Blackwell's favorites as a first course at luncheon is eggs *en cocotte*, this dish often followed by a daintified version of shepherd's pie, the lamb minced very fine, and with this a cole slaw made with sour cream.

EGGS EN COCOTTE

Heat as many *cocottes,* or individual long-handled earthenware casseroles, as are required. Pour 1 tablespoon hot cream into each. Break 1 egg into each, and add salt, pepper, and ½ teaspoon of butter. Put the *cocottes* in a wide, shallow pan of hot water, cover the pan, and let the eggs poach until the whites are set and the yolks done to taste.

Mrs. Harold E. Talbott

The late Secretary of the Air Force and Peggy Talbott came as close to being family to me as any people I have ever known. For the past fifteen years, I have always lunched with them on the traditionally family holidays of Thanksgiving and Christmas. Peggy was a wonderful wife, she is a wonderful friend, and tops as a hostess. Three of her favorite recipes:

COLD EGGS WITH HAM AND TARRAGON

Cover the bottom of a silver or glass serving dish with a fine meat jelly, set the dish in ice and refrigerate until the jelly is stiff. Cover the jelly with thin slices of ham and a poached egg on each slice. Decorate the eggs with tarragon leaves and truffles, or red pimentos, and let the whole get very cold. Then cover the eggs with a thick meat jelly so that the jelly stays around the eggs. Put back into the icebox for about 30 minutes before serving.

SPINACH SOUFFLÉ
(6 servings)

Pour 2 cups hot medium white sauce into 3 beaten egg yolks, stirring constantly. Add 1 teaspoon chopped onion, if desired. Cool. Add 1 cup cooked, sieved spinach; and when this is well mixed, carefully fold in 3 stiffly beaten egg whites. Turn into a greased casserole, set casserole in pan of hot water, and bake in 375° oven for 45 to 50 minutes. Serve with Hollandaise sauce.

BALLOONS

(6 to 8 servings)

Put ¼ cup butter into 1 cup boiling water. Add 1 cup flour. Stir over the fire for 3 minutes. Cool. Add 4 slightly beaten eggs, one at a time. Then beat the whole mixture for 5 minutes. Drop with a spoon into hot lard. They take about 8 or 10 minutes to puff up and are then done. Serve with the following sauce: boil together for 5 minutes 2 tablespoons butter, 1 cup brown sugar, ½ cup thin cream. Serve very hot.

Mrs. Josh Logan

Nedda and Josh are partial to very rare roast beef for the main dish at dinner, and they like to serve a delicious salad made with fresh, raw spinach, and mixed with a sour cream and bacon dressing. A first course might be chopped raw mushrooms served in a salad dish with a dressing of oil, lemon juice, and salt and pepper. The mushrooms for this must be very fresh and crisp. One of their favorite desserts is crepes Canarius.

CREPES CANARIUS

(6 servings)

Make crepes by sifting together ⅔ cup of flour, 1 tablespoon sugar, and a little salt. Add 2 whole eggs and the yolks of 2 eggs which have been beaten together. Then add 1¾ cups of milk and stir until batter is smooth. Add 2 tablespoons melted butter, and 1 tablespoon brandy or rum. Cook the crepes in a skillet in bubbling butter until golden and done, about 1 minute on each side. Stack one on top of another until ready to fill. Make a filling of equal parts lard, sugar, and ground almonds. Roll each crepe around a tablespoon of this filling, and place in a crepes suzette dish in which hot butter is sizzling. Pour over equal amounts of orange curaçao, Cointreau, and Triple Sec. Ignite and serve.

Mrs. Byron Foy

A typical winter dinner menu at the Foys' might start with a good hot consommé, then lobster soufflé, after that *poulet sauté Anna,* and for dessert, Jamaica ice made from a native recipe.

POULET SAUTÉ ANNA

(4 to 6 servings)

Make a bouillon by cooking the neck, feet, back, and gizzard of 1 frying chicken in water. Add 1 carrot, 1 onion, 3 leeks, salt and pepper. Simmer until bouillon is reduced and strong. Strain, and set aside ready for use. Heat 3 tablespoons olive oil and 2½ tablespoons butter in a skillet. Cut 2 shallots and 1 medium-sized onion into tiny pieces. Fry them, together with the serving pieces of the chicken, over a hot fire for about 10 minutes. Lower the flame and cook for 25 minutes more. Then remove pieces of chicken to a warm dish. Add the bouillon to the fat in the skillet. Add 3 cups of heavy cream, and 3½ tablespoons of fine champagne. Cook over low flame until sauce thickens. Add a little lemon juice and salt and pepper to taste. When the sauce is ready, place the chicken in it and let it stand in a warm oven until ready to serve. It must not boil.

JAMAICA ICE

(10 to 12 servings)

Chop 1 small pineapple, 2 oranges, 2 grapefruits, 2 tangerines,

2 bananas, ½ can of apricots (or use fresh, if available). Add
the juice of 2 tangerines and the milk of 2 coconuts. Sweeten
to taste. Add 1 cup of cream, and freeze.

Mrs. T. Reed Vreeland

A consommé that Diana Vreeland serves as a first course at
dinner is a savory legacy from the recipe collection of Elsie de
Wolfe, at whose house I first tasted it. The sweetbreads, with
salade Parisienne, make an excellent main course at luncheon.

CONSOMMÉ VERT-PRÉ

Make a very good rich bouillon. Add enough spinach juice
to color it green, and just before serving add finely chopped
fines herbes. Serve hot or iced.

RIS DE VEAU À LA LYONNAISE
(Sweetbreads Lyonnaise)
(*4 servings*)

Parboil 2 pairs of sweetbreads in salted water for 20 minutes.
Drain, cut away all tubes and membranes, and cool between two
plates, weighted on top. Slice the sweetbreads diagonally and
lard each slice with 1 or 2 small bits of bacon or salt pork.
Sauté the sweetbreads to a light golden brown in 3 tablespoons
of hot butter, turning them once. Add 1 clove of garlic,
chopped, 1 good teaspoon each of chopped parsley and chives,
½ teaspoon dried tarragon, 1 clove mashed in a mortar (or a
pinch of ground cloves), and 1 cup chicken stock. Simmer for
3 or 4 minutes. Strain the sauce into another pan and thicken
it by blending in 1 scant tablespoon butter, creamed thoroughly
with 1 tablespoon flour and 1 egg yolk. Cook the sauce over a

low flame for 3 minutes, stirring constantly. Add a few drops of lemon juice, pour the sauce over the sweetbreads, and serve very hot.

SALADE PARISIENNE
(*4 to 6 servings*)

Slice thinly equal amounts of cooked beets, celery root, and potatoes to make 4 cups. Season these with salt and pepper, and a marinade of 1 part wine vinegar to 3 parts olive oil. Let stand awhile. Mash the yolks of 5 hard-cooked eggs through a fine sieve into a bowl. Blend in 2 tablespoons anchovy paste and add gradually about ¼ cup of olive oil, stirring until smooth. Add 1 teaspoon French mustard, a little tarragon vinegar, 4 tablespoons diced tuna fish, 2 tablespoons diced sour pickles, the diced white of the hard-cooked eggs, a pinch of red pepper, and 1 teaspoon chopped fresh tarragon. Drain the marinated vegetables, mix all together, and arrange in a serving dish.

Mrs. William F. R. Ballard

Fashion consultant Bettina Ballard claims that her method of having good food is to have a good cook. Maybe, but she is a first-rate cook herself — let Ballard Fish Soup speak for her. This soup ("the simplest dish to make in the whole world," according to Bettina) goes on the menu as a first course for a winter dinner, followed often by veal with tarragon. The cold curried chicken is a summer dinner favorite.

BALLARD FISH SOUP

(6 servings)

Take 2½ pounds of scrod, left in big pieces, and put them in the bottom of a large earthenware casserole. Salt and pepper this, using a pepper mill. Gently fry about 2 tablespoons of shallots in butter. Add two 7½-ounce cans of minced clams, including juice, to the scrod. Add the shallots and then 1 quart of heavy cream. Sprinkle a few bread crumbs on top. Cook the soup about 30 minutes in a 350° oven. Serve into soup dishes from the same earthenware casserole at the table.

VEAL WITH TARRAGON

(6 servings)

Have your butcher pound 2½ pounds of veal cutlets until they are very thin. Cut into serving pieces. Salt and pepper the veal and roll in *very little* bread crumbs. Sauté the veal in a generous amount of butter — about ¾ of a stick — until nicely browned on both sides. When almost done, add a lot of fresh tarragon, chopped, and ½ cup of dry white wine.

COLD CURRIED CHICKEN

(4 to 6 servings)

Roast a 4-pound chicken until done. Take out of oven and let cool. Bone the chicken and cut into slices. Put the pieces on a platter and cover with curry sauce. Cool in the ice box. Serve on the same platter.

CURRY SAUCE: Fry 1 tablespoon of chopped onion until soft. Fry ½ cup of chopped apple in the same pan until tender. Add 1 tablespoon of flour and 2 tablespoons of curry powder to onions and apples. Add half of a 6-ounce can of tomato paste, 1 cup of chicken stock, and 1 cup of heavy cream. Cook together until thick. Pour over the chicken.

Claudette Colbert

SNAILS

(6 servings)

Remove 6 dozen snails from their shells. Boil shells in soda water, rinse well, and dry. Cream 1 pound of sweet butter, add 3 cloves of garlic, mashed, ¾ cup chopped parsley, ½ teaspoon of salt, and a little pepper. Put a little of this mixture into each shell. Then put in a snail. Then fill up shell with mixture. Bake in a 400° oven until butter melts and bubbles, and serve *very* hot.

Joan Fontaine

Creole fish gumbo, as Joan does it, has such a name around Hollywood that when word goes out that the soup kettle is being readied for it Mike Romanoff, for one, instantly puts in his bid to be there for the dishing out. Joan serves the gumbo in a large chafing dish, from which guests ladle it out themselves into deep ceramic soup bowls. Steaming rice accompanies it, hot French bread, green salad, and a good white wine. Cold Andalusian *gazpacho* comes first on a summer menu, served with cheese straws. After this, stuffed artichoke hearts, a main dish such as tenderloin of beef with red wine and mushroom sauce, then hot bean sprout salad, with chilled fruits and Italian coffee to finish off.

CREOLE FISH GUMBO

Boil 2 crabs and 2 lobsters for 15 minutes, starting with *cold* salted water. Add 1 pound of shrimps and continue cooking for 4 minutes more. Remove from fire. Remove shells and heads, and put these back into pot with water they were boiled in. Add to pot 1 carrot, 2 stalks celery, 1 onion, 1 bay leaf, a few pepper corns, parsley sprigs, and 6 fresh or 1 large can tomatoes. Simmer for at least 30 minutes. Strain through sieve, and replace stock in pot. Now fry 2 slices of bacon. When done, crumble and leave in the skillet with fat. Add to bacon 2 stalks of chopped celery, 2 cloves of crushed garlic, 2 chopped onions (preferably red), 1 chopped green pepper, and 1 tablespoon chopped parsley. Brown these ingredients and add 1 pound of halibut cut into 1-inch chunks. Add ¼ cup of olive oil and cook 2 minutes, or until the fish is just done. Add all this to the stock pot, with ½ cup tomato paste, ½ cup white wine, juice of 2 lemons, 1 tablespoon of sugar, 2 tablespoons saffron, 2 tablespoons Worcestershire, 2 teaspoons Tabasco, 2 cups okra, 1 tablespoon gumbo filé (this is sassafras and may be purchased at a pharmacy), 1 pint of clams, the crabs, lobsters, and shrimps, and cayenne, salt, and paprika to taste. Simmer until well blended, thickening if necessary with a *roux* made by browning 3 tablespoons of flour in 3 tablespoons of butter.

ANDALUSIAN GAZPACHO

(*4 servings*)

Place the following in a bowl: 4 small cucumbers, seeded and finely chopped; 6 ripe tomatoes, peeled and coarsely chopped; 1 green pepper, finely minced; 1 clove garlic, finely mashed; 2 tablespoons grated carrot; 2 tablespoons grated onion. Add cold water to cover, with 2 tablespoons lemon juice, or lime juice (I greatly prefer the latter); 1 teaspoon dry mustard, dash Tabasco, salt and pepper to taste. Chill thoroughly at least 8 hours. Serve in individual bowls with a dab of sour cream — about 1 tablespoon — on top.

STUFFED ARTICHOKES AU GRATIN
(6 servings)

Boil 6 artichokes with ½ lemon and 1 onion, quartered. Drain, remove leaves and chokes and put hearts aside to keep warm. Make a white sauce with 2 tablespoons butter, 4 tablespoons flour, 1½ cups creamy milk. Blend butter and flour together in double boiler. Slowly add milk and stir constantly until thick and smooth. Add salt and pepper to taste. Remove from fire and blend in 1 cup grated cheese, and 2 tablespoons sherry. Add 1½ cups cooked shrimps (the baby Seattle shrimps, if possible). Spoon this mixture into artichoke heart cups, sprinkle bread crumbs over the tops, and cook until thoroughly heated — about 15 minutes in a 350° oven. Garnish with lemon and watercress.

BEAN SPROUT SALAD
(4 servings)

Fry 3 slices of bacon with 1 clove mashed garlic. Remove bacon and put aside to dry. Remove garlic from pan, and add 1 tablespoon dry mustard, 1 tablespoon Worcestershire, salt, and freshly cracked pepper to sizzling bacon fat. Blend. Remove pan from fire and slowly add ¾ cup red wine vinegar, blending well. Crumble bacon and add crumbs to 1 pound fresh bean sprouts that have been quickly blanched under hot water tap.

Pour the hot dressing over this, toss quickly, and serve immediately. I usually line the salad bowl with red lettuce for color.

Rosalind Russell

VEAL IN SOUR CREAM

(6 servings)

Cook 6 pieces of bacon in large frying pan, and set bacon aside. Brown 3 pounds of boneless stew veal in the bacon fat. Cook ½ pound of sliced mushrooms and 2 large onions, chopped, in same fat. Mix 1 cup of white wine with 1 cup of sour cream. Put veal, mushrooms, and onions in buttered casserole. Season to taste with salt and pepper. Pour on wine and cream. Crumble bacon over top. Simmer, covered, 1½ hours, either in a 325° oven, or on top of the stove over a low flame with an asbestos mat under the casserole. For variety, a good addition is 1¼ pounds boiled ham, diced and browned with the vegetables. In that case, skip the bacon and use other bacon fat.

Mrs. Ronald Colman

Benita contributed this recipe with the comment that its main distinction is that it is about the only dessert she has ever seen Ronnie enjoy. He has good reason to.

CHEESE PIE

Combine four 3-ounce packages of cream cheese, 2 eggs, ¾ cup sugar, 2 teaspoons vanilla, and ¼ teaspoon almond flavoring. Whip until smooth and light. Make a Graham cracker crust as follows: combine 14 Graham crackers, crumbled with ¼ cup melted butter, and use the mixture to line a pie pan. Pour filling into crust and bake 15 minutes in a 350° oven. Remove from oven and allow to cool for 5 minutes. Make a topping as follows: blend together 3½ tablespoons of sugar, 1 teaspoon vanilla, ¼ teaspoon of almond flavoring, and 1 cup sour cream. Pour topping over pie and return to oven to bake 10 minutes longer. This should be left in refrigerator for at least 5 hours and served on a yacht.

Mrs. Darryl Zanuck

"I have made this fudge for Darryl and hundreds of soldiers for many years," said Virginia, "and if the directions are followed exactly you will find it is the best."

FUDGE

Put 2 cups white sugar and 2 large tablespoons Baker's cocoa in saucepan, mixing with hands until sugar and cocoa are thoroughly mixed, with all tiny lumps of sugar eliminated. Add 1 small can Carnation milk (don't substitute another brand), and 2 large tablespoons of butter. Stir all together and put on stove, keeping flame under pan always even. The trick is to stir constantly in one direction until mixture thickens. Test by dropping a small amount of fudge into cold water. It should form a soft ball that holds together between the fingers. Never stop stirring. Now turn flame lower and add 1 teaspoon vanilla, 1 cup chopped walnuts, and a pinch of salt. By this time the fudge should have thickened. Have enough cold water in the sink so that when the pan is set in it the lower half is submerged. Keep stirring. Fudge should now be very thick. Pour

onto buttered platter. Wait 10 minutes. Fudge is then ready
to be cut into squares. Never put in icebox. Fudge can be
eaten warm or put in candy container. You will find this fudge
will never be sugary but will have a creamy texture and
should keep the same freshness for two weeks.

Loretta Young

Rice fixed in this way makes an excellent accompaniment to
almost any creamed meat or fish dish.

RICE PILAFF

(4 servings)

Cook, wash, and drain 1 cup of rice. Dry out in colander
over boiling water. Melt 4 tablespoons butter in a skillet, add
rice, and cook over low heat for about 10 minutes, or until
rice is browned. Add two or three puréed tomatoes, or one
6-ounce can tomato paste, 3 cups seasoned bouillon, and a dash
of marjoram. Cover and let cook slowly 45 to 60 minutes, or
until rice has absorbed all the liquid.

Claude Philippe

Philippe relaxes from his six-day week at the Waldorf in
busman fashion: Sundays he spends at his farm near Peekskill,
New York, playing host to as many as a hundred friends who
may drop in for lunch — all of whom, incidentally, are required to lend a hand either in preparing the meal or, when
the kitchen gets too crowded, weeding the garden. *Pot-au-feu*
is a classic French dish, on the hearty side, wonderful for a
midday Sunday meal on a brisk day.

POT–AU–FEU
(6 *servings*)

Cut 4 or 5 carrots, 3 white turnips, 6 leeks, and 1 green cabbage into 1-inch-long and ¾-inch-thick strips. Bring 3 pounds of fresh plate ribs of beef, the neck, wings, and gizzards of 4 large fowls, and 1 marrow bone tied in a muslin bag to a boil in a 6-quart earthenware pot. Cool. Remove water. Now fill the pot to 2 inches from the top with cold water, bring to a boil and let boil slowly until the beef is cooked — about 2 hours. Make a bunch of 2 celery stalks and a few parsley roots. Put into pot. Add 1 tablespoon of salt, 3 peppercorns, and 2 medium-sized onions with a clove in each. Bring to a boil and let boil slowly for another hour. Add cut carrots, turnips, leeks and cabbage. Boil slowly for another hour, to keep the broth clear. Test the broth and correct seasoning. Before serving, remove the extra fat from the top of the pot. Garnish attractively with sliced toasted rolls and Parmesan cheese.

Henri Soulé

The Pavillon may not be the only restaurant in New York that serves Billibilli, but I doubt that Soulé's recipe for it could be matched anywhere. This soup was a great favorite of the Aga Khan's, who liked to serve it as a preliminary course to one of his curry dinners. The Mousse de Sole Pavillon is pretty grand for the average menu just any time, but well worth the trouble when you're in the mood to be elegant. At the Pavillon it is served at dinner between soup and main course, these usually kept to the simple side because of the richness of the mousse. I gave a small dinner of *adieu* for Dickie Gordon before she sailed for France last spring, and left the menu to Soulé. Beluga caviar came first, then a strong clear consommé, followed by the Mousse de Sole; this followed by a plain delicately roasted chicken. A *gratin* of vegetables accompanied the chicken, then fresh asparagus, served, as it always is in France, as a separate course. Dessert was a Bombe Regina with fresh strawberries and little cakes.

BILLIBILLI

(6 *servings*)

Place the following ingredients in a large saucepan: 3 pounds of fresh, cleaned mussels, 1 onion and 3 shallots (chopped), 3 parsley branches, 2 tablespoons butter, 1 pint dry white wine, and 1 quart heavy cream. Add salt and pepper and a dash of cayenne. Cook for 10 minutes and strain through cheesecloth. Serve very hot with cheese straws.

MOUSSE DE SOLE PAVILLON

(8 *servings*)

Pound the meat of 2 pounds of English sole (about 4 soles, boned) with 3 teaspoons salt and a little pepper. Gradually add the whites of 4 eggs. Strain mixture through a fine sieve and place it in a saucepan on ice. Then work it up with a wooden spoon and gradually fold 1 quart of heavy cream into it. Mold the mousse into a buttered mold and cook in oven over hot water, with a low flame, for 1 hour. Serve with the following sauce:

SAUCE CHAMPAGNE: Take the bones from the soles used for the mousse and place them in a buttered pan with ½ chopped onion, 2 chopped shallots, salt and pepper. Cover with white dry wine or champagne. Boil slowly. Cook mixture down until reduced. Thicken with 2 or 3 spoons of *velouté* of fish or, if unable, 2 or 3 spoons of béchamel (white cream sauce) and add 1 pint heavy cream, finally adding 2 tablespoons fine butter, and lemon juice. Strain the sauce and pour over the mousse. Decorate with strips of truffles.

Valerian Rybar

ARTICHOKES À LA GRECQUE

(6 *servings*)

Clean 6 choice, large artichokes, and snip off the tip of each leaf. Mix ½ cup of bread crumbs with salt, pepper, ½ clove of finely chopped garlic, and 2 tablespoons of finely chopped parsley. Then stuff each leaf. Place the artichokes in a pan and add ½ cup of water, taking care not to spill any on the artichokes. Pour 3 tablespoons of pure olive oil over each artichoke. Salt and pepper lightly, and let simmer for 2 hours, replenishing water when necessary. Serve lukewarm.

MONT BLANC

(8 *servings*)

Boil 2 pounds of large chestnuts until soft, then peel. Place them in blender with 2 tablespoons Jamaica rum, ½ cup sugar, 1 tablespoon vanilla, and 1 teaspoon of grated orange rind. Mix and blend thoroughly. Squeeze mixture through a potato ricer onto serving platter, form into shape of mountain, topping it with 1 cup heavy cream, sweetened and thickly whipped. Chill and serve.

Cole Porter

Kedgeree originated in India, where the British found it,

added fish to the native rice and vegetable recipe, and took to serving it for breakfast. It makes a fine main dish for a simple luncheon. Mrs. Lytle Hull likes to serve it for lunch, followed by a salad, or cold asparagus, or artichokes, then a dessert of mixed fresh fruit cut into large pieces. Kedgeree may be made in a number of ways: Cole's recipe is the English version. The cherry and wine compote is particularly good as a finale to a heavy dinner.

KEDGEREE
(4 servings)

Boil 1½ pounds of any kind of fish (cod is good, or haddock or hake). Remove bones and flake fish. Put 4 tablespoons of Patna rice into salted, fast-boiling water. Boil until tender. Drain rice in colander and allow plenty of cold water to run over it to wash it well from all starch. Let rice stand awhile, then place it evenly on a flat tin and dry it gradually in a slow oven. Hard-boil 3 eggs and, when they are cold, shell them and chop them up finely. Then mix fish, rice, and eggs well together. Season with a little salt and pepper. Melt 2 or 3 ounces of butter in a saucepan, add the fish mixture, and heat, stirring until hot through.

CHERRY COMPOTE WITH RED WINE
(6 servings)

Make a sirup by bringing to a boil 2 cups of red wine, 1 cup of sugar, the juice of two No. 2 cans of black Bing cherries, a little lemon peel, and 2 cinnamon sticks. Boil for 15 minutes. Mix 1 teaspoon arrowroot or cornstarch with 1 tablespoon of cold water and add to the sirup. Simmer for a few minutes longer, and flavor with Kirschwasser. Pour the sirup over the cherries and serve warm.

Alfred Lunt

Alfred gave me this recipe with the comment: "This may sound too simple to include in your book, but if made quickly and deftly the whole process should not take more than five minutes. It is really quite delicious." And it is.

BEEF PATTIES WITH CAPERS
(*2 servings*)

Beat together 1 pound of top round steak — from which all fat has been removed, and the beef ground at least twice — 1 teaspoon salt, and ½ cup heavy cream. When thoroughly combined form into 4 or 6 plump patties and fry very quickly in ⅛ pound of hot butter. Turn only once. Do not overcook; they must be pink inside. Remove to serving dish, grind pepper over patties, and keep warm. Add 2 tablespoons chopped capers to butter in pan. Stir them about and add a very, *very* little hot water. Pour this over the patties and serve at once.

Arthur Hornblow, Jr.

A somewhat more extravagant beef dish, this, but even simpler to prepare. Arthur's comment: "The Viennese call it 'schlemmer-schnitte' and it can be found superbly prepared at Luchow's. But one can well do it for oneself quite easily, and I have given it the name Caviar Cardinal. Perhaps it is most appropriately served as a first course but, depending upon the size of the portion, it can take its place either as a main dish at lunch or as a handsome hors d'œuvre cut into smaller slices, or as an after-theater supper treat."

CAVIAR CARDINAL

Grind fine 1 pound of sirloin from which all bits of fat have been trimmed. Spread ½ of this freshly ground meat in a flat circle on each of two cold plates. Cover each cake of raw meat with a generous layer of *fresh* Russian caviar. Sprinkle the caviar with a light layer of finely chopped onion if desired. Serve with crisp rye or white toast on the side, and a bit of lemon for those who may like it. Any beverage goes well with Caviar Cardinal, perhaps especially cold beer.

Clark Gable

This isn't the dish that won Clark first prize at my cooking party, but it sounds good enough to, if he's willing to try again.

STUFFED BIRDS
(6 to 8 servings)

Make a stuffing using 1 package of wild rice, cooked according to directions on the box, and mixed with 2 chopped onions which have been sautéed in ¼ pound of butter until limp. Salt and pepper 6 or 8 birds (quail or dove or squab) inside and out, stuff, truss, and shake in paper bag with flour. Arrange birds in oven dish and pour over enough chicken broth to cover. Bake at 350° for 1¾ hours. Make a cream sauce, using ¼ pound butter, ½ cup flour, and 1 quart milk (part broth if desired). Remove birds from oven, pour sauce over them. Sprinkle with 1 package blanched, slivered almonds, and brown lightly under broiler, Serve on toast with 1 slice of Canadian bacon under each bird.

$\mathcal{I}$ndex